TREASURED
ISLANDS

PETER NALDRETT

TREASURED ISLANDS

*The explorer's guide to over 200
of the most beautiful and intriguing
islands around Britain*

CONWAY

LONDON · OXFORD · NEW YORK · NEW DELHI · SYDNEY

CONWAY
Bloomsbury Publishing Plc
50 Bedford Square, London, WC1B 3DP, UK
29 Earlsfort Terrace, Dublin 2, Ireland

BLOOMSBURY, CONWAY and the Conway logo are trademarks of Bloomsbury Publishing Plc

This edition published in Great Britain 2021

A catalogue record for this book is available from the British Library

Library of Congress Cataloguing-in-Publication data has been applied for

ISBN: PB: 978-1-8448-6592-5; ePDF: 978-1-8448-6594-9; ePUB: 978-1-8448-6593-2

2 4 6 8 10 9 7 5 3 1

Typeset in Geometric 415 BT Lite by Susan McIntyre
Printed and bound in India by Replika Press Pvt. Ltd.

To find out more about our authors and books visit www.bloomsbury.com
and sign up for our newsletters

CONTENTS

Overview map

Faroe Islands

Scotland

Northern
Ireland

Isle of Man

Ireland

England

Wales

Isles of Scilly

Channel Islands

| 0 | 50 | 100 | 150 km |
| 0 | 50 | 100 | 150 miles |

INTRODUCTION

Living in Sheffield, where day trips to the Peak District, York and Alton Towers are easier to arrange than a journey to the seaside, it's easy to forget that we dwell on an island. Britain is, after all, 1,407km (874 miles) from head to toe and that epic journey from Land's End to John O'Groats can take weeks for those pedalling or walking. Home to over 60 million people, this sceptred isle is no tropical desert paradise where people end up chatting with a volleyball called Wilson. And yet, from Blackpool to Blackburn and from Wrexham to Wick, everybody living in Britain has at least one thing in common – they are an islander. And being an island nation has shaped Britain's history, culture and politics for thousands of years. From Viking and Norman invasions to the defensive structures built to keep out Hitler. From the rise of seaside resorts encircling our coast to the floods and erosion that can destroy it. From the tragic tales of sea-bound migrants trying to reach our shores to the 'go it alone' decision to approve Brexit. Being an island has shaped us and continues to do so.

Calling yourself an 'islander' is to put yourself on a spectrum; the term means different things in different parts of the country. At one end of the spectrum, I'm an islander in South Yorkshire and I know this because I have to fly, sail or journey through a tunnel to reach France. At the other end of the spectrum are those who live in small communities on tiny islands with just a handful of people. Being an islander to them means having to get on a boat to reach even a small supermarket or take their dog to the vet. And there are plenty of islands that fit on this spectrum. Estimates differ, but there are thought to be over 6,000 islands in the United Kingdom. As many as 196 are inhabited. Some disappear at high tide, others are too rocky to be reached. Some were abandoned in the 1930s because life became too hard, others thrive due to tourism and farming. Some islanders never see the sea, some spend their working lives on the waves. We are all islanders, but some are more islander than others.

Sitting in my Sheffield home, whenever I hear the words 'and now the Shipping Forecast…' it means two things. First, I'm about to become lost in a mesmerising world of exotic and little-known place names, each one igniting my curiosity. Rattray Head. Gibraltar Point. Cape Wrath. Shetland. Viking. North Utsire. Each has a melody of data linked to it, describing current visibility, wind speed and state of the sea. I draw up a mental map of where the storms are around Britain, where people are sleeping safely and where folks are battening down the hatches. When the dreamy notes of 'Sailing By' introduce the final shipping forecast of the day at 00:48, they are a coastal beacon indicating that we are all going on a journey together. Second, hearing those words and that tune means I have stayed up far too late and it's past time to head off to bed.

I'd become a fan of BBC Radio 4's Shipping Forecast long before I started researching this book, but of course it meant very little to me, miles from the coast in my South Yorkshire inland bubble. I started to look upon it differently, though, when planning visits to the islands featured in the book. Suddenly, the late night announcement, so impeccably delivered, became an important friend, informing me what sea conditions would be like and, sometimes, whether I would be able to journey out to the small communities off the coast. It was also a lifeline that would tell me whether I was likely to get back; many of our island communities can be isolated for days on end in rough weather. If I was lucky, the wind would be at force 6 or below. When it gets up to 8, 9, 10 and beyond, you know you're in for a rough ride.

'How are your sea legs?' a friend asked me as I was about to venture off on the first of my island adventures.

Perhaps surprisingly for somebody who had just agreed to visit the islands of Britain, Ireland and the Faroe Islands, my ability to cope with stormy seas was not something I'd really considered. I'd been on a boat before, of course, and couldn't remember any adverse side effects. But I suddenly became aware that things might get a little choppier for me heading to Shetland and Orkney than on a cross-Channel ferry or a tourist cruise around Loch Ness. Perhaps I should have considered seasickness earlier on in the project and not as my bags were packed, ready to head off to the Isle of Man. The travel advice that people, for some reason, wanted to offer me started rolling in like crashing waves once my journeys began in earnest. Some of it was valuable and some confusing and contradictory: Go out on deck. Get some fresh air. Don't use binoculars. Stare at the horizon. Focus on one object. Eat a hearty breakfast. Don't eat anything. Stay inside. Go to the front of the boat. Sit at the back of the boat. If at all possible, lie down. Don't lie down. Everybody seemed to have an opinion on how to combat seasickness, and a combination of their advice helped me out on some of the rougher trips. That journey back from the Isle of Man was a testing one; I started off with the intention of writing the chapter on deck, but ended up staring determinedly at lighthouses and light vessels as the boat nauseatingly rocked from side to side. The trip back from the Isles of Scilly on a boat nicknamed 'The Vomit Comet' was also challenging, although the time seemed to pass quickly up on deck as I kept an eye on the horizon. But by far the roughest seas I encountered were on leaving Iceland for the Faroe Islands. Fortunately, on this long journey I had a cabin and so headed straight for bed. Once horizontal, the rough lurching felt more like gentle swaying and I soon nodded off, rising again when the storm had passed.

As it turns out, the weather was not the biggest barrier to writing this book. When I set out, my aim was to visit every single island included here, to photograph it and speak to colourful local characters. Stormy seas and cancelled boats meant some plans had to be aborted, but the unexpected arrival of COVID-19 brought travel to its knees, forcing me to scrub several trips from the list. In the end, I visited over 150 of the islands – each one unique in its culture and scenery. Where circumstances meant I couldn't reach the island environment, I made sure I spoke to somebody who had a particular fondness for it. Through my research, I've learned how communities interact with wildlife, have a valuable but often troubled relationship with tourism, develop their own unique cottage industries and are frequently at the mercy of the weather. Every one of these islands is a special place, for both the residents and the visitor. I hope you enjoy reading about them and are able to plan your own trips to some of these wonderful destinations.

How to use this book

With so many different islands providing a wealth of adventurous opportunities, finding the trip you're looking for can be a little daunting. We've categorised the islands in several ways to make it easier for you to navigate your way around the book. Firstly, they fall under the relevant country or dependency – such as England, Scotland or the Isle of Man. Once you go to that section of the book, you'll find the islands subdivided further into groups. For example, in Scotland you'll find islands in the Outer Hebrides or Shetland grouped together. In some cases, a further subdivision is needed. In the Inner Hebrides, for example, islands around Mull and Skye are grouped together. The islands are therefore joined together and subdivided in a similar way to documents in your computer folders. This will help you to explore and find out about islands that are close to each other and perhaps share some cultural characteristics. Use the map, contents and index to find the page number of specific islands you are looking to discover, before branching out to those located close by.

Acknowledgements

The word 'adventure' doesn't seem to do justice to the epic time I have had visiting and writing about these islands. It's been the biggest writing project I've undertaken so far and I am so grateful to my wife, Nicola, who has been dragged as far south as the Isles of Scilly and then north to the Faroe Islands. My two children, Toby and Willow, have been incredible, taking everything in their stride and never complaining – not even on the 60 hour ferry journey to Tórshavn. Thanks you guys!

Key to the icons

 Architecture & monuments

 Arts & crafts

 Flora & fauna

 Food & drink

 Geology

 Great views

 History & museums

 Local industry

 Popular culture

 Stand-out beaches

 Walks

 Watersports

 Wellbeing

TOP TEN ISLANDS FOR...

FOODIES

1. Some of Scotland's finest oysters are just one of the delicacies to be found on the **Isle of Skye** (page 54).
2. When it comes to fantastic peaty whisky, you'll be spoilt for choice on **Islay** (page 27).
3. Satisfy your sweet tooth by indulging in the chocolate made on the religious retreat of **Caldey Island** (page 223).
4. Add **Anglesey**'s fiery chilli chutneys to your meal and you'll be tackling hot fruit grown on the island (page 210).
5. The Outer Hebrides island of **Grimsay** is famous for delicious lobsters and other seafood from local seas (page 115).
6. Tuck in to some of the tastiest cheese imaginable on the Isle of **Arran**, channelling mustards and pickles (page 76).
7. Head to **Mull** and enjoy a freshly caught Tobermory trout, served with an egg on top (page 42).
8. Enjoy the food of a traditional Irish pub on **Arranmore** while listening to live music (page 250).
9. See the goats being milked on **Cape Clear Island** before enjoying the ice cream they help to produce (page 261).
10. Visit the chocoholic paradise of **Sark** for some of Caragh's sweet treats (page 314).

WILDLIFE

1. Bird life can be seen in abundance when you take a boat trip to the **Farne Islands** (page 162).
2. Birdwatchers from all over the world head to **Fair Isle** to see many migrating species (page 128).
3. You're likely to spot seals and dolphins on a pleasure cruise to **Puffin Island**, along with puffins of course (page 217)!
4. Journey to Vestmannabjørgini on **Streymoy** in the Faroe Islands and be amazed at the steep cliffs and guillemots soaring overhead (page 234).
5. Tigers and lions aren't the natural fauna of Ireland, but they are found on **Fota** – home to the rarity that is an island wildlife park (page 268).
6. Prepare to be dive-bombed by great skuas, known as bonxies by the locals, on walks around **Papa Westray** (page 98).
7. The sheep of **Foula** provide the distinctively coloured wool used in a range of clothing (page 134).
8. Keep your eyes peeled for the diminutive ponies that get their name from their native **Shetland** (page 136).
9. Deer, otters and badgers are all to be found on the wildlife-rich island of **Eriska** (page 23).
10. Brent geese are just one of the visitors to **Two Tree Island**, a former landfill site that is now a rich wildlife reserve (page 207).

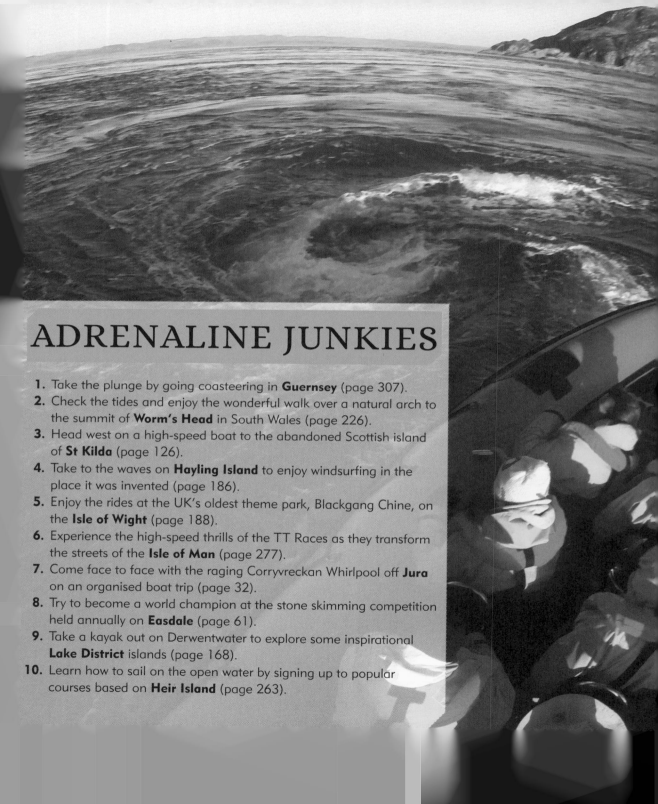

ADRENALINE JUNKIES

1. Take the plunge by going coasteering in **Guernsey** (page 307).
2. Check the tides and enjoy the wonderful walk over a natural arch to the summit of **Worm's Head** in South Wales (page 226).
3. Head west on a high-speed boat to the abandoned Scottish island of **St Kilda** (page 126).
4. Take to the waves on **Hayling Island** to enjoy windsurfing in the place it was invented (page 186).
5. Enjoy the rides at the UK's oldest theme park, Blackgang Chine, on the **Isle of Wight** (page 188).
6. Experience the high-speed thrills of the TT Races as they transform the streets of the **Isle of Man** (page 277).
7. Come face to face with the raging Corryvreckan Whirlpool off **Jura** on an organised boat trip (page 32).
8. Try to become a world champion at the stone skimming competition held annually on **Easdale** (page 61).
9. Take a kayak out on Derwentwater to explore some inspirational **Lake District** islands (page 168).
10. Learn how to sail on the open water by signing up to popular courses based on **Heir Island** (page 263).

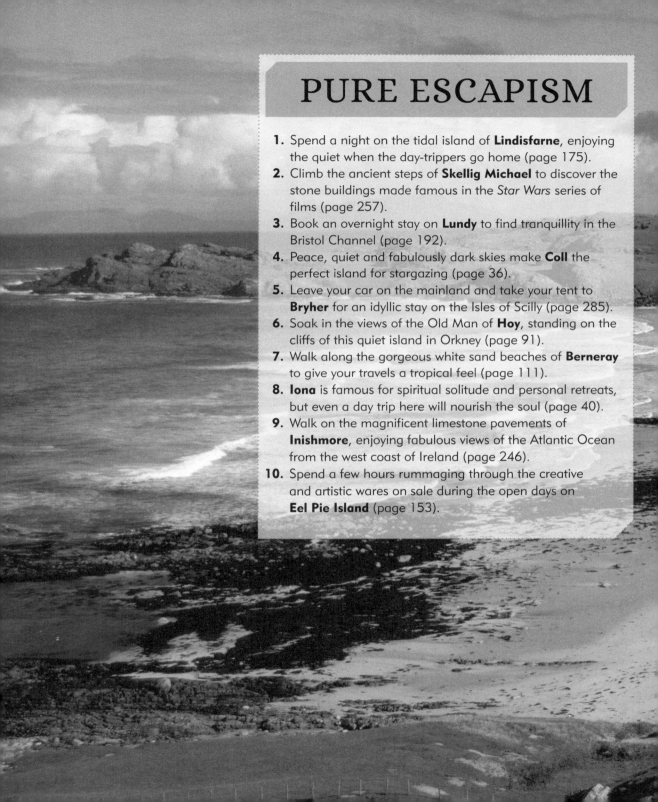

PURE ESCAPISM

1. Spend a night on the tidal island of **Lindisfarne**, enjoying the quiet when the day-trippers go home (page 175).
2. Climb the ancient steps of **Skellig Michael** to discover the stone buildings made famous in the *Star Wars* series of films (page 257).
3. Book an overnight stay on **Lundy** to find tranquillity in the Bristol Channel (page 192).
4. Peace, quiet and fabulously dark skies make **Coll** the perfect island for stargazing (page 36).
5. Leave your car on the mainland and take your tent to **Bryher** for an idyllic stay on the Isles of Scilly (page 285).
6. Soak in the views of the Old Man of **Hoy**, standing on the cliffs of this quiet island in Orkney (page 91).
7. Walk along the gorgeous white sand beaches of **Berneray** to give your travels a tropical feel (page 111).
8. **Iona** is famous for spiritual solitude and personal retreats, but even a day trip here will nourish the soul (page 40).
9. Walk on the magnificent limestone pavements of **Inishmore**, enjoying fabulous views of the Atlantic Ocean from the west coast of Ireland (page 246).
10. Spend a few hours rummaging through the creative and artistic wares on sale during the open days on **Eel Pie Island** (page 153).

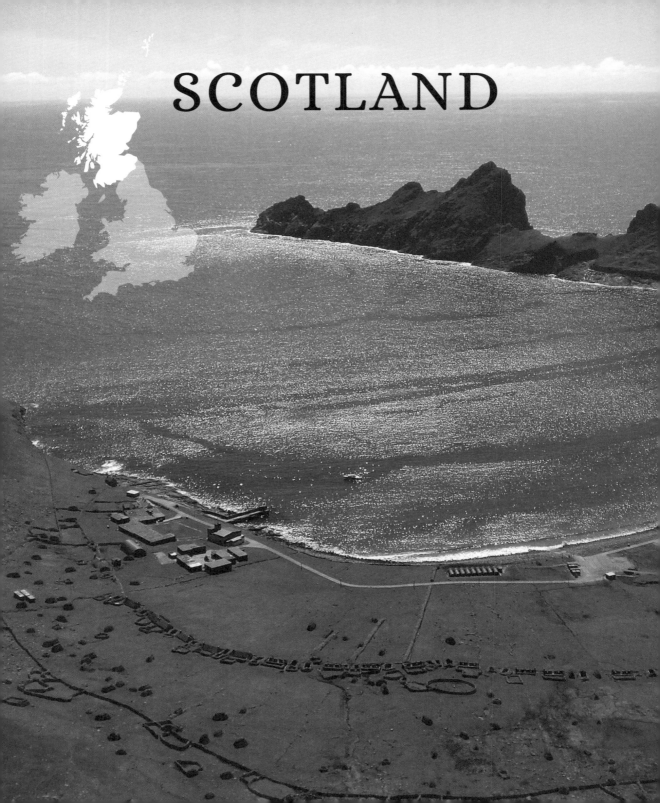

SCOTLAND

Nearly half the chapters of this book are Scottish, a reflection of how many islands make up this amazing country and how important they are to its culture and economy. Visits to the 'Highlands and Islands' of Scotland are hugely popular, and if you have the time to explore them in depth it will mean studying ferry timetables as you hop from one idyllic location to another. If there is a downside to discovering the wealth of Scottish islands, it's simply that it is tough to know where to start. Should you stick close to the mainland by investigating the Inner Hebrides, Small Isles and islands of the Clyde? They are certainly popular and within easy reach. Or should you push the boat out, as it were, and venture further afield to explore the Western Isles or the wilds of St Kilda? Journeys to the far north – on overnight ferries to Shetland and Orkney from Aberdeen – are perhaps the most extreme version of Scottish island hopping and your reward will be an introduction to friendly communities, stunning landforms and incredible historical ruins.

Wherever you head, you're in for a treat. You'll become familiar with stunning views, fall in love with the accents of the locals and revel in the amazing food and drink on offer. Freshly caught fish is available on many of the islands, and for a tipple of world-famous whisky be sure to hit the islands of Islay, Skye and Orkney. When you visit the gorgeous Scottish islands you'll become enchanted, and so a return visit is inevitable.

DON'T MISS

- Exploring the abandoned island of St Kilda on an unforgettable day trip across the sea
- Travelling back in time by visiting the archaeological wonders of Orkney
- Posing for photographs next to the charming coloured houses of Tobermory harbour on Mull
- Sampling the wide range of peaty whisky distilled on Islay
- Walking on the beautiful beaches of Berneray and looking out for otters

◄ *The smooth amphitheatre of Village Bay on Hirta with its historic landscape.*

The idyllic Shoe Bay at sunset.

EILEAN SHONA

Scotland's Neverland

The privately owned Eilean Shona is one of 17 tidal islands in Scotland and it has a stunning setting on the west coast. To gain access you'll need to holiday at one of the seven self-catering cottages on this small piece of land that sits at the entrance to Loch Moidart. Once on Eilean Shona, it is best to stay for the duration of your trip and take advantage of the wonderful isolation found here. As well as a handful of folk on holiday, you'll be sharing the island with red squirrels, pine martens, deer and otter. The island is car-free, meaning you can indulge in wilderness activities that get back to nature. Paddling in the sea, crabbing, kayaking or cooking meals on campfires is the stuff of dreams but very much the reality on Eilean Shona. No wonder this idyllic Scottish island retreat has provided inspiration for a literary great. Eilean Shona was a summer haunt for JM Barrie in the 1920s, along with some of his family and friends. While based on the island, he worked on the screenplay for the 1924 silent film version of his classic children's book, *Peter Pan*.

LOCATION: 56.7968°N 5.8583°W

GRID REFERENCE: NM645739

POPULATION: 4

SIZE: 5.3km²

GETTING THERE: A short causeway allows access to the island at low tide for those staying in the cottages and at other times the trip involves a short boat ride.

WHERE TO STAY: A range of self-catering accommodation is available on the island (**T:** 01967 431249, **W:** www.eileanshona.com).

Why I Love...
Eilean Shona

'Eilean Shona, the enchanted isle where all the senses tingle as your ears retune themselves from the ambient noise of cars and planes to birdsong and rustling leaves. Where your eyes adjust to the dark nights and the stars not only shine bright in the sky but are reflected in the sump oil blackness of the still loch. Where the summer days are without an end and winter nights fill you with wonder.'

Vanessa Branson,
entrepreneur and
arts patron

ERISKA

Wildlife on a Viking Island

Eriska's name is wrapped up in Viking history. When the Norsemen swept through west Scotland in the 10th century, they were led by, among others, Erik the Red and it's after him the island is named.

Eriska is a small, flat tidal island dominated by the luxury hotel that sits on it. The hugely impressive house was built in 1884 in traditional baronial style, and designed by architects who had worked on features at Edinburgh Castle. While much of the original design remains, the house now accommodates guests in what has become one of Scotland's great retreats.

Expect to have one or two wildlife encounters during your visit here. A wander around the wooded island may reveal a roe deer, and otters are often spotted on the west of the island from Rowan Tree Point. Look out for the life-size bronze sculpture of

an otter on a rock, known as the Guardian of Eriska. There are also several badger setts on the island.

LOCATION: 56.5311°N 5.4131°W

GRID REFERENCE: NM902429

POPULATION: 0

SIZE: 1.5km²

GETTING THERE: Access is via a causeway close to the A828, north of Oban.

WHERE TO STAY: The Isle of Eriska Hotel, Benderloch, PA37 1SD, **T:** 01631 720371, **W:** www.eriska-hotel.co.uk

WHERE TO EAT: Food is available at the hotel.

The Isle of Eriska Hotel and Spa.

Looking south-west from the hotel.

COLONSAY

LOCATION: 56.0651°N 6.2076°W	
GRID REFERENCE: NR381937	
POPULATION: 124	
SIZE: 40.7km²	

Bag a MacPhie!

You'll probably have heard of people trying to tick off the Munros – the list of Scotland's highest mountains – but may be less familiar with the idea of MacPhie bagging. The Isle of Colonsay's must-do list of peaks – known as the MacPhies – is similar to the Munros but a lot smaller, not nearly as strenuous and far less time consuming. There are 22 smaller peaks on the official list, with each of the qualifying summits rising over 300ft (92m) above sea level. Some have completed all the MacPhies in one lengthy walk, making it an ambitious way to spend a day going up and down in Colonsay.

Beach Time

Venture to Colonsay and one thing will remain with you forever – you'll be telling your friends about the incredible beaches for years to come. With clear waters and beautiful sandy stretches, you could be forgiven for thinking you've landed on a tropical island rather than an island in the Inner Hebrides. Of course, the weather will most likely extinguish any dreams of a Caribbean paradise, but if you catch Scotland's clear skies and a few hours of sunshine there are few places that can match the appeal of Balnahard Beach and Kiloran Bay in the north of this lovely island.

GETTING THERE: Ferries arrive at Colonsay from Oban (2hr 20min) and Islay (1hr 10min). See www.calmac.co.uk for more details.

WHERE TO STAY: The Colonsay Hotel, Isle of Colonsay, PA61 7YP, **T:** 01951 200316, **W:** www.colonsayholidays.co.uk. Island Lodges, Holmfield House, Kilchattan, Isle of Colonsay, PA61 7YR, **T:** 01951 200320, **W:** www.colonsay.eu.

WHERE TO EAT: The Colonsay Pantry, Scalasaig, Isle of Colonsay, PA61 7YW, **T:** 01951 200325, **W:** www.thecolonsaypantry.co.uk. Colonsay Pub, Isle of Colonsay, PA61 7YP, **T:** 01951 200316, **W:** www.colonsayholidays.co.uk.

Experience the beautiful beaches of Colonsay.

A TASTE OF HONEY

A taste of Colonsay's wildflower honey, made by the native black bees around the island, will leave you buzzing. The wildflower sources contributing to this rare honey include heathers and thyme from the machair.

Colonsay Book Festival

A literary lock-in like no other, this is one of the most remote book festivals in the world, creating a homely, cosy atmosphere few can match. There has always been a passion for a good book on the island and by 2012, the Colonsay Book Festival was up and running. The annual two-day event, held in the island's village hall, brings together writers and bibliophiles to share their stories and experiences.

DANNA

A Truly Scenic Area

Right at the end of the Tayvallich Peninsula near the charming town of Tayvallich, a stone causeway makes the link to Danna. It's a bit of a trek to find it, with the road winding 20km (12 miles) or so down a single-track road. Danna is a tiny island with a small population to match, but like the Knapdale area in general, it has a big reputation for wildlife and nature. The island is part of the Ulva, Danna and the MacCormaig Isles Site of Special Scientific Interest and is also in the Knapdale Scenic Area. Most of this low-lying island is given over to pastoral farming, with a small area of woodland breaking up the fields. The island is not short of good views across Loch Sween or towards other islands over the Sound of Jura.

LOCATION: 55.94°N 5.69°W

GRID REFERENCE: NR695785

POPULATION: 1

SIZE: 3.2km²

GETTING THERE: Danna is connected to the Tayvallich Peninsula and accessible via a causeway. Check the tides, as the causeway has been known to flood.

WHERE TO STAY: Kilmartin Hotel, Kilmartin, Lochgilphead, PA31 8RN, **T:** 01546 510250, **W:** www.kilmartin-hotel.com. The Horseshoe Inn, Kilmichael Glassary, Lochgilphead, PA31 8QA, **T:** 01546 606369, **W:** www.horseshoeinn.biz.

By the time this youngster tastes his first Islay dram, the whisky in these barrels will be well matured.

Loch Sween and the island of Danna.

ISLAY

LOCATION: 55.7572°N 6.2862°W

GRID REFERENCE: NR311598

POPULATION: 3,228

SIZE: 619km²

Welcome to the Whisky Island!

Although Islay is home to just over 3,000 people, the reputation for distilling on the island spreads right the way around the globe. Mention Islay to discerning drinkers from Japan to Johannesburg and they'll tell you the island is synonymous with whisky. This is one of Scotland's key whisky regions and has its name protected by law, so only the distilleries based here can claim to produce an Islay single malt. And there is no shortage of distilleries on Islay for you to explore, with no fewer than nine shipping their prized spirit around the world as Scotland's most popular export. Even if you spend a week on Islay on a whisky-based holiday, you won't run short of interesting, informative tours to take.

GETTING THERE: Ferries to Islay leave the mainland from Kennacraig, and arrive at either Port Askaig or Port Ellen. Ferries also connect Islay with Jura and Colonsay. Visit www.calmac.co.uk for more information. Islay Airport (www.hial.co.uk/islay-airport) has regular connections with Edinburgh and Glasgow.

WHERE TO STAY: Islay House, Bridgend, PA44 7PA, **T:** 01496 810287, **W:** www.islayhouse.co.uk. Port Charlotte Hotel, Port Charlotte, PA48 7TU, **T:** 01496 850360, **W:** www.portcharlottehotel.co.uk.

WHERE TO EAT: The Harbour Inn, Bowmore, PA43 7JR, **T:** 01496 810330, **W:** www.bowmore.com/harbour-inn. SeaSalt Bistro, 57 Frederick Crescent, Port Ellen, PA42 7BB, **T:** 01496 300300, **W:** www.seasalt-bistro.co.uk.

TASTE TEST...

Of all the Scottish whisky regions, Islay is far and away my favourite. And up there with the best of them is the 12-year-old Bowmore. As soon as the lid comes off and it hits the glass, an air of peaty smoke can be sensed. Pick up traces of honey and enjoy the long finish it provides, ideal for winter nights by the fire.

Those familiar with their whisky will be able to pick out an Islay dram without any problem at all. The Islay taste is highly distinctive and considerably different from those of the other whisky regions in Scotland, and is famous for having a very strong, peaty and smoky flavour, particularly the whiskies produced in the south of the island at Ardbeg, Laphroaig and Lagavulin. The taste becomes slightly lighter as you head north to Bowmore, Bruichladdich, Caol Ila, Ardnahoe and Bunnahabhain. Tours offer glances into the nuances that make each of the distilleries and their whiskies unique. They do, of course, offer tasting sessions and the opportunity for you to buy a bottle or two. My time on Islay was greeted with a spell of harsh weather. Sampling the island's whisky next to a log fire was the perfect antidote.

An American Monument

Perched on the 131m (430ft)-high cliffs of the Oa Peninsula, the huge monument to two shipping disasters looks like a lighthouse from a distance. As you get closer, you see it is made out of rock and stands here to commemorate the loss of two ships carrying US troops in 1918. The *Tuscania* was making its way from Nova Scotia to France when it was torpedoed by a German U-boat, 11km (7 miles) from this spot. Of 2,000 soldiers and 300 crew, 230 of them lost their lives. Eight months after this tragedy, in October 1918, HMS *Otranto* collided with HMS *Kashmir* during a heavy storm off the island, leading to the loss of 400 lives.

Fine Sand

Reserve some time on Islay for a trip to the coast. Take off your shoes and socks for a walk on Machir Beach, in the north-west of the island. This secret sweeping bay contains one of the finest sandy beaches in the country and is an experience not to be forgotten.

The beaches on Islay provide a haven for all ages to play and relax, with long, sandy beaches and rocks combining to make an atmospheric setting in all weathers.

Why I Love...
Islay

'Islay has a mysterious pull. It may be the rich heritage and culture; the fascinating history with the beautiful colours of the landscapes, from the green hills to the white sandy beaches to the sea and the clean air. Peace and quiet with friendly locals and some of the world's best single malt whiskies.'

David Turner,
Bowmore Distillery
Manager

ISLE OF GIGHA

LOCATION: 55.6844°N 5.7447°W

GRID REFERENCE: NR647498

POPULATION: 110

SIZE: 14km²

An Independent Community

The sense of community on Gigha is incredible and there is a real pride in what has been achieved here. With an emphasis on sustainability, the population is on the rise once more after a steady fall during the 20th century. A turning point in the island's history came in 2002 when the local population organised a buyout with the help of grants and loans. The island community now owns Gigha through a specially developed Trust, having bought it from private landlords. The sale went through on 15 March – a day now light-heartedly seen as the island's 'Independence Day'.

Fish You Were Here?

No trip to Gigha is complete without sampling the local delicacy, smoked halibut (www.gighahalibut.co.uk), harvested from tanks fed by the surrounding Atlantic Ocean. Established in 2006, this island business is a relatively recent one but it has quickly become a classic. The tasty and sustainably sourced fish is cured for a day before being traditionally smoked using oak chips from Islay whisky barrels. Freshness combines with peaty whisky smoke to give Gigha halibut a unique taste – one that is vacuum packed and distributed across Europe and the United States.

Garden Roam

Gigha benefits from a warm microclimate, a meteorological factor that drove Colonel Sir James Horlick to establish Achamore Gardens on the island in 1944. As unusual as it is peaceful, the 54-acre site has many species from all over the planet. The woodland walks are especially memorable, and you can wander among rhododendrons, azaleas, camellias and New Zealand tree ferns. It's an exotic oasis in the middle of a remote Scottish island, the location making the gardens even more remarkable. The garden also provides a stunning viewpoint, where you can gaze longingly over the sea and begin dreaming up a trip to Islay and Jura.

GETTING THERE: The ferry for Gigha leaves from the Kintyre peninsula at Tayinloan and takes 20 minutes (www.calmac.co.uk).

WHERE TO STAY: Gigha Hotel, Isle of Gigha, Argyll, PA41 7AA, **T:** 01583 505254, **W:** www.gighahotel.com. Springbank Bed and Breakfast, Isle of Gigha, Argyll, PA41 7AD, **T:** 01583 505047.

WHERE TO EAT: The Boathouse, Isle of Gigha, Argyll, PA41 7AG, **T:** 01583 505123, **W:** www. boathouseongigha.com. Gigha Hotel, Isle of Gigha, Argyll, PA41 7AA, **T:** 01583 505254, **W:** www.gighahotel.com.

The CalMac ferry runs services to and from the island.

Why I Love... Gigha

'It is an idyllic, peaceful wee island, surrounded by pristine waters, making it the perfect place to bring up our halibut. It's only a 20-minute ferry ride from the mainland but in its landscape is the secret to complete tranquillity.'

Amanda Anderson,
Sales and Marketing Manager,
Gigha Halibut

JURA

LOCATION: 55.9550°N 5.8638°W

GRID REFERENCE: NR589803

POPULATION: 196

SIZE: 367km²

In a Whirl

The waters just to the north of Jura are some of the most hazardous in the British Isles and the famous Corryvreckan Whirlpool is at the heart of the danger. This is the third biggest whirlpool in the world and it's a formidable sight – one you won't want to get up close and personal with. It occurs here thanks to water travelling through a narrowing channel called the Sound of Jura and it is squeezed out the other end in a mile-wide gap – the Gulf of Corryvreckan. The surging water encounters some extreme features beneath the surface – not least a 219m (720ft)-deep hole and a 130m (427ft)-tall pinnacle. All this combines to create fast currents and the circular whirlpool, which is an awesome sight. It's possible to get as close as is safely viable on a RIB trip (www.juraboattours.co.uk from Jura and www.seafari.co.uk from the mainland). You'll be able to experience the differences in water level and see the currents raging in a terrifying dance.

GETTING THERE: A high speed RIB connects Jura to the mainland during the summer, leaving from Tayvallich and arriving at Craighouse. To reach the island from Islay, a small car ferry leaves Port Askaig and completes the ten-minute journey about 14 times a day.

WHERE TO STAY: Jura Hotel, Craighouse, Jura, PA60 7XU, **T:** 01496 820243, **W:** www.jurahotel.co.uk. Feolin Farmhouse Holiday Cottage, Craighouse, Jura, PA60 7XG, **T:** 01285 720247. Barnhill, Jura, PA60 7XW, **T:** 01786 850 274, **W:** www.escapetojura.com/Barnhill.

WHERE TO EAT: The Antlers Bistro, Craighouse, Jura, PA60 7XP, **T:** 01496 820123. Jura Hotel, Craighouse, Jura, PA60 7XU, **T:** 01496 820243, **W:** www.jurahotel.co.uk

A WEE DRAM

Set aside some time to enjoy a visit to Jura Distillery and sample a taste of the whisky that has made Jura a household name around the world. Many of the islanders took part in a TV ad for the whisky in late 2020.

▲ Corryvreckan Whirlpool.
▶ A sunny day on the peat-covered moorlands.

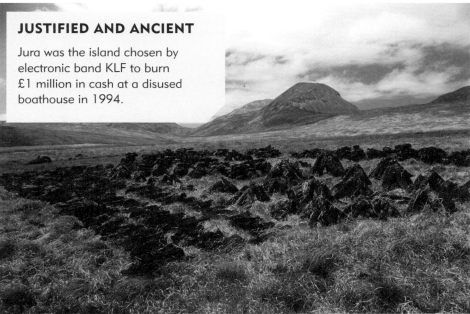

JUSTIFIED AND ANCIENT

Jura was the island chosen by electronic band KLF to burn £1 million in cash at a disused boathouse in 1994.

Where the Clocks Strike 13...

In the late 1940s George Orwell wanted to get away from it all to write what would be his final novel. Somewhere that was difficult to reach, somewhere to absorb the isolation, somewhere to be inspired by nature – Jura ticked all the boxes and the house he chose, Barnhill, was a 6.5km (4 mile) hike up a dirt track from the nearest road. There, without electricity, he penned what would become a dystopian masterpiece – *Nineteen Eighty-Four*. But the novel that brought us the TV programmes *Room 101* and *Big Brother*, as well as myriad cultural and language references that are still in use today, almost wasn't finished, after a near-fatal incident at Corryvreckan Whirlpool. Out on a trip with his son, Orwell and his boat were sucked into the whirlpool and the pair had to swim to a nearby cave. It was hours later when a fisherman rescued them. The cottage where Orwell stayed is now let out to holidaymakers and is largely in the same state as it was when the novel was written, save for an electricity generator. The Orwell Society puts on trips to the cottage every two years or so, and has even taken the author's son back to the spot. On this part of the island you're unlikely to come across any other people, but you can expect to see plenty of deer. While fewer than 200 residents live on Jura, there are over 5,500 deer – roughly 28 deer for every person.

Why I Love...
Jura

'I was brought up on the Isle of Jura and after 36 years in the military I was drawn back to its beauty. The place has a magnetism and there is an abundance of wildlife. I love seeing the minke whales, dolphins, red deer and porpoise on my sea tours.'

Robert Henry,
owner of Jura Boat Tours

ORONSAY

LOCATION: 56.0222°N 6.2527°W

GRID REFERENCE: NR350891

POPULATION: 8

SIZE: 6.4km²

Tidal Tranquillity

Home to just a handful of people, this tidal island on the southern tip of Colonsay can be accessed at low tide and provides perhaps the most isolated experience in the Inner Hebrides. The occasional place to stay and eat on next-door Colonsay makes that island look like Las Vegas in comparison. But the appeal of remote Oronsay is exactly that – you'll be alone with the seals, choughs, corncrakes and bees, enjoying a view of the Paps of Jura in the distance.

GETTING THERE: From Colonsay, you are able to walk across to Oronsay at low tide.

WHERE TO STAY: The Colonsay Hotel, Isle of Colonsay, PA61 7YP, **T:** 01951 200316, **W:** www.colonsayholidays.co.uk. Island Lodges, Holmfield House, Kilchattan, Isle of Colonsay, PA61 7YR, **T:** 01951 200320, **W:** www.colonsay.eu.

▼ *Cloud over the island of Oronsay, near Fiskavaig.*

Why I Love...
Coll

'There are no streetlights, not even in the village of Arinagour, you can stay cosy in bed or step out onto the doorstep and still enjoy the Milky Way overhead. As the winter days are shorter you've got plenty of time to enjoy our Dark Sky, and the milder winter temperatures experienced by the island may surprise you if you've just come from the frosty mainland.'

Alison Jones,
Assistant Manager,
Coll Bunkhouses

COLL

The Sky at Night

This is the place to come for any budding astronomers wanting to get an unobstructed view of the night sky. Coll was awarded Dark Sky status in 2013 – the second place in Scotland to achieve this – in recognition of the spectacle overhead when the sun has set. The designation puts Coll on the same astronomy footing as Death Valley in the United States. There are no streetlights on Coll and other sources of light pollution are minimal, making this an ideal place to bring binoculars and telescopes – or simply to lie down and take it all in with the naked eye. This is also a place to keep watch for Northern Lights activity. Strong displays – and a number of apps and websites let you know when these are on the way – are often visible here on Coll. Of course, the biggest obstacles are the clouds and they block the night sky all too often. But if there's a magic combination of no cloud, no moon and rampant Northern Lights activity, you're in for an unforgettable treat. Other night-sky features clearly seen from here include the Orion Nebula.

During the daytime, Coll is a haven for wildlife. There's an RSPB reserve on the west coast with corncrakes, but as usual you're more likely to hear than see them. Keep an eye open for all kinds of wildflowers and for basking sharks off the coast.

LOCATION: 56.6338°N 6.5564°W

GRID REFERENCE: NM207584

POPULATION: 195

SIZE: 76.9km²

GETTING THERE: From the mainland, the ferry leaves from Oban (2hr 30min). If you are taking a car, you'll need to make a reservation. See www.calmac.co.uk for more details. Coll has an airport, with frequent flights to Oban and Tiree.

WHERE TO STAY: Coll Bunkhouse, Arinagour, Isle of Coll, PA78 6SY, **T:** 01879 230217, **W:** www.collbunkhouse.com. Coll Hotel, Arinagour, Isle of Coll, PA78 6SZ, **T:** 01879 230334, **W:** www.collhotel.com.

WHERE TO EAT: The Island Café, First Port of Coll, Shore Street, Arinagour, Isle of Coll, PA78 6SY, **T:** 01879 230262, **W:** www.theislandcafe.business.site.

Coll Bunkhouse.

ERRAID

LOCATION: 56.2943°N 6.3686°W

GRID REFERENCE: NM298199

POPULATION: 6

SIZE: 1.8km²

Kidnapped!

The tiny island of Erraid is found off the south-western tip of Mull and is home to a community that is part of the Findhorn Foundation. Those wanting to get away from it all for a meditative retreat can plan to come and spend the week here. Transport to the island is by a small boat, which must be arranged in advance with those living here. In rough weather, a walking route is available when the tide is out.

A young Robert Louis Stevenson visited the island while his father, Thomas, was in the region building lighthouses. Erraid went on to appear in his novel *Kidnapped*, with the character of David Balfour being marooned here after a shipwreck.

Why I Love... Erraid

'I love Erraid because of its raw, wild beauty. The fact you can walk onto the island, yet there are no roads or cars. The chance to live in a community with a close connection to nature, combined with living closely with people from many different countries. The island is made of granite, shaping the land in a dramatic way in places.'

Arran Skinner,
member of the Erraid Community and custodian of the island

GETTING THERE: Travel for those visiting the island community on Erraid needs to be arranged on an individual basis. See www.erraid.com for more details.

WHERE TO STAY: Week-long retreats are available with the Findhorn Foundation on Erraid, running Saturday to Saturday.

WHERE TO EAT: Those staying for a week on Erraid have their meals provided.

GOMETRA

LOCATION: 56.4904°N 6.2888°W

GRID REFERENCE: NM361414

POPULATION: 2

SIZE: 4.1km²

GETTING THERE: A ferry service operates between Mull and Ulva and on the far side of Ulva a bridge takes you to Gometra.

WHERE TO STAY: Search Gometra on www.airbnb.com and you'll find basic bothies available, with simple decoration and outside toilets.

Glorious Gometra

Getting to Gometra is an Indiana Jones-style adventure in itself. The journey is difficult and you need to plan ahead, beginning with the trip to Mull from the mainland. From there you'll get transport on Mull to the ferry for Ulva, then complete a walk of up to four hours to the other side of Ulva. Here you'll find a bridge taking you to Gometra.

There are plenty of clues to this tiny island's busier life in centuries past. Today, sheep farming is the mainstay for the small community that is still here. A shop stocks basic food supplies for people visiting in the summer months. On a clear day, the views from Gometra are sublime. You can see from South Uist in the Outer Hebrides right down to Islay and Jura.

Why I Love... Gometra

'I loved Gometra from the first moment I came, a quarter of a century ago. Gometra House was deserted and collapsing, its lawns covered in thistles and stags, but it was of staggering beauty. I felt I had returned home, and decided to live here with my child.'

Roc Sandford,
proud Ghomesdreach

IONA

Is This an Abbey I See Before Me?

Around 130,000 visitors take the passenger ferry to Iona every year, drawn in by the island's reputation as a spiritual destination and peaceful place of retreat. It is an enchanting island to visit and many sailing across the water to experience the unique community are returning visitors who are only too pleased to come back. Yes, there are stunning views and an impressive range of wildlife to be enjoyed on Iona, but the principal purpose of many tourists is to learn about the island's religious background and role as the 'Cradle of Christianity' in Scotland. Columba arrived here in 563 with 12 companions and founded a monastery, introducing Iona to Christianity. The monastery survived Viking raids and remained in place until around 1200, when the Benedictine abbey was built. The modern abbey you see today was rebuilt in the 20th century when Rev. George MacLeod founded the Iona Community and set about restoring several other structures on the island that lay in ruin.

As well as exploring the abbey, a visit to Iona should take in some of the crosses that have stood on the island for centuries. St Martin's Cross overlooks the roadside outside the abbey, in the same place it has stood since the 8th century. A replica of St John's Cross can be found in the abbey's entrance, with the original being in the adjacent Infirmary Museum. Unsurprisingly, given its religious status, Iona has been a popular place to bury kings down the centuries – former leaders of Ireland, France and Norway are said to be buried in the abbey grounds. Scotland, of course, has the highest number of kings believed to have chosen Iona as a final resting place. Some suggest as many as 48 Scottish kings are laid to rest here, including the protagonist of one of Shakespeare's most famous plays – *Macbeth*.

LOCATION: 56.3342°N 6.4104°W

GRID REFERENCE: NM275245

POPULATION: 177

SIZE: 8.8km²

GETTING THERE: After arriving on Mull, drive to Fionnphort for the ten-minute crossing to Iona. You don't need to book, simply turn up. Most vehicles aren't allowed across and those that are need a permit. For more details visit www.calmac.co.uk.

WHERE TO STAY: Argyll Hotel, Iona, PA76 6SJ, **T:** 01681 700334, **W:** www.argyllhoteliona.co.uk. St Columba Hotel, Iona, PA76 6SL, **T:** 01681 700304, **W:** www.stcolumba-hotel.co.uk.

WHERE TO EAT: Martyr's Bay Restaurant, Iona, PA76 6SJ, **T:** 01681 700382, **W:** www.martyrsbay.co.uk. Iona Heritage Centre Garden Café, Iona, PA76 6SJ, **T:** 01681 700576, **W:** www.ionaheritage.co.uk.

ISLE OF MULL

LOCATION:	56.4489°N 5.9122°W
GRID REFERENCE:	NM590354
POPULATION:	2,990
SIZE:	875.3km²

Wouldn't You Like to Go?

One of the most popular islands among tourists to Scotland, Mull is easily accessible from the mainland at Oban and encompasses all the popular features of the Scottish isles – beaches, castles, towns, mountains, wildlife, lovely food and remote landscapes are all in plentiful supply. There's a great sense of community here, too. We arrived in Tobermory with the fuel gauge at rock bottom and the petrol station having closed ten minutes earlier – but people were keen to help and the owners opened up again to fill us up!

Thousands of children have grown up asking the question 'What's the story in Balamory?' Only four series of the children's TV programme *Balamory*, which was filmed largely in the village of Tobermory, were made, between 2002 and 2005, but they were produced at an alarming rate; some 254 episodes of the island-based show were completed and are still aired today. I spoke to people in the tourist information office who seemed somewhat bewildered by the long-lasting appeal of the show. But as a parent of kids who grew up singing songs with PC Plum, I get why young fans still flock to Tobermory to take selfies outside the multi-coloured waterfront 'homes' of Josie Jump, Spencer and Miss Hoolie!

A Taste of Mull

Unsurprisingly, fish features on the menu in many homes and restaurants on Mull. The local speciality is smoked trout, which the Tobermory Fish Company (www.tobermoryfish.co.uk) sells locally and distributes throughout the country. Tobermory Trout, which featured in an episode of *All Creatures Great and Small*, is a tasty dish caught in the clear waters of the Inner Hebrides. The Isle of Mull has one whisky distillery, also based in Tobermory (www.tobermorydistillery.com). It produces two very different single malts, allowing you to choose between the non-peated Tobermory and a bottle of the heavily peated Ledaig.

Taste Test

A slice of Tobermory's famous smoked trout makes a wonderful breakfast snack. The Tobermory Fish Company recommends placing the trout on sourdough toast, covering it with rocket and adding a poached egg on top. It's a fresh, smoky breakfast that is as much a treat at home as it is on Mull.

GETTING THERE: The most popular way to reach Mull is by the ferry, which leaves Oban and arrives in Craignure 46 minutes later. Bookings are recommended for this route, but you can simply turn up for the sailing between Lochaline and Fishnish and also the ferry linking Kilchoan with Tobermory. See www.calmac.co.uk for more details. Flights to Mull are available from Glasgow.

WHERE TO STAY: The Tobermory Hotel, Main Street, Tobermory, Isle of Mull, PA75 6NT, **T:** 01688 302091, **W:** www.thetobermoryhotel.com. Glengorm Castle, Tobermory, Isle of Mull, PA75 6QE, **T:** 01688 302321, **W:** www.glengormcastle.co.uk.

WHERE TO EAT: Ninth Wave Restaurant, Bruach Mhor Fionnphort, Mull, PA66 6BL, **T:** 01681 700757, **W:** www.ninthwaverestaurant.co.uk. Café Fish, Main Street, Tobermory, Isle of Mull, PA75 6NU, **T:** 01681 301253, **W:** www.thecafefish.com.

▶ *Glengorm Castle sits high on a hill, enjoying great views out to sea.*

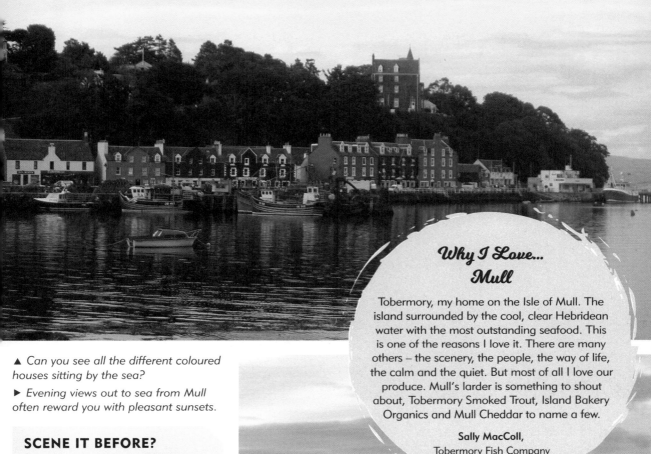

▲ *Can you see all the different coloured houses sitting by the sea?*

▶ *Evening views out to sea from Mull often reward you with pleasant sunsets.*

Why I Love... Mull

Tobermory, my home on the Isle of Mull. The island surrounded by the cool, clear Hebridean water with the most outstanding seafood. This is one of the reasons I love it. There are many others – the scenery, the people, the way of life, the calm and the quiet. But most of all I love our produce. Mull's larder is something to shout about, Tobermory Smoked Trout, Island Bakery Organics and Mull Cheddar to name a few.

Sally MacColl,
Tobermory Fish Company

SCENE IT BEFORE?

Apart from Balamory, Mull has had other moments on the screen:

- Several scenes in the 1971 thriller *When Eight Bells Toll*, starring Anthony Hopkins, were filmed on the island.
- *I Know Where I'm Going* explored many Scottish customs and was mainly filmed on the island.
- Catherine Zeta-Jones and Sean Connery filmed parts of the 1999 movie *Entrapment* in Duart Castle.

LISMORE

LOCATION: 56.5095°N 5.5119°W

GRID REFERENCE: NM840408

POPULATION: 192

SIZE: 23.5km²

GETTING THERE: The ferry to Lismore takes an hour from Oban. For more information get in touch with Calmac. **T:** 01457 650397, **W:** www.calmac. co.uk. A shorter foot passenger ferry operates from Port Appin.

WHERE TO STAY: The Bunkhouse, Baleveolan Croft, Lismore, PA34 5UG, **T:** 07720 975433.

WHERE TO EAT: Isle of Lismore Café, Port Acharrin, Lismore, PA34 5UL, **T:** 01631 760020, **W:** www.lismoregaelicheritagecentre. org/the-cafe.

Great Garden

If you take your car to Lismore, make sure you have enough fuel because there isn't a filling station on the island. Many people agree the best way to explore the island is on two wheels, and you can take bicycles on the ferry without charge. You can also hire bikes on the island from Kara and Mark (call 07376 425996). The island has plenty of paths and tracks crossing it, making it easy to explore on foot as well. Whether you choose to explore Lismore on two legs or with pedal power, you'll soon discover why it got its name. In Gaelic, Lismore means 'Great Garden', which hints at its reputation for lush wildflower landscapes. Over 300 species of flowering plants grow wild on the island and around 130 species of bird regularly visit.

History buffs will also get a lot out of a visit to Lismore. Like many islands in the region, this was an important destination for pilgrims. It was once the seat of the bishops of Argyll and a church has been based here since the 13th century. Look out for the ruined Viking fort as well.

And on a clear day, the views from this small island are stunning. Sandwiched between the mainland and other islands, there are spectacular vistas of Ben Nevis, Glencoe and the mountains of Mull.

◄ *Looking east from the island of Lismore across the waters of Loch Linnhe.*

► *Fingal's Cave.*

STAFFA

LOCATION: 56.4354°N 6.3443°W

GRID REFERENCE: NM323355

POPULATION: 0

SIZE: < 1km²

Must-See Trip to Fingal's Cave

The approach to Staffa, an isolated island of dramatic rocks and hexagonal basalt columns visible from the Isle of Iona, is as spectacular as it is bumpy. Formed as basaltic lava cooled over time, the rocks here are similar to those found in Iceland and at the Giant's Causeway in Northern Ireland. Rising sharply from the sea in dramatic fashion, Staffa's columns are a world-class natural formation and are most impressive at the much-loved Fingal's Cave. Depending on the sea conditions, boat trips can get you onto the island and allow time to explore the wonder of Fingal's Cave. The flat tops of the hexagonal columns sit just above the high-water mark and make for an ideal walkway. It's inspiring stuff. Take your camera, but no shot can really do justice to the enormity of the spiritual wonder you feel when in the cave entrance.

Nobody lives on Staffa today, but the island has been inhabited in the past. During the latter years of the 18th century, a single family on Staffa was surviving on a very basic diet but left because of winter storms.

GETTING THERE: Several boating companies organise trips that get you up close to Staffa and Fingal's Cave, including www.staffatours.com and www.seafari.co.uk.

WHERE TO STAY: Trips leave from several places, including Tobermory, Iona and Oban. Accommodation is available near all the points of departure.

Fingal's Cave in the Arts

There aren't many natural landforms in the UK that have had an overture written for them, but there is none more deserving than Fingal's Cave. Felix Mendelssohn visited the island in 1829 and was blown away by the experience, so much so he wrote the titular piece of music after being inspired by the echoing acoustics of the sea cave. Those having seen the James Bond-style adventure *When Eight Bells Toll* – starring Sir Anthony Hopkins – will recognise the famous opening to the cave in one of the film's thrilling scenes. Fingal's Cave has been painted countless times, including by JMW Turner, and has been the inspiration for creative writing by Jules Verne and William Wordsworth.

TIREE

LOCATION: 56.5082°N 6.8797°W

GRID REFERENCE: NL999458

POPULATION: 653

SIZE: 78.2km²

Tiree Five-0

There are good reasons why Tiree is known as the 'Hawaii of the North'. The long sandy beaches here enjoy more sunshine hours than many places in the UK and are battered by some terrific waves, making conditions ideal for surfing. There's fun to be had all year round on Tiree, but the eyes of the surfing world are on the island come October when it holds the Tiree Surf Classic, a week-long festival of wave-based sport and the world's longest standing professional surfing competition. Kitesurfing, paddleboarding and sea kayaking are other popular ways to have fun on the water, giving Tiree a formidable reputation for outdoor watersports.

GETTING THERE: The ferry from Oban calls at Coll before arriving at Tiree, and takes four hours. See www.calmac.co.uk for more details. Flights connect Tiree with several airports, including Glasgow, Birmingham and London Stansted.

WHERE TO STAY: Tiree Lodge Hotel, Gott Bay, Kirkapol, Isle of Tiree, PA77 6TW, **T:** 01879 220329, **W:** www.tireelodge.co.uk. Rockvale Guest House, Balephetrish, Isle of Tiree, PA77 6UY, **T:** 01879 220675, **W:** www.rockvaletiree.co.uk.

WHERE TO EAT: Beachcomber Craft Café, Crossapol, Isle of Tiree, PA77 6UP, **T:** 01879 220590.

ULVA

Ulva's Ghosts

A walk around the rugged, remote island of Ulva can be a fairly upsetting experience. The ruined remains of 16 small townships tell the history of the island, which once prospered thanks to the kelp industry and later suffered under the rapid clearances inflicted by infamous landlord Francis William Clark. The summer kelp industry saw tons of the seaweed collected, dried and burnt to produce fertiliser and other products. During this time the island was home to a thriving community of over 800 people, but Clark's purchase of the island in 1835 led to a rapid downturn. In the 1840s, his clearance policy, combined with the Highland Potato Famine, saw the number of people living on Ulva drop to little more than 100. Today, the island's ghostly feel is a reminder of how the policies of some landowners had a huge impact on ordinary families living on the Scottish islands. In perhaps the greatest postscript to the story, Ulva is now community-owned after a recent buyout.

LOCATION: 56.4770°N 6.2076°W

GRID REFERENCE: NM410396

POPULATION: 6

SIZE: 19.9km²

GETTING THERE: A ferry service operates from the Isle of Mull, taking foot passengers and bicycles across the narrow strait to Ulva.

WHERE TO STAY: Lip na Cloiche B&B, nr Ulva Ferry, Isle of Mull, PA73 6LU, **T:** 01688 500257, **W:** www.lipnacloiche.co.uk.

WHERE TO EAT: The Boathouse, Visitors Centre, Oskamull, Ulva, PA73 6LZ, **T:** 01688 500241, **W:** www.theboathouseulva.co.uk.

EILEAN DONAN

Famous Fort

One of the best-loved, most photographed views in Scotland, Eilean Donan is breathtaking because of its setting and beautifully constructed castle. Named after Bishop Donan – a 6th-century Irish saint – this stunning tidal island is a magnet for international tourists and a must-stop destination of any good tour of Scotland. A fort first appeared on the island in the 13th century, and various expansions and contractions of the defences took place down the centuries. The castle is thought to have been at its largest during the medieval period, when it occupied most of the island. However, the castle's involvement in the Jacobite risings of the 17th and 18th centuries proved destructive. In 1719, a three-day bombardment by three English frigates and the subsequent landing of soldiers overwhelmed Spanish supporters of the Jacobites who were holding the castle at the time. Any remains were blown away by the hundreds of barrels of gunpowder the Spaniards had in their possession. And it was in this ruinous state that the castle remained for most of the following two centuries.

It wasn't until Lt Colonel John Macrae-Gilstrap bought the island in 1911 that the castle's fortunes started to change. He set about on an ambitious rebuilding programme, working to surviving plans, which saw the castle restored to former glories by the summer of 1932.

Today, the island and castle are staples of the Scottish tourism industry and it's an excellent location to spend the afternoon. Whichever angle you view the bridge and castle from, it's worth posing for a photograph with them – they manage to look magnificent and incredibly atmospheric no matter what the weather.

LOCATION: 57.2740°N 5.5157°W

GRID REFERENCE: NG881258

POPULATION: 0

SIZE: <1km²

GETTING THERE: The island is located off the A87 as it heads towards the Kyle of Lochalsh. There is a **car** park on the mainland, with a footbridge over to the island.

WHERE TO STAY: The castle has a cottage and apartments for those wanting to stay within easy reach of the island's incredible setting (www. eileandonancastle.com).

WHERE TO EAT: The visitor centre has a well-stocked café.

Eilean Donan Castle is one of the most iconic scenes in Scotland.

SCENE IT BEFORE?

- The castle was famously the setting for the 1986 film *Highlander*.
- James Bond fans may recognise the castle from *The World is Not Enough* (1999), which starred Pierce Brosnan as the famous secret agent.
- Eilean Donan also featured in *The New Avengers* (1976) and *Loch Ness* (1999).

ISLE OF EWE

Love Island

Try saying 'Isle of Ewe' out loud and you'll soon find yourself declaring 'I Love You.' This sandstone island in the middle of Loch Ewe is privately owned, but paddling around it in a kayak or canoe is a popular activity for romantics. Even radio comedians The Goons used it as an 'I love you, too' gag in one of their 1950s episodes.

Ewe Loch is a beautiful place to explore and a journey around the shore of the Isle of Ewe delivers peace, tranquillity and stunning views. Among the quiet solitude, make time to lean in and whisper 'Isle of Ewe' to your loved one.

LOCATION: 57.8300°N 5.6100°W

GRID REFERENCE: NG855885

POPULATION: 7

SIZE: 3.1km²

GETTING THERE: Kayaks are available to paddle around the island. Visit www.gairlochkayakcentre.com or www.ewecanoe.co.uk for more information.

WHERE TO STAY: Gairloch Sands Hotel, Gairloch, IV21 2BL, **T:** 01445 712001. Shieldaig Lodge, Badachro, Gairloch, IV21 2AN, **T:** 01445 741333, **W:** www.shieldaiglodge.com.

EILEAN BÀN

Underneath the Bridge

If it is possible for an island to be a 'stepping stone' then Eilean Bàn surely fits the bill. The island was used to help span the gap between mainland Scotland and the Isle of Skye during the construction of the Skye Bridge (1992–95). This tiny island is now dominated by the roadway that passes overhead, saving both locals and tourists the hassle of boarding a ferry. The bridge proved controversial on opening because islanders were charged to use it, which led to protests and some locals refusing to pay the toll. The Scottish government scrapped the fee in 2004 and today it is free to cross the bridge.

Eilean Bàn was the final home of author Gavin Maxwell, whose book *Ring of Bright Water* (1960) centred on his house in the West Highlands, where he kept several wild otters as pets. It is also home to a distinctive lighthouse, built by the Stevenson brothers in 1857. Kyleakin Lighthouse ceased operation in 1993 when the Skye Bridge led to it being decommissioned. Today the island is owned by the Eilean Bàn Trust and cottages are available to book if you fancy a week beneath the bridge.

LOCATION: 57.2800°N 5.7400°W

GRID REFERENCE: NG746271

POPULATION: 0

SIZE: >1km²

GETTING THERE: Eilean Bàn lies to the west of the Kyle of Lochalsh, part way along the bridge to Skye. There is lay-by parking on the island before passing on to the main part of the bridge.

WHERE TO STAY: Holiday cottage accommodation is available on the island. Visit www.eileanban.org for more information.

Skye Bridge.

ISLE OF SCALPAY

An Island Retreat

Those lucky enough to be heading to the Isle of Scalpay for a short stay won't forget the peaceful isolation to be found just a few minutes across the water from Skye. Views of the Cuillin Mountains frame the scene and on the island itself you're more likely to see red deer and otters than humans – only four people call this place home. There are no roads, so you leave your car on Skye and let the hours and days slip away in one of the rare places in Britain where time stands still.

It's important not to get your Isle of Scalpays mixed up, though; this privately-owned island just off the Isle of Skye in the Inner Hebrides shouldn't be confused with the other Scalpay, off the Isle of Harris in the Outer Hebrides.

LOCATION: 57.3110°N 5.9786°W

GRID REFERENCE: NG605315

POPULATION: 4

SIZE: 24.8km²

GETTING THERE: Those staying on the island arrange a boat to collect them when they are ready. See www.isleofscalpay.com for more information.

WHERE TO STAY: Three holiday cottages can be booked on the island. See www.isleofscalpay.com for more details.

WHERE TO EAT: Raasay House, Raasay, IV40 8PB, **T:** 01478 660300, **W:** www.raasay-house.co.uk. A pop-up café operates in the community hall – check www.raasay.com for times.

RAASAY

LOCATION: 57.3813°N 6.0295°W

GRID REFERENCE: NG579395

POPULATION: 161

SIZE: 62.4km²

Single Malt

This thin island that points a crooked finger north of Skye is home to one of the newest distilleries in the country, producing both whisky and gin. Established in 2017, the Isle of Raasay Distillery is also the first to produce whisky on this remote Hebridean island. At least, it's the first to produce it legally. When the Excise Acts of 1788 outlawed stills under 100 gallons, some smaller producers in the Highlands and Islands began hiding their wares. It's thought illicit distilling took place on Raasay, with a still being found in a local rock shelter at the time.

As with establishing any distillery, there's a lag time until the first batches are available, and the first bottles of Isle of Raasay Single Malt whisky went on sale in 2020. After you've visited the distillery, take time to drive between Brochel Castle and Arnish on what has become known as Calum's Road. Local crofter Calum MacLeod built this 2.8km (1.75 mile) route singlehandedly over ten years. The feat has been celebrated in books, songs and a radio drama.

GETTING THERE: Ferries depart for Raasay from the Isle of Skye at Sconser, taking 25 minutes to make the trip. Visit www.calmac.co.uk for more information.

WHERE TO STAY: Raasay House, Raasay, IV40 8PB, **T:** 01478 660300, **W:** www.raasay-house.co.uk. Isle of Raasay Distillery, Raasay, IV40 8PB, **T:** 01478 470178, **W:** www.raasaydistillery.com.

WHERE TO EAT: Raasay House, Raasay, IV40 8PB, **T:** 01478 660300, **W:** www.raasay-house.co.uk. A pop-up café operates in the community hall – check www.raasay.com for times.

SKYE

What Does Skye Taste Like?

Several thriving companies produce food on Skye, ensuring the island very much has a taste of its own. As you pass through Portree on the island's main road, you can practically taste the produce as the smell wafts out of the old woollen mill. Established by a South African couple who fell in love with Skye on a tour of Scotland, the Isle of Skye Baking Company (www. isleofskyebakingco.co.uk) is a key place to get hold of many Scottish favourites – including Scottish tablet, oatcakes and shortbread. Head a little further north, to the port of Uig, and you'll find something to wash it all down. The Isle of Skye Brewing Company (www. skyeale.com) has its origins in a pub meet-up between old schoolteacher friends who lamented the lack of a brewery on the island. That was in 1992, and five years later they won the CAMRA Champion Beer of Scotland. Many of their beers are named after the local Cuillin Mountains and their first brew – Red Cuillin – is so popular that it's still produced to the original recipe.

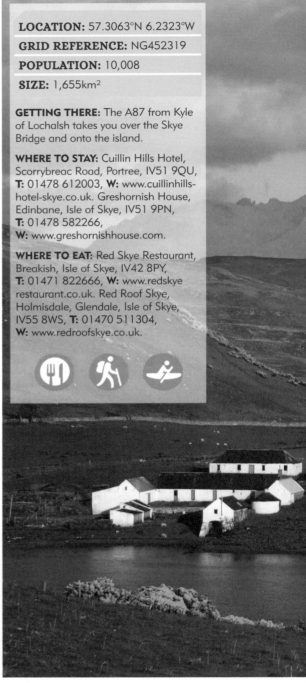

LOCATION: 57.3063°N 6.2323°W

GRID REFERENCE: NG452319

POPULATION: 10,008

SIZE: 1,655km²

GETTING THERE: The A87 from Kyle of Lochalsh takes you over the Skye Bridge and onto the island.

WHERE TO STAY: Cuillin Hills Hotel, Scorrybreac Road, Portree, IV51 9QU, **T:** 01478 612003, **W:** www.cuillinhills-hotel-skye.co.uk. Greshornish House, Edinbane, Isle of Skye, IV51 9PN, **T:** 01478 582266, **W:** www.greshornishhouse.com.

WHERE TO EAT: Red Skye Restaurant, Breakish, Isle of Skye, IV42 8PY, **T:** 01471 822666, **W:** www.redskye restaurant.co.uk. Red Roof Skye, Holmisdale, Glendale, Isle of Skye, IV55 8WS, **T:** 01470 511304, **W:** www.redroofskye.co.uk.

Journey to the south of Skye for all things seafood at The Oyster Shed (www.theoysterman.co.uk). Here you can sample what are considered by many to be the island's finest oysters along with plenty of other treats from the sea, such as crab, langoustine and salmon. Nearby is the island's only distillery, which is perhaps a little surprising given the size of the place. But Talisker (www.malts.com) is a big hitter. It's a giant of the whisky world and many people look to it as the greatest of them all, each dram a celebration of peaty smokiness.

The mountains of Skye frame the view from the mainland.

Munro Bagging

If you're a keen hiker there are routes on Skye to match all levels of fitness. From coastal strolls to challenging climbs atop extraordinary mountains, this island punches above its weight when it comes to sheer natural beauty. You may be familiar with the Munros – a tick list of Scottish mountains above 3,000ft, named after Sir Hugh Munro. You may not have realised how many of these iconic peaks are found on the Isle of Skye in the famous Cuillin range – no fewer than 12 of Skye's mountains feature on the Munro list, making it a key place to return to if you're bagging them all. The Holy Grail of Skye's Munros is Sgùrr Dearg – the Inaccessible Pinnacle. Claiming the scalp of this peak sees hardy climbers get up close and personal with a formidable slab of rock rising up from the Cuillin ridge.

Go Wild!

The increasing popularity of wild swimming has seen one of Skye's natural attractions become a hot destination. The incredible Fairy Pools are fed by a series of waterfalls and provide a crystal-clear setting for a plunge. Free to access, the pools are reached via a 2.5km (1.5 mile) walk from the car park near Carbost. Bring your cossie and camera for a chilly dip to remember.

SOAY

A New Home for the Evicted

From the air, Soay looks like a tree in a plant pot. It's a figure-of-eight type island, almost split in two by the sea at one point, and is a quiet place of retreat for those who have made the decision to live here. Far from the nearest shops and services, Soay is well and truly cut off by Soay Sound. Hard to imagine, then, that 158 people once lived here in 1851. The Highland Clearances on Skye in the 19th century saw many crofters come to Soay, the key factor leading to the tiny island's peak population. Numbers have dwindled down the decades to the handful still here today.

The island's most famous resident was the naturalist and author Gavin Maxwell (see also Eilean Bàn, page 51). After the Second World War, Maxwell set up a basking shark fishery but the project wasn't successful and didn't last long. The former headquarters can still be seen on the island and the badly planned tale is told in his book *Harpoon at a Venture* (1952).

LOCATION: 57.1499°N 6.2293°W

GRID REFERENCE: NG443145

POPULATION: 3

SIZE: 10.4km²

GETTING THERE: There is no regular ferry service, but some boating companies (such as www.bellajane. co.uk) arrange trips that call at and sail close by Soay.

WHERE TO STAY: Suilven Elgol B&B, Elgol, Isle of Skye, IV49 9BL, **T:** 01471 866379, **W:** www.elgolbedandbreakfast. wordpress.com. Bayview B&B, Elgol, Isle of Skye, IB49 9BL, **T:** 07975 957785, **W:** www.bayviewelgol.com.

SOUTH RONA

Freedom and Foraging

Just 8km (5 miles) long, the wide range of terrain on South Rona is fascinating. Days spent roaming the island bring you across woods, rocky outcrops, enchanting coast, hidden lochs and exposed hills.

But then, after a day enjoying the wilderness and wildlife, attention will turn towards satisfying the appetite you've built up. People staying in the self-catering cottages can rustle up their own treats. But the lodge offers a 'supper club', where island produce is the order of the day. The emphasis is on seasonal availability, so expect free-range eggs, seafood, wild rhubarb, wild mushrooms and other fresh ingredients. The island is most famous for its Rona venison, processed and freshly frozen on the island. Those staying can get involved with creating the meals if they wish, from making venison sausages to going out on the water in search of langoustine, lobster and crab.

South Rona is also known simply as 'Rona' but sometimes has the 'South' placed before it to distinguish it from North Rona, which is an island sitting far to the north of the Western Isles. Isle of Rona postage stamps are also on sale, helping to subsidise the charter boat that delivers the island's mail.

▶ *Across the sea on Skye, famous mountain The Storr stands proud.*

▼ *Visitors enjoy a rocky view from the shoreline.*

LOCATION: 57.5339°N 5.9795°W

GRID REFERENCE: NG619563

POPULATION: 3

SIZE: 9.3km²

GETTING THERE: Boats are on hand to transport people who have arranged to stay on South Rona.

WHERE TO STAY: Three cottages are available to rent on the island. See www.isleofrona.com for more information.

WHERE TO EAT: The cottages are self-catering, but the owners of Rona Lodge also offer meals using local produce.

Why I Love...
Rona

'Rona is home to a host of wildlife, including otters, sea eagles, dolphins, porpoises, minke whales and basking sharks. The red deer are a magnificent spectacle in autumn when you can listen to the stags roar and return to enjoy a dram by the fire. But the beauty of Rona is that just "doing nothing" is an experience in itself.'

Bill Cowie,
Rona Island Manager

BELNAHUA

LOCATION: 56.2515°N 5.6934°W	
GRID REFERENCE: NM713127	
POPULATION: 0	
SIZE: >1km²	

Ghosts of Industry

Belnahua is an intriguing ghost island, giving an insight into the rich heritage of the Slate Islands. Now uninhabited, a journey around its shores takes you back in time to when these Slate Islands were an industrial powerhouse, roofing buildings all over the world. At its height, around 200 people lived and worked on Belnahua, extracting slate from the ground and shipping it to the mainland. The scene is now that of an industrial wasteland, but with an eerie and beautiful charm given its fabulous setting. Despite the many ruined buildings that once housed the workers and the pocked landscape once the focus of quarrying, it's hard to imagine Belnahua was a hive of activity before the First World War. Although some tourist and fishing trips are sometimes seen landing on the island, most people enjoy the view from their vessel.

GETTING THERE: Several boating companies run trips from the mainland that take you up close to Belnahua and explain about its rich history. The trips can be combined to see other islands, too. For more details visit www.seafari.co.uk.

WHERE TO STAY: See Seil, page 64.

EASDALE

LOCATION: 56.2929°N 5.6618°W

GRID REFERENCE: NM735172

POPULATION: 59

SIZE: >1km²

Skimming the Surface

This small, little-known Scottish island is just a stone's throw from the mainland – and there's more stone throwing going on here than you may think! In 1983, islander Albert Baker started what was to become one of the world's most curious competitions – the World Stone Skimming Championships. Today, upwards of 300 competitors head for the island in late September to skim a stone across a lake in an old slate quarry. There are lots of flat stones around for those taking part, and anybody can join in and help raise funds for charity, but you'll need to follow the strict rules! The stone must bounce twice on the water to qualify as a skim, and once it does the judges measure the distance to the point it sinks. Competitors are limited to just three attempts and a range of awards are given at the end of the event – some of them made from slate, of course! There's live music to keep non-skimmers entertained and you'll probably be able to spot the odd journalist and film crew; media interest in this unusual event is high and it has made a quirky feature on several TV shows and in national newspapers.

GETTING THERE: A regular ferry service from Ellenabeich makes the short trip across the sea to Easdale.

WHERE TO STAY: Easdale Island B&B, Easdale Island, PA34 4TB, **T:** 01852 300509, **W:** www.easdaleisland.scot. Garragh Mhor, Easdale, PA34 4RF, **T:** 01852 300513, **W:** www.garraghmhor.co.uk.

WHERE TO EAT: The Puffer Bar, Easdale Island, PA34 4TB, **T:** 01852 300022, **W:** www.pufferbarandrestaurant.co.uk.

Abandoned

This tiny island used to be home to over 450 people, with the economy driven by the slate industry. However, a ferocious storm in 1881 flooded the quarries and changed the fate of Easdale. With the jobs gone and the future looking bleak, people soon made the decision to head elsewhere and look for work.

◀ *The unmistakable outline of the remarkable island of Belnahua.*

▶ *Your stone must skim the surface twice to count in the Championships.*

KERRERA

LOCATION: 56.3833°N 5.5667°W

GRID REFERENCE: NM828287

POPULATION: 34

SIZE: 12.1km²

GETTING THERE: Passenger ferry departing from Gallanach, just south of Oban (www.calmac.co.uk).

WHERE TO STAY: Don Muir, Pulpit Hill, Oban, PA34 4LX, **T:** 01631 570078, **W:** www.donmuir.co.uk. The Manor House, 6C Gallanach Rd, Oban, PA34 4LS, **T:** 01631 562087, **W:** www.manorhouseoban.com.

◄ *With Oban in the distance, the small ferry heads to and from the island.*

▼ *Walkers can loop around the island, passing isolated farmhouses along the way.*

A Joyful Walk

A popular day trip for those wanting to escape the crowds of Oban, the short ferry journey across the Sound of Kerrera from Gallanach takes a dozen passengers at a time to the walker's paradise of Kerrera. A slippery, sloping jetty leads the way to the small ferry, which doesn't have seats but does have a much-needed little shelter for inclement weather. With great views and a real sense of seclusion, the island measures just 7km (4.3 miles) by 2km (1.2 miles), so it's possible to complete a full circuit during a visit. Head around to the western side of the island and you'll be rewarded with great views of Gylan Castle. This attractive ruin, where Scottish King Alexander II died in 1249, benefited from a partial restoration in 2006.

The small population is mainly split into two settlements, one in the north and another in the south. Some islanders living here tend to keep a 4x4 on the island because of the rough terrain, and have a smaller car on the mainland so they can avoid taking vehicles on the small boat. A postal worker arrives once a day, riding a quad bike along the tracks to distribute letters and parcels. During the tourist season, a tea room serves food and drink for those trekking their way around Kerrera.

LUING

What's Your Beef?

The long island of Luing is separated from Seil by the Cuan Sound, a narrow stretch of water with a ferry service that provides a lifeline for those living here and allows a steady flow of day-trippers. The island's coastline is beautifully rugged and best explored on foot; many visitors come here to get away from it all and stretch their legs in idyllic surroundings.

Today, the main sources of employment on Luing are tourism and lobster fishing. Beef farming is also rising in importance as the island makes a name for itself producing high-quality meat products. In the postwar period, a local farmer's breeding programme developed Luing cattle – a hardy hornless cow breed able to rear its young in the island's harsh weather. The number of farmers rearing Luing cattle has increased over recent years and the breed is now well established across the UK, Ireland, Canada, Australia and South America. It was officially recognised by the government in 1965, about the time when the island's slate industry lost its significance. Earlier, there had been good-sized quarries at Toberonochy and Cullipool, and Luing slate was used on the roof of Iona Abbey.

LOCATION: 56.2348°N 5.6503°W

GRID REFERENCE: NM740100

POPULATION: 195

SIZE: 14.3km²

GETTING THERE: Just 200m (656ft) separates Luing from the island of Seil and a regular ferry bridges the gap. The service is run by Argyll and Bute Council, with details of crossings found on www.calmac.co.uk.

WHERE TO STAY: Creagard Country House, Cullipool Village, Isle of Luing, PA34 4UB, **T:** 0141 639 4592. Gorsten B&B, Toberonnochy, Isle of Luing, PA34 4TZ, **T:** 01852 314213, **W:** www.gorstenbnb.business.site.

WHERE TO EAT: Atlantic Islands Centre, 23 Cullipool, Isle of Luing, PA34 4UB, **T:** 01852 314096, **W:** www.isleofluing.org/atlantic-islands-centre.

◄ *A member of the crew on My Tara carrying a creel aboard the boat off the island of Luing.*

▼ *Luing cattle.*

SEIL

LOCATION: 56.2933°N 5.6505°W

GRID REFERENCE: NM742172

POPULATION: 551

SIZE: 13.7km²

GETTING THERE: Seil is linked to the mainland by the B844 road.

WHERE TO STAY: Morvargh B&B, Clachan-Seil, Isle of Seil, PA34 4TJ, **T:** 01852 300206. Oban Seil Farm, Clachan-Seil, PA34 4TN, **T:** 01852 300245, **W:** www.obanseilfarm.com.

WHERE TO EAT: The Oyster Bar, Isle of Seil, PA34 4RQ, **T:** 01852 300121, **W:** www.oysterbareasdale.com. The Fisherman's Kitchen, Tigh Ian, Isle of Seil, PA34 4TF, **T:** 01852 300578, **W:** www.fishermanskitchen.co.uk.

Bridge Over the Atlantic

To get to Seil, you must cross over a lovely single-arched stone bridge set over the tiny stretch of water that separates Seil from the mainland, making it an island. The quaint construction, which dates way back to 1792, has been referred to inventively as the 'Bridge over the Atlantic'.

The main village on Seil is Ellenabeich, at the end of the road from the mainland. It's sometimes referred to as Easdale because of its proximity to the island of the same name, so don't let this dual naming confuse you. With a background of slate quarrying, the village has a rich industrial history that is now explored at the Scottish Slate Islands Heritage Trust, based in the cottage of a former quarryman. Ellenabeich is a great place to go off exploring other islands with the Seafari company based here.

Donald, Where's Your Troosers?

After the Battle of Culloden (16 April 1746), the wearing of kilts was banned across Scotland. But the hardy folk of Seil defied the new rule and stuck to their guns when on their own ground. They would, however, ditch the kilt and change into trousers if they were crossing the bridge to the mainland. The quick change would take place in the pub near the bridge, now called Tigh-an-Truish – which translates as House of Trousers.

Oyster Source

Seil is renowned as one of the best places to sample locally sourced oysters, with the Oyster Bar in Ellenabeich being a particular favourite. You can also enjoy views of surrounding islands, including Jura and Scarba, from this family-run restaurant.

Why I Love... Seil

'Seil island, connected to the mainland since 1792 by a fine stone bridge, is the most accessible of the Inner Hebrides, but retains its insular culture and ambience. It lies among a romantic scatter of neighbouring islands, including Easdale island, to which it's connected by a passenger boat, and Luing, which is served from Seil by a vehicle ferry. Seil is rich with remnants of a long, varied history and boasts outstanding scenery and fine people.'

The Hon. Michael Shaw,
former MP

▲ *Sea cliffs and harbour on the Isle of Seil.*

▶ *Clachan Bridge (Bridge over the Atlantic): single-arched, hump-backed masonry bridge spanning the Clachan Sound.*

SHUNA

LOCATION: 56.2116°N 5.6137°W

GRID REFERENCE: NM760080

POPULATION: 3

SIZE: 4.5km²

Sustainable Shuna

Just 20 minutes across the water from the pier at Arduaine, a working farm oversees care of the island's sheep and six holiday cottages. Spending time on this small island, you get to take a break from the stresses of mainland life and have a truly magical experience. Cars are left on the mainland and you won't find any roads – or even telephones – here. Visitors can explore Shuna to their heart's content, sharing the land with the red deer. The ruined castle was built in Victorian times by an architect thought to have died in the *Titanic* disaster of 1912.

Although it's one of the Slate Islands, Shuna is different from its neighbours because it doesn't contain all that much slate. What it does have is a thirst for sustainability; all the island's electricity is generated through solar panels and a wind turbine.

GETTING THERE: People who have arranged to stay on the island are ferried across from the mainland by the accommodation owners.

WHERE TO STAY: A small range of holiday accommodation is available. Visit www.islandofshuna.co.uk for more information.

The boathouse on Shuna sits in an idyllic woodland location.

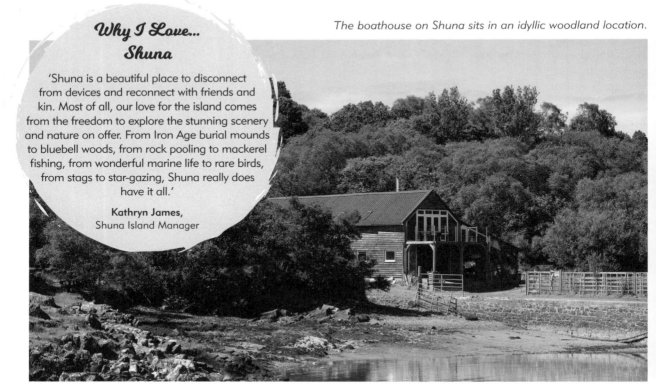

Why I Love... Shuna

'Shuna is a beautiful place to disconnect from devices and reconnect with friends and kin. Most of all, our love for the island comes from the freedom to explore the stunning scenery and nature on offer. From Iron Age burial mounds to bluebell woods, from rock pooling to mackerel fishing, from wonderful marine life to rare birds, from stags to star-gazing, Shuna really does have it all.'

Kathryn James,
Shuna Island Manager

CANNA

LOCATION:	57.0605°N 6.5476°W
GRID REFERENCE:	NG244058
POPULATION:	18
SIZE:	11.4km²

Sand and Stone

If the weather is kind and the ferry from Mallaig allows you to get over the sea to the Isle of Canna, you're in for a real treat – especially if you arrange to stay and experience the overnight isolation of this special place. There's a hubbub of activity when the boat arrives with new visitors, returning friends and important deliveries, but once that vessel sails back to the mainland a quiet hush descends again and you're alone in a tantalising environment. This is a tiny island and is easily explored through a series of short walks, but there are some very special attractions waiting to be discovered. Black Beach gets its name from the colour of the volcanic sand found here, and the magnificent Prison Rock stack provides a perfect backdrop. Legend has it a local woman called Marion Macleod was imprisoned here in the 17th century for being unfaithful to her husband. More grim tales are found near the site of what was once Canna's main settlement, A'Chill. The 'Punishment Stone' was used to dish out sentences to local offenders; their thumb was wedged into the small gap and they were left to reflect on their actions for as long as was seen fit. Nearby, the Christian Cross is a neatly decorated landmark dating back to the 7th century. The two arms of the cross are missing – sadly thought to have fallen victim to target practice during the Napoleonic Wars.

GETTING THERE: Passenger ferries run from Mallaig to Canna. See www.calmac.co.uk for more details.

WHERE TO STAY: Canna Campsite, Isle of Canna, PH44 4RS, **T:** 01687 462477, **W:** www.cannacampsite.com. Tighard Guest House, Isle of Canna, PH44 4RS, **T:** 01687 462474, **W:** www.tighard.com.

WHERE TO EAT: Café Canna, West Bothy, Isle of Canna, PH44 4RS, **T:** 01687 482488, **W:** www.cafecanna.co.uk.

Canna You Run?

One of the world's most remote and isolated organised runs takes place on Canna in May – and places fill up quickly because plenty of people want to take part in the 10km event. There's a small registration fee and of course the obligatory T-shirt is available for those who finish the off-road course. If you've still got the energy after running around the scenic route, there's a celebratory ceilidh at night to get the blood pumping once again.

EIGG

LOCATION: 56.9035°N 6.1471°W

GRID REFERENCE: NM476868

POPULATION: 87

SIZE: 30.5km²

Eigg takes Some Beating

For such a tiny place, Eigg is a leader among Scottish islands. With the help of the Scottish Wildlife Trust, it was the first island, on 12 June 1997, to successfully achieve a buyout from its private landowner and therefore change the population's relationship with the island. To mark the historic date, a raucous ceilidh is held for the people of Eigg. This tiny island was also the world's first community to be powered entirely from renewable sources, leading the fight against climate change.

To discover what life was like before these records were broken, head to Cleadale's Museum of Crofting Life. The Campbell family moved to the island in 1907 and the island-run museum, set in their croft, has a number of artefacts to show what family life was like on Eigg at that time in a small but homely display. Before hopping on board the ferry back to the mainland, hang out at Galmisdale Café to get a feel for Eigg's vibrant community.

GETTING THERE: Passenger ferries run from Mallaig to Eigg. See www.calmac.co.uk for more details.

WHERE TO STAY: Kildonan House, Isle of Eigg, PH42 4RL, **T:** 01687 482446, **W:** www.kildonanhouseeigg.co.uk. Glebe Barn, Isle of Eigg, PH42 4RL, **T:** 01687 315099, **W:** www.glebebarn.co.uk.

WHERE TO EAT: Galmisdale Bay Café, The Pier, Isle of Eigg, PH42 4RL, **T:** 01687 482487. Dinner can be enjoyed at Lageorna B&B, Isle of Eigg, PH42 4RL, **T:** 01687 460081, **W:** www.lageorna.com.

◀ The island offers some tasty footpaths.

▼ Welcome to Eigg, one of our greenest islands.

Arrivals tend to come from Mallaig, from where Calmac's small ferries bring day-trippers and a much smaller number of travellers who decide to stay over. Many tourists visit to marvel at the island's sublime geology, which is interwoven with its history. Eigg is essentially formed by basalt – a volcanic rock. You can discover the magnificent igneous landscape as you cross the island, which is quickly covered because it's only 8km (5 miles) long and 4.9km (3 miles) wide. At low tide, a cave that formed in the rocks along the southern shore is accessible, but it's not for the faint-hearted! In 1577, members of Skye's MacLeod Clan lit a fire in the cave's entrance, suffocating 396 of Eigg's inhabitants – all but one of the island's population – who were hiding inside. Reaching Massacre Cave, as it came to be known, is a bit of a scramble, and signs warn you not to enter due to the danger from falling rocks.

A more jolly exploration of the island's geology is the beach of the singing sands, not far from Cleadale in the island's crofting north. The titular 'singing' is created by quartz grains on the beach, which seem to squeal as you walk on them.

If you have energy left, save it for the climb to An Sgurr. At 393m (1,289ft), it's not a massive climb, but it is the highest point on the island. You'll also be visiting the largest piece of pitchstone lava in the UK, a landform that impressively dominates the island's skyline on the ferry's approach. For such a tiny place, Eigg is a geologist's dream!

▲ *The chilling entrance to Massacre Cave.*

▼ *Approaching Eigg with its distinctive outline.*

MUCK

LOCATION: 56.8335°N 6.2509°W

GRID REFERENCE: NM408794

POPULATION: 27

SIZE: 6km²

Where There's Muck...

It's not the most attractive of names, but despite sounding like it needs a spring clean, the beautiful island of Muck still manages to pull in plenty of visitors on the ferry from Mallaig. For such a small island, there's a wealth of activities available here. Cycling is an ideal way to get around and visitors are encouraged to bring their push bikes – there is no charge for them on Calmac ferries. Diving enthusiasts also make a splash when they head to the island and explore the waters and marine life during the summer months. Other water activities are also popular in the sea around Muck, so expect to see plenty of people escaping the humdrum of mainland life and sailing the waters when calm.

GETTING THERE: Ferries visit Muck and the other Small Isles from Mallaig. See www.calmac.co.uk for more details, noting day trips are not possible every day.

WHERE TO STAY: Port Mòr House Hotel, Isle of Muck, PH41 2RP, **T:** 01687 460001, **W:** www.isleofmuck.com. Gallanach Lodge, Isle of Muck, PH41 2RP, **T:** 01687 462365, **W:** www.gallanachlodge.co.uk.

WHERE TO EAT: The Craft Shop, The Bothy Portmhor, Isle of Muck, PH41 2RP, **T:** 07908 965822, **W:** www.isleofmuck.com.

Grey seals.

Wildlife Wonders

Don't forget your binoculars! The waters around Muck are well known for hosting seals and porpoises, which always add a welcome spectacle to the journey from the mainland.

Over 40 species of birds breed on the island, making this a very important wildlife habitat. Add to that minke whales and basking sharks, which can sometimes be spotted off the coast, and you may well be enjoying some of the most stunning wildlife watching in the country.

History buffs will gain plenty from a visit to Muck.

Ancient cairns built here date back to 2000 BC, while a recently discovered Norse building and a prehistoric fort add a timeless sense that people have occupied this island for millennia. No fewer than five sites on Muck have been designated as ancient monuments by the Royal Commission.

I'm in the Mood for Dancing

Throughout the year, ceilidhs are held at the island's community centre. Visitors are welcome, and if there's one that coincides with your trip it's really not to be missed.

RUM

LOCATION: 56.9938°N 6.3483°W

GRID REFERENCE: NM360976

POPULATION: 22

SIZE: 104.6km²

The Textile Castle

Stepping onto the Isle of Rum, you'll feel a million miles away from the 'dark satanic mills' of Victorian northern England. But the textile factories of 19th-century Lancashire have left their mark on this corner of the Small Isles in the form of the imposing and dominating Kinloch Castle. Clothing giant Sir George Bullough used his factory fortune to buy the island as a summer shooting haven. The enormous castle he commissioned was completed in 1900 and it still stands as a category A listed building. Now owned by Scottish National Heritage, it used to operate as a hostel but today you'll need to be on one of the organised summer tours to see inside the most famous building on the island. The guided visits escort island hoppers into what is essentially an Edwardian time capsule, calling in at well-preserved bedrooms and halls that reveal how the wealthy textile mogul entertained friends and family over a century ago. There's no need to book on the tours, which are timed to set off with the arrival of the ferries and will even wait if the boat is late.

GETTING THERE: Ferries run from Mallaig to Rum. See www.calmac.co.uk for more details.

WHERE TO STAY: Rum Bunkhouse, Kinloch, Isle of Rum, PH43 4RR, **T:** 01687 460318, **W:** www.rumbunkhouse.com. Ivy Cottage Guest House, Isle of Rum, PH43 4RR, **T:** 01687 462744, **W:** www.ivycottageisleofrum.co.uk.

WHERE TO EAT: Kim's Kitchen operates in the village hall during the summer months, **E:** isleofrumteashop@gmail.com.

Rum Running

Many experienced hikers and Munro baggers recommend the longer trails on Rum as the most thrilling walking environment found on any of the Scottish islands. The towering mountains are impressive from a distance as the ferry approaches and are simply stunning up close. The gorgeous scenery and far-reaching views across the sea to the mainland, Skye and the other Small Isles are your reward for trekking up to one of Rum's much-loved summits. But walking the entirety of the Rum Cuillin, despite being a potentially epic adventure, comes with a considerable warning: you'll need to scramble over rocks and allow at least 12 hours to reach all five major peaks in one

go. This is a summer activity that must be approached with respect and the correct equipment; there is no mountain rescue team on the island and there'll be a delay getting trained teams in from the mainland. The weather on Rum is also famously challenging, featuring more changes than a Kylie concert. Be prepared, as the scouts say.

Otterly Brilliant

A well-signed short walk from the harbour brings you to a popular otter hide, where it's possible to hole up for some time in efforts to spot the beautiful creatures on the shore. Bring your binoculars to get the most from your visit.

SANDAY

LOCATION: 57.0493°N 6.4835°W

GRID REFERENCE: NG282043

POPULATION: 9

SIZE: 1.8km²

School and Skuas

Connected both physically and socially with its larger neighbour, the tidal island of Sanday harbours a small community of its own but is often referred to jointly with Canna. In the early 20th century, children from both islands went to school on Sanday and so a footbridge was built to make the journey much easier. After standing firm for a century, the bridge was destroyed by a storm in 2005 and the replacement, built the year after, now allows vehicles to make the crossing between Canna and Sanday. It's a crucial link between the two islands, both of which are owned by the National Trust for Scotland.

Spend time on Sanday and you're likely to get an appreciation for the wildlife visiting at different times of the year. Look out for the thriving bird population, which includes Manx shearwater, puffins and great skua. Keep your eye on the latter – they show no fear of humans and repeatedly dive-bomb if they feel you're too close to their territory.

GETTING THERE: Sanday is linked to Canna via a bridge and is accessible across sandbanks at low tide. Passenger ferries run from Mallaig to Canna. See www.calmac.co.uk for more details.

WHERE TO STAY: See Canna, page 67.

PRIEST ISLAND

LOCATION:	57.9632°N 5.5093°W
GRID REFERENCE:	NB925025
POPULATION:	0
SIZE:	1.2km²

Priest Island is one of the noted breeding locations for storm petrels.

An Old Retreat

The outermost of all the Summer Isles, uninhabited Priest Island was once a Christian retreat and there have been several discoveries of stone circles here. It is now owned and managed by the RSPB as a nature reserve, hosting one of the largest storm petrel colonies in the country and providing an environment for the likes of otters and shrews. Getting to the island is dangerous and only for the experienced sailor, but it is possible to visit the rugged coastline and bird population on a tour of the Summer Isles.

GETTING THERE: Trips around the Summer Isles are available with Shearwater Cruises, leaving from Ullapool and taking a voyage around Priest Island.

WHERE TO STAY: Base yourself in Ullapool for the trip to sea. The Arch Inn, 10–11 W Shore St, Ullapool, IV26 2UR, **T:** 01854 612454, **W:** www.thearchinn.co.uk. The Stonehouses, Mill Street, Ullapool, IV26 2UN, **T:** 01854 613838, **W:** www.thestonehouses.co.uk.

TANERA MÒR

LOCATION: 58.0039°N 5.3999°W

GRID REFERENCE: NB992067

POPULATION: 4

SIZE: 3.1km²

Herring Boom and Herring Bust

Once a thriving community of 118 people at the end of the 19th century, Tanera Mòr today is a holiday haven for those wanting to escape for a week or two. At its peak the island was a hotbed of activity for herring fishing, with two settlements – Ardngoine and Garadheancal – growing around the industry. But when the herring trade suffered a stark decline in the early decades of the 20th century, the island's population endured the same fate. All those who had been dependent on Tanera Mòr's fishing industry moved off the island. A handful of people lived on the island in the postwar years, but today the focus is on redeveloping the abandoned houses and creating holiday accommodation for those seeking a remote vacation.

GETTING THERE: Trips around the Summer Isles are available with Shearwater Cruises, leaving from Ullapool and making a stop on Tanera Mòr.

WHERE TO STAY: For opportunities to stay on the island, visit www.summer-isles.com.

Inspiring a Cult Classic

If the name of the Summer Isles seems familiar, you may recognise it from the 1973 film *The Wicker Man*. Although it wasn't filmed here – shooting took place on Skye and the mainland – it's thought Tanera Mòr was the inspiration for the fictional Summerisle, where the horror story is set.

▼ *The ruins of the former herring factory.*

ISLE OF ARRAN

LOCATION:	55.5735°N 5.2533°W
GRID REFERENCE:	NR949358
POPULATION:	4,629
SIZE:	432.5km²

Stretch Your Legs

One of the best resources for walkers on Arran is the well-signed footpath that wraps its way right around the shore. At 107km (66.5 miles) long, the Arran Coastal Trail was officially opened in 2003 and has been heralded as one of the best long-distance routes in Scotland. Because the trail circles the island, you can start and finish at any point, but most people tackling it start from where their ferry arrives. Of course, you can use small sections of the coastal path for a stroll lasting just a few hours.

Hikers looking for a climbing challenge can tackle Goat Fell. At 874m (2,867ft) above sea level, this is a steep and strenuous climb, but a popular one nonetheless. The most-used route sets off from near Brodick Castle. Leaving the coastline and passing through forests, moorland, various plant species and onwards towards a formidable mountain, it's no wonder this island cross-section has led to Arran's nickname, 'Scotland in Miniature'.

Machrie Moor

The standing stones on this remote, atmospheric moorland date back 4,000 years and provide a moment of spirituality for many visitors. In magnificent surroundings, enjoying views to the mainland and a skyline of fine mountains, the significance of this hilltop for Scottish history

GETTING THERE: There are two options for reaching Arran on the ferry. The longer route leaves Ardrossan and heads for Brodick, taking 55 minutes. On Kintyre, ferries leave from Claonaig and link with Lochranza at the north of the island. See www.calmac.co.uk for more details.

WHERE TO STAY: The Douglas Hotel, Shore Road, Brodick, Isle of Arran, KA27 8AW, **T:** 01770 302968, **W:** www.thedouglashotel.co.uk. The Lagg Hotel, Lagg, Brodick, Isle of Arran, KA27 8PQ, **T:** 01770 870255, **W:** www.lagghotel.com.

WHERE TO EAT: The Lighthouse, Pirnmill, Isle of Arran, KA27 8HP, **T:** 01770 850240, **W:** www.thelighthousearran.co.uk. Café Thyme, Machrie, Isle of Arran, KA27 9EB, **T:** 01770 840227, **W:** www.oldbyre.co.uk/cafethyme.irs.

◄ *Beautiful Glen Rosa attracts walkers and those seeking a wild dip.*

► *The mysterious and inspiring standing stones on Machrie Moor.*

is immense. The stones placed around this lonely landscape were sites of religious and ritualistic importance, and in Neolithic times the island's stone circles – six of them in total – were once the location of cremations and burials. Archaeologists have made historically significant findings here but vast areas of the moor have still to be examined. It makes you wonder what else is down there beneath your feet.

More Taste, Less Speed

Foodies heading to Arran are in for a delicious time. The island is a treasure trove of small producers selling tasty treats. Spend a few days here tucking into local food and drink, and feel the pace of life slow down. Here is a selection of Arran tastes for you to savour:

- Milk from island dairy cows is used to make a range of award-winning flavours at Arran Ice Cream (www.arranicecream.co.uk).

- For a small brewery, big beers are in plentiful supply at Arran Brewery, which is a joy to visit (www.arran brewery.co.uk).

- Hints of mustard and pickle make the cheese made on the island memorable (www.arranscheeseshop.co.uk).

- Fancy a wee dram that's been distilled on the island? Make time for a visit to Lochranza distillery or its sister site at Lagg (www.arranwhisky.com).

- No holiday is complete without a good chocolate shop. Thankfully, James of Arran is here to oblige (www.jamesofarran.com).

DAVAAR

LOCATION: 55.4225°N 5.5412°W

GRID REFERENCE: NR760200

POPULATION: 0

SIZE: <1km²

The Land That Time Forgot

The walk across to Davaar from the mainland must be attempted only at low tide, and you need to make sure you are off the island in ample time. Rising up from the sea and quickly reaching a height of 115m (377ft), Davaar looks like the inspiration for a fantasy movie. The island's lighthouse was built in 1854 by Thomas Stevenson. The lighthouse keeper's cottage is now a holiday home, as is another building known as The Lookout, which housed naval crews during the Second World War.

GETTING THERE: Davaar can be reached on foot at low tide along a causeway that twists and turns out into the Clyde from near to Campbeltown on the Mull of Kintyre.

WHERE TO STAY: There are two holiday cottages on Davaar. Visit www.kintyrecottages.com for more details.

The island's highlight is an artistic work found inside a cave and once thought to be a miracle. This painting of the crucifixion was discovered by local fishermen in 1887, who immediately presumed it had been placed inside the cave by God. It was, though, created by art teacher Archibald MacKinnon, who believed the idea came to him in a dream. The painting certainly caused a stir when it was found. MacKinnon returned to the cave a couple more times to add touches when the paint started to fade. Restoration work to the painting has continued and it was certainly needed in 2006, after a graffiti artist replaced the image of Christ with one of Che Guevara.

GREAT CUMBRAE

LOCATION: 55.7534°N 4.9257°W

GRID REFERENCE: NS164550

POPULATION: 1,376

SIZE: 11.6km²

I Want to Ride My Bicycle

With quiet roads, idyllic scenery and a relatively flat route around its perimeter, Great Cumbrae is an ideal destination for those wanting to leave the car on the mainland and venture out on bikes. Whether you bring your own on the ferry or hire them in Millport, pedalling the island's cycle route is the best way to see Great Cumbrae. Alternative cycle routes are available that loop around the middle of the island, but these are more hilly and harder work. Expect to do a steady 14.5km (9 miles) while navigating a full circuit of the island.

Crocodile Rock

No, not the 1970s Elton John pop classic! Great Cumbrae is famous for a much older Crocodile Rock, which is popular among families due to its charming smile. One of Scotland's quirkier landmarks, the distinctive rock at Millport has had a painted makeover transform it into a crocodile. We're often out and about and see unusually shaped rocks that look like animals or objects – but you'll be left in no doubt about where the eyes and jaws are of this rocky beast. You may be surprised to learn that this is not a new addition to the coast of Great Cumbrae. Far from it. While the exact date is a mystery, the painting on Crocodile Rock is believed to be over 100 years old as it was documented back in 1913. Today, the community is extremely proud of its special rock; it gets a fresh lick of paint every few years and big centenary celebrations were held here in 2013!

GETTING THERE: Ferry sailings take around 10 minutes to reach Millport from Largs. There's no need to book – just turn up and go on the next available boat. See www.calmac.co.uk for more details.

WHERE TO STAY: Royal George Hotel, Quayhead, Millport, Great Cumbrae, KA28 0AP, **T:** 01475 530301, **W:** www.royalgeorgehotelmillport.com. Craigard Guest House, Craig Street, Millport, Great Cumbrae, KA28 0DR, **T:** 01475 530532, **W:** www.craigardmillport.co.uk.

WHERE TO EAT: Crocodile Chippy, Glasgow Street, Millport, Great Cumbrae, KA28 0DL, **T:** 01475 530916. Frasers Bar, 9 Cardiff Street, Millport, Great Cumbrae, KA28 0AS, **T:** 01475 530518.

HOLY ISLAND

Island Meditation

A sacred spring – or holy well – was said to have healing properties on this island, one of several around Britain that has the same name. Found just off the east coast of Arran, Holy Island is reached via a short crossing over Lamlash Bay and visitors are welcome during the summer months. This Holy Island was home to the hermit monk St Molaise in the 6th century and a monastery in the 13th century. It continues to be an important base for meditation today; in the south of the island a community of nuns are completing their three-year retreat and in the north you will be greeted by Tibetan flags at the Centre for World Peace and Health. Run by a Tibetan Buddhist master, the centre holds several retreats and courses for those wanting to develop their inner peace.

Expect to encounter plenty of wildlife on the island, whether you visit for a day or longer. As well as plenty of seabirds, Holy Island is home to Eriskay ponies, Soay sheep and Saanen goats.

A challenging annual swim takes place once a year from Arran to Holy Island for those wanting to test their stamina. Dozens of people get their wetsuits and swimming caps on before taking to the sea for the Two Island swim. Visit www.vigourevents.com for more information.

LOCATION: 55.5225°N 5.0700°W

GRID REFERENCE: NS063297

POPULATION: 31

SIZE: 2.5km²

GETTING THERE: The ferry to Holy Island leaves from Lamlash, Arran, between April and October. The departure times link with the ferries arriving on Arran from the mainland.

WHERE TO STAY: Retreats are available at the Centre for World Peace and Health, Holy Isle, KA27 8GB, **T:** 01770 601100, **W:** www.holyisle. org.

ISLE OF BUTE

LOCATION: 55.8379°N 5.0554°W

GRID REFERENCE: NS087647

POPULATION: 6,498

SIZE: 122km²

A Gothic Wonder

Scotland boasts many gothic homes, but you'll have to do a lot of searching before you find one as intricately detailed and visually stunning as Mount Stuart. This is a Victorian gem, home to the Stuarts of Bute, descendants of the Royal House of Stuarts. The lavish, cathedral-style family home was designed and built at the end of the 19th century after the previous Mount Stuart was gutted in a fire. The influences that went into making the fabulous sandstone mansion are varied – including astrology and mythology – and the entire scene is framed by 300 acres of impressive gardens, completing what is considered to be one of the finest buildings on any of the British islands.

West Island Way

The first long-distance footpath to be established on a Scottish island is a great way to see Bute and get some exercise at the same time. The 48km (30 mile) route is split up into four distinct sections, making it easy to organise a two-, three- or four-day trip to complete the walk. There'll be plenty of wildlife to spot along the trail, and it's also an ideal way to appreciate the varied landscapes on offer. You'll walk through forests, farmland, moors and along the coast. The Isle of Bute also has several brilliant beaches, ideal for dog walking, going for a run or playing with the family. Scalpsie Bay is a particular favourite, with Stravanan Bay and Lubas Bay being worthy alternatives.

GETTING THERE: Two ferry routes connect the Isle of Bute to the mainland, the shortest from Colintraive to the wonderfully named Rubodach, taking 5 minutes. Closer to Glasgow, ferries leave Wemyss Bay for the 35-minute sailing to Rothesay. See www.calmac.co.uk for more details.

WHERE TO STAY: Cadillac Kustomz Hotel, 23 Marine Place, Rothesay, Ardbeg, Isle of Bute, PA20 0LF, **T:** 07341 811278, **W:** www.cadillac-kustomz-hotel.co.uk. Sunnyside Guest House, 12 Argyle Place, Rothesay, Isle of Bute, PA20 0BA, **T:** 01700 502351.

WHERE TO EAT: Harry Haw's, High Street, Rothesay, Isle of Bute, PA20 9AS, **T:** 01700 505857, **W:** www.harryhawsbute.co.uk. Sea Dragon, 4 East Princes Street, Rothesay, Isle of Bute, PA20 9DL, **T:** 01700 502094.

▲ *The ferry to the Isle of Bute, ready to take cars across the short stretch of water.*

▶ *The fabulous Mount Stuart is one of the island's key attractions.*

Jazz Hands

Some of the biggest names in jazz – including Acker Bilk – have performed at the island's annual jazz festival over the years. Beginning in 1988 with just six performers, the festival has grown in stature and is a firm fixture on the jazz calendar. Events centre on the Rothesay Pavilion, which is transformed in May when music lovers make a beeline for Bute.

INCHCOLM

LOCATION: 56.0303°N 3.3029°W	
GRID REFERENCE: NT189827	
POPULATION: 2	
SIZE: <1km²	

Abbey Days

Most people crossing the Firth of Forth won't notice the tiny island of Inchcolm below them as they thunder north in cars and trains. Back when this crossing relied on ferry services, a great deal more activity took place on Inchcolm, which lies a quarter of a mile off the northern shore. With nearby road and rail bridges providing a stunning modern-day backdrop, there are two ferry companies that take you across to the island from South Queensferry. A journey out onto the water from here is worth it just to get up close to the world-famous rail bridge and enjoy views of the local seal population. But on reaching the island it's all about getting to know the rich religious history of Inchcolm Abbey, which has earned Inchcolm the nickname 'Iona of the east'. The fabulous abbey, in such a stunning setting, is now managed by Historic Scotland. The first Augustinians settled here during the 1100s and were drawn by the island's peaceful location. Despite being relatively isolated, though, Inchcolm's position in the Firth of Forth drew unwanted attention from military forces in England from the 1300s. Because of these raids on Inchcolm, the brethren were spending more

GETTING THERE: Two ferry companies leave for Inchcolm from Hawes Pier at South Queensferry. For more information, contact Forth Tours (**T:** 0131 331 3030, **W:** www.forthtours.com) or Maid of the Forth (**T:** 0131 331 5000, **W:** www.maidoftheforth.co.uk).

WHERE TO STAY: The Queens Bed and Breakfast, 8 The Loan, South Queensferry, EH30 9NS, **T:** 0131 331 4345, **W:** www.thequeensbandb.co.uk. Premier Inn, Builyeon Road, South Queensferry, EH30 9YJ, **T:** 0333 777 4683, **W:** www.premierinn.com.

time on the mainland and the Reformation in 1560 finally brought the monastic way of life on the island to an end.

Exploring the ruins of the abbey is an astonishing experience. It's the best-preserved group of monastic buildings in Scotland and there are plenty of gems to discover. Alexander I decided to build a monastery here to show thanks, it is thought, for his life, after he sought refuge on the island from a terrible storm. He died soon after so the job fell to his brother, David I, and the abbey status was granted a year later. Look out for the incredible fresco of a funeral procession in one of the tomb recesses and the stone screens placed to separate the choir from the nave.

Inspiring the Bard

Inchcolm was well known as a burial ground back in Shakespeare's day, so much so that it even gets a mention in *Macbeth*. In the famous Scottish play, Macbeth buys off a Danish king with gold and gives the Danes the option to bury their dead on Inchcolm for 'ten thousand dollars'.

AUSKERRY

Ripping Yarns

One of the most interesting of Britain's island cottage industries is found on tiny Auskerry, where the skin, wool and horns of native Orkney sheep are used to make a range of products that are shipped to all corners of the world. Uniquely coloured sheepskin rugs, woven blankets, knitting and crochet kits, and balls of naturally coloured wool yarn are all available on the Auskerry Island website (www.isleofauskerry.com). Wool from the island's sheep is hand clipped with shears and sent off to a Scottish mill to be spun into yarn, which is then returned to Auskerry, some hand-dyed into a range of subtle colours. The sheepskins are cured on the island and even the horns of the sheep are not wasted – they are made into buttons and sold. The sheep living on Auskerry are hardy creatures and form the second largest flock of the rare North Ronaldsay breed. Well adapted to the sometimes harsh environment, they have kept this tiny island thriving. One of the most popular products are the Auskerry blankets, which are made from 100% island wool and spun to the owner's pattern at a Speyside Mill.

LOCATION: 59.0342°N 2.5579°W

GRID REFERENCE: HY675165

POPULATION: 4

SIZE: <1km²

GETTING THERE: There are no regular ferry services to Auskerry, but trips are available from companies based in the harbour in Kirkwall.

WHERE TO STAY: St Ola Hotel, Harbour Street, Kirkwall, KW15 1LE, **T:** 01856 875090, **W:** www.stolahotel.co.uk. The Shore, Shore Street, Kirkwall, KW15 1LG, **T:** 01856 872200, **W:** www.theshore. co.uk.

▲ *The hard work put into the sheep products of Auskerry make them very popular items.*

BROUGH OF BIRSAY

Home to Norse and Picts

Time your visit to match low tide and you'll be able to make the short stroll across to this magical and historical island, framed by the waves crashing onto stunning, jagged rocks. Make the steep climb up to the lighthouse to enjoy the sweeping views out to sea. The biggest reason for getting to this tiny island is to see the incredible remains of a Pictish and Viking settlement that greet you as soon as you make it across. The outlines of homes, places of work, barns and drainage systems can still be made out at this hugely atmospheric and historically significant site, where you'll also find a replica of a carved Pictish symbol stone.

LOCATION: 59.1364°N 3.3300°W

GRID REFERENCE: HY239284

POPULATION: 0

SIZE: <1km²

GETTING THERE: Walk across from Orkney Mainland at low tide on the causeway.

WHERE TO STAY: Lindisfarne B&B, Stromness, KW16 3EX, **T:** 01856 850082, **W:** www.stayinstromness. co.uk/lindisfarne. Asgard B&B, Stromness, KW16 3JS. **T:** 01856 851699, **W:** www.stromness-orkney. co.uk.

◄ *The remains of a Viking settlement are an unforgettable, yet low key, attraction.*

▼ *The rock-strewn causeway is a popular spot for creating stacks.*

BURRAY

LOCATION: 58.8507°N 2.9375°W

GRID REFERENCE: ND460963

POPULATION: 409

SIZE: 9km²

GETTING THERE: Burray is connected to Orkney Mainland and South Ronaldsay by road.

WHERE TO STAY: The Sands Hotel, Burray, KW17 2SS, **T:** 01856 731298, **W:** www.thesandshotel.co.uk. Peedie Waaness, Burray, Orkney, KW17 2SX, **W:** www.waanessorkney.co.uk.

WHERE TO EAT: Orkney Fossil and Heritage Centre, Viewforth, Burray, KW17 2SY, **W:** www.orkneyfossilcentre. co.uk.

Several wrecks can be spotted close to the Churchill Barriers, scuttled to block the entrance to Scapa Flow.

The Churchill Barriers

Despite their remote location, the islands of Orkney were of key strategic importance in both world wars, from the scuttling of German ships at the end of the First World War to the posting of servicemen and arrival of POWs in the Second World War. The causeways linking Burray, Mainland, Lamb Holm and Glimps Holm have their roots in the sea battle between Britain and Germany. In 1939, the Royal Navy battleship HMS *Royal Oak* was sunk by a German U-boat while moored in the natural harbour of Scapa Flow. In an attempt to stop further destructive attacks, Churchill ordered the construction of a series of barriers between the islands. It became a mammoth undertaking; some 250,000 tons of rock was taken from Orkney quarries and dropped into place, filling in the sea, which was nearly 18m (60 ft) deep in some

places. Construction started in 1940 and at the peak of activity in 1943 over 2,000 people were put to work on the project. Many were Italian POWs who had been captured in North Africa; approximately 1,300 of them were brought to Orkney and around 700 were placed in two camps on Burray.

New Displays and Old Fossils

The Orkney Fossil and Heritage Centre in Burray does exactly what it says on the sign. Visitors to this popular attraction can be sure to learn heaps about the island's geology and rich history. On the geological side of things, you'll get the opportunity to see and handle the fossilised remains of creatures living on the island some 385 million years ago. The history section has great information about both wartime and peacetime, though stories of the former are most intriguing.

EDAY

LOCATION: 59.1885°N 2.7718°W

GRID REFERENCE: HY560338

POPULATION: 130

SIZE: 27.5km²

GETTING THERE: Ferries for Eday leaving Kirkwall on the Orkney Mainland, with the route taking 1 hour 15 minutes (**T:** 01865 872044, **W:** www.orkneyferries.co.uk).

WHERE TO STAY: Eday Hostel, London Bay, KW17 2AB, **T:** 07447 460169, **W:** www.hostellingscotland.org.uk/hostels/eday.

Ancient Eday

People have been living on Eday for 5,000 years, meaning there is plenty of history to explore here. Chambered tombs of the island's early farming community are now monuments of significant historical value. It is thought that many of these tombs were communal burial locations for the communities living nearby and you'll still see them dotted about Eday today.

Another key feature of Eday's landscape is the peat moorland that has been an important resource for Orkney. Large amounts of peat have been exported to peatless islands nearby for use as fuel. In the past, some of Eday's peat was even sent to distilleries on the mainland for use in the smoking process.

Birdlife

Eday is referred to as the heart of northern Orkney. It's certainly the beating pulse of the wildlife scene. All year round there are thousands of birds in these coastal waters, including guillemots, razorbills and puffins. Short-eared owls and kestrels are found inland on the moors. Binoculars will help you to spot otters as well as grey and common seals – visit in the summer and there's a chance of seeing newborn seal pups.

The Last Pirate

Take a tour of Carrick House, a 17th-century laird's house, to learn more about piracy in the region. In 1725, John Gow, Britain's last pirate, and his ship *The Revenge* ran aground on the island. He asked the laird for help but he got no joy and was stabbed as he tried to escape – the blood stain from the struggle can still be seen on the floor of Carrick House. Gow was captured and held captive before being transported down to London for the customary torturing and execution. The house is also home to many portraits of the lairds who lived here and an exhibition of artefacts from the Stone Age and the Iron Age. There's also a collection of mounted African animal heads that will divide opinion.

◄ *A pile of freshly cut peat to be used for fuel.*

EGILSAY

LOCATION: 59.1543°N 2.9283°W

GRID REFERENCE: HY470301

POPULATION: 26

SIZE: 6.5km²

Orkneyinga Saga

The population of the small island of Egilsay has fallen slightly in recent decades, bucking the trend of many islands, which have seen their numbers stabilise and increase. Egilsay may be a tiny island and tricky to reach, but spending time here is to take a stroll through history. The skyline is dominated by a stunning 12th-century kirk. Although ruined and without a roof, the church of St Magnus is in surprisingly good shape for a building of its age and is currently looked after by Historic Scotland. Aside from the cathedral in Kirkwall, this is the best example of a Norse church on the Orkney Islands and is a constant reminder of the influence the Vikings had on the region. The story of the church features in the *Orkneyinga Saga*, the medieval narrative of the islands that features Viking dealings with both Scotland and Norway. The tale goes that Magnus Erlendsson – then Earl of Orkney – arrived to settle a dispute but was murdered. The Bishop of Orkney made him a saint and the church was built at the scene of the crime.

GETTING THERE: Ferries leave Orkney Mainland from Tingwall, arriving at Egilsay via Wyre and Rousay. For more information contact Orkney Ferries (**T:** 01856 872044, **W:** www.orkneyferries.co.uk).

WHERE TO STAY: Accommodation on Orkney Mainland close to the ferry terminal includes Woodwick House, Evie, KW17 2PQ, **T:** 01856 751330, **W:** www.orkney.com/listings/woodwick-house.

Egilsay is one of many islands in the region that is riddled with fantastic history.

FLOTTA

Naval History

The name 'Flotta' comes from the Norse for 'flat isle'. This small island is, indeed, generally low-lying but gently rises as you head inland. When you find high ground, you get a 360-degree view that is quite spectacular. The larger hills on Orkney are visible, as well as the beautiful seascape of Scapa Flow. Situated as it is at the southern entrance to this famous body of water, Flotta holds a phenomenally strategic position, and there is no shortage of war stories emanating from here. With a population of less than 100 today, it's hard to imagine the sheer numbers of troops that were stationed here during both world wars. But evidence shows no fewer than 10,000 men watched a boxing bout here in the First World War. King George V arrived to visit soldiers in 1915 and his son – who was to become King George VI

– watched a film in the island's wartime cinema. A more tragic turning point saw the loss of 1,000 servicemen following the accidental explosion aboard the battleship HMS *Vanguard*, which was moored in Scapa Flow, in 1917. The island was once again used as a military base when the world went to war anew in 1939. More of the island's maritime history is explored in the small but well presented Peerie Museum, which also does a good job of conveying Flotta's wider heritage.

Today the island is dominated by the oil terminal on the northern shore. Operational since the 1970s, the unmistakable 68m (223ft)-tall flare stack is perhaps one of the most glimpsed, if less attractive, of Orkney icons. Flotta is home to the second biggest terminal for North Sea oil, surpassed only by Sullom Voe in Shetland.

LOCATION: 58.8267°N 3.1239°W

GRID REFERENCE: ND352938

POPULATION: 80

SIZE: 8.8km²

GETTING THERE: Ferries leave Houton on Orkney Mainland for Flotta, with the trip taking 1 hour 10 minutes. For more information contact Orkney Ferries (**T:** 01856 872044, **W:** www.orkneyferries.co.uk).

WHERE TO STAY: Scorrabrae Inn, Orkney, KW17 2RP, **T:** 01856 811483. Westrow Lodge B&B, Orphir, Orkney, KW17 2RD, **T:** 01856 811360, **W:** www.rovingeye.co.uk/westrowlodge.html.

▼ *The skyline of Flotta looks like a sci-fi movie set in places.*

GRAEMSAY

An Underrated Isle

Sandwiched between Orkney Mainland and Hoy, Graemsay is relatively well served by ferry services calling at the island as they make their way between the two larger islands. But despite having a reputation as the 'Green Isle' due to its lush countryside, this small area of land is far from overrun by tourists. In fact, you're more likely to have large sections of the coastal path to yourself rather than having to share the beautiful views with strangers. True, there's nothing in the way of facilities for visitors, but this curious little island does provide a great opportunity for a lovely walk. The most notable landmarks are the two lighthouses, Hoy High Light and Hoy Low Light, guiding ships into Hoy Sound from the Atlantic Ocean. The lighthouses are of a similar design, but seafarers can tell them apart by their different heights and lights.

LOCATION: 58.9302°N 3.2958°W

GRID REFERENCE: HY255055

POPULATION: 28

SIZE: 4.1km²

GETTING THERE: Graemsay is close to both Orkney Mainland and Hoy, with ferries linking to Stromness and Moaness. For more information contact Orkney Ferries (**T:** 01856 872044, **W:** www.orkneyferries.co.uk).

WHERE TO STAY: A range of accommodation is available in Stromness near the ferry terminal. Orca Hotel, Victoria Street, Stromness, KW16 3BS, **T:** 01856 850447. Brinkies Guest House, Brownstown Road, Stromness, KW16 3JN, **T:** 01856 851881.

HOLM OF PAPAY

Neolithic Tomb

Visits to Holm of Papay leave every day thanks to the ranger on Papa Westray. Book in advance to make sure you secure your spot and hope that the weather plays along with your plans. The main reason to make the voyage is to explore the incredible Neolithic South Cairn. Accessed through a ladder, you can descend into the tomb and see the stunning underground passage, some 20.4m (67ft) long. There are 14 chambers down here and decorations carved on the wall. It's a stunning location for this historical gem, on a tiny atmospheric island where birds easily outnumber visitors.

LOCATION: 59.3505°N 2.8686°W

GRID REFERENCE: HY507519

POPULATION: 0

SIZE: <1km²

GETTING THERE: Trips to Holm of Papay run from Papa Westray every day during the summer. Call the ranger on Papay for more details on 07931 235213.

WHERE TO STAY: Papa Westray Hostel, Beltane House, Papa Westray, KW17 2BU, **T:** 01857 644321, **W:** www.papawestray.co.uk/beltane-house.

HOY

LOCATION: 58.8459°N 3.2788°W

GRID REFERENCE: ND263961

POPULATION: 419

SIZE: 143km²

The Old Man of Hoy

Standing tall, proud and a little crooked, the Old Man of Hoy has watched over the eastern seas of Orkney for over 250 years. The Old Man is one of the most famous examples of a sea stack in Britain and, at 137m (450ft), it's also one of the tallest. At the right angle and with a certain amount of imagination, you can see how the stack was named after a human. The head shape towards the top of the stack is perhaps the most easily identifiable feature. The Old Man of Hoy used to have two feet at the base of the column, separated by an arch in the middle that made the rock look even more man-like. The rock in these parts, though, is made of old red sandstone, which is quick to erode, and one of the old man's legs was worn away by the waves and collapsed in the 19th century. Many think the Old Man's days are numbered and those wanting to see him should get a move on – cracks have been spotted in the stack and huge amounts of rock could fall into the sea at any time. Sea stacks, of course, are lonely fingers of rock that used to be part of the main cliff but were battered by waves. After the energy of the sea formed a cave, an arch soon followed and the stack was created when the roof of the arch collapsed. The Old Man of Hoy remains a popular place for climbers wanting to scale the challenging vertical ascent first ticked off by Sir Chris Bonington in 1966. A good footpath from Rackwick Bay goes over the cliffs and leads to a great vantage point of the stack – keep well back from the edge, though! The view from the beach at Rackwick is also fabulous, with huge boulders and majestic cliffs creating a stunning backdrop.

Power Tower

In the early 19th century when the threat of war from Napoleon's forces was strong, a series of Martello towers were built around Britain's coastline. Many were concentrated in south-eastern England, where the danger was thought to be greater. But strategic spots elsewhere around the coast also received the protection of a tower and Hoy is home to one of the three remaining in Scotland. Crockness Tower affords a great view towards Scapa Flow, which has long been an important naval site. Inside the tower you can find out about the military history of the building and learn more about the ceilidhs that have been held here!

GETTING THERE: Two ferry routes are available to reach Hoy. Boats leave Houton on Orkney Mainland, arriving on Hoy via Flotta. A service also sets out from Stromness on Orkney Mainland (**T:** 01865 872044, **W:** www.orkneyferries.co.uk).

WHERE TO STAY: The Hoy Hotel, Lyness, Hoy, KW16 3NT, **T:** 01865 791377, **W:** www.hoyhotel.co.uk. Hoy Hostel, Hoy, KW16 3NJ, **T:** 01865 850907, **W:** www.orkney.gov.uk.

WHERE TO EAT: Beneth'ill Café, Hoy, KW16 3NJ, **T:** 01865 791119, **W:** www.benethillcafe.co.uk.

▼ *The views north and south along the coast from the Old Man are dramatic.*

LAMB HOLM

The Italian Chapel

After their capture in North Africa, more than 1,200 Italian prisoners of war were transported to camps in Orkney and there they stayed between 1942 and 1945. Many were put to work on the new Churchill Barriers (see Burray, page 85) that linked three islands – including Lamb Holm – to Orkney Mainland and stopped enemy boats gaining access to Scapa Flow. Prisoners were prohibited from working on projects that were part of the war effort, but the causeways conveniently had the dual aim of improving communications and transport between the islands.

The camps themselves are no longer here, but one stunning building remains from the period. In 1943, an agreement was reached between the priest in Lamb Holm's Camp 60 and the commandant to provide a place of worship for the devoutly religious Italian POWs. Two huts were cobbled together, but the prisoners created a remarkable church out of practically nothing – the drab interior was plastered and then painted in staggeringly beautiful ornate detail, with a concrete altar added for services. The original architect, Domenico Chiocchetti, returned in the 1960s to oversee a restoration project.

LOCATION: 58.8869°N 2.8934°W

GRID REFERENCE: HY486003

POPULATION: 0

SIZE: <1km²

GETTING THERE: Lamb Holm is connected to Orkney Mainland via road.

WHERE TO STAY: Graemeshall House, Graemeshall Road, Orkney, KW17 2RX, **T:** 01856 781220, **W:** www.graemeshall-house.co.uk. The Inn, St Mary's, Orkney, KW17 2RT, **T:** 01856 781786, **W:** www.orkneytheinnguesthouse.co.uk.

Today, you're more likely to see a church of this breathtaking nature in the centre of Rome, and it's the juxtaposition of its location on this tiny remote island that gives the spectacle added wow factor.

After marvelling at the intricate internal decor of this Category A listed building, don't neglect the exterior; the work that went into disguising the fact this was just a couple of huts stuck together is as significant. A concrete façade,

The Italian façade of the chapel has a surreal quality in the island's surroundings.

NORTH RONALDSAY

The detail inside the chapel is more Rome than Lamb Holm.

painted white with lovely detail around the door and a bell, gives the island of Lamb Holm a truly Mediterranean feel. This is undoubtedly one of the top sights to see on Orkney, attracting in the region of 100,000 people a year. It's also one of the nation's most symbolic – and yet lesser known – examples of countries coming together during conflict. Many of the POWs who built this chapel revisited the site in the decades after the war, while their descendants continue to make their own pilgrimages to the island.

Northern Lights

At the north-eastern extremity of Orkney, North Ronaldsay has traditionally been one of the more difficult of the island group to reach. Dangerous currents and hidden reefs surround the island and the notorious North Ronaldsay Firth has claimed many ships down the years. The 18th century was a particularly torrid time for losing people at sea in shipwrecks. Air travel, of course, has changed that, and generous discounts are offered to travellers who spend the night on the island, so boosting the local economy.

There's still very much a feeling of being 'out on a limb' on North Ronaldsay, and justifiably so. To the north, it's a 40km (25 mile) journey to Fair Isle and 80km (50 miles) to Shetland. The 72 people living here are scattered around on sheep-farming crofts. Visitors arriving on this tiny, flat island are welcomed by those working in tourism. Families have been encouraged to settle on North Ronaldsay in an attempt to boost the population and maintain services, such as the important local school that educates a handful of the island's children.

With little shelter, prepare to be battered by strong winds that blow across this Orkney outpost from rough seas. Grey skies blend into the water and practically the only things to venture up from the horizon are the lighthouses – one on Holland House and two at Dennis Head. The New Lighthouse is the tallest on any land in Britain and as well as climbing over 30m (100ft) to the top, you can also enjoy the exhibition about local life and have a cuppa in the café.

LOCATION: 59.3733°N 2.4258°W

GRID REFERENCE: HY759542

POPULATION: 72

SIZE: 6.9km²

GETTING THERE: Flights and ferries link North Ronaldsay with Kirkwall on Orkney Mainland. For more information contact Orkney Ferries (**T:** 01856 872044, **W:** www. orkneyferries.co.uk) or Loganair (**T:** 0344 800 2855, **W:** www.loganair. co.uk).

WHERE TO STAY: The North Ronaldsay Bird Observatory offers hostel and guesthouse accommodation as well as camping, at Twingness, North Ronaldsay, KW17 2BE, **T:** 01857 633200, **W:** www.nrbo. org.uk.

WHERE TO EAT: The Bird Observatory (see above) serves meals. The Lighthouse also has a café, **T:** 01857 633297, **W:** www.northronaldsay. co.uk.

For the Birds

The main reason many pay a visit to North Ronaldsay is to spend time at the Bird Observatory. The island has an international reputation for attracting species; some of the more famous rarities to have flown here include Siberian blue robin, yellow-browed bunting and Cretzschmar's bunting. Since the observatory was built in the 1980s, it has recorded visits from over 340 different bird species. Some of these have attracted a great deal of media attention and seen large numbers of birdwatchers flock to the island.

I Sea Ewe

One of the more unusual sights on 'North Ron' is the island's unique breed of goat-like sheep paddling around the shoreline and eating seaweed. The diet gives their meat a rich taste and their wool a thick texture. Yarn from these sheep is much sought-after and available in a range of colours from www.northronaldsayyarn.co.uk.

ORKNEY MAINLAND

Immerse Yourself in History

By far the largest of the island group, Orkney Mainland is where it all happens. Kirkwall is the 'bright lights, big city' of Orkney, boasting an enviable array of facilities and the majority of Orkney's accommodation. While the bulk of archaeological wonders are in the more remote areas of the island, Kirkwall is a great place to come for a taste of history – and whisky! Some of the island's most treasured and unusual exhibits are to be found in Kirkwall's Orkney Museum opposite the cathedral. Look out for the whalebone plaque discovered on a Viking boat and a witch's spell box. Across from the harbour, the cosy Wireless Museum is packed with fascinating radio antiques. Because these waters saw a lot of action in the two world wars, many of the exhibits were washed up on the islands by the tides.

LOCATION: 59.0242°N 3.1339°W

GRID REFERENCE: HY350158

POPULATION: 17,162

SIZE: 523km²

GETTING THERE: Ferry services operate overnight between Kirkwall and Aberdeen, and over a shorter distance between Stromness and Scrabster. Contact Northlink Ferries for more information (**T:** 0845 6000 449, **W:** www.northlinkferries.co.uk). Flights from several UK airports head for Kirkwall with Loganair (**T:** 0142 642 9407, **W:** www.loganair.co.uk).

WHERE TO STAY: Ayre Hotel, Ayre Road, Kirkwall, Orkney, KW15 1QX, **T:** 01856 873001, **W:** www.ayrehotel. co.uk. Kirkwall Hotel, Harbour Street, Kirkwall, Orkney, KW15 1LE, **T:** 01856 872232, **W:** www.kirkwallhotel.com.

WHERE TO EAT: Eviedale Bistro and Bakehouse, Evie, Orkney, KW17 2PJ, **T:** 01856 751714, **W:** www.eviedale-cottages.co.uk. Helgi's, 14 Harbour Street, Kirkwall, Orkney, KW15 1LE, **T:** 01856 879293, **W:** www.helgis. co.uk.

The Standing Stones of Stenness are a worthy rival to Stonehenge.

North Star

Ask whisky fans what their favourite dram is and you're sure to spark a heated discussion. I alternate between four; interestingly enough, they are all produced on Scottish islands, and one originates in the northernmost whisky distillery in the country. Highland Park's home is in Kirkwall, but the bottles are distributed all over the world. A tour around the distillery typically takes an hour, although lengthier ones are available for those needing more detail. There's also the usual tasting and shop experience to round it off (www. highlandparkwhisky.com).

Your Country Needs You

Featuring the pointing finger and the slogan designed to encourage young people to join the war effort, the Your Country Needs You posters are famous for playing their part in Britain's First World War conscription campaign. They worked, of course, with thousands presenting themselves for action – many before they were old enough to do so. But the man behind the poster, Lord Kitchener, was one of the many who did not make it through the war years. He died just off the coast of Orkney along with over 600 others when HMS *Hampshire* struck a mine. Kitchener was on his way to meet the Russian Tsar in a secret meeting when disaster struck. A memorial tower is dedicated to him at Marwick Head.

Festival Island

Several festivals take place throughout the year, including the County Show in August and the St Magnus Arts Festival. The one that appeals to music lovers and grabs most media coverage is the Orkney Folk Festival towards the end of May. It began as a small event in 1982 but has grown to be of international significance, pulling in visitors and performers from across the globe. As well as music, there's also a good programme of dance and storytelling (www.orkneyfolkfestival.com).

AN EPIC SAGA

Relive the bloodthirsty tale of how Norsemen conquered the islands at the Orkney Saga Centre. The historic stories – known as the *Orkneyinga Saga* – were written by an Icelandic author around AD 1200 and tell the story of Viking history in the region.

▶ *The ancient remains of Skara Brae on the Orkney Mainland were uncovered by a devastating storm in 1850 that claimed over 200 lives. The Neolithic settlement dates back around 5,000 years and is a must-visit.*

Why I Love...
Orkney

'The Orkney Mainland has been inhabited for 8,500 years and wherever you step you feel a connection with the long human history of the islands and the people who lived here in the centuries and millennia before. From Kirkwall's towering cathedral to the winding flagstone street along the Stromness shore, from Neolithic village to Nissen hut, Stone Age tomb to standing stone, from palace to cairn to concrete causeway, all endure together in this close living landscape.'

John Peterson,
Orkney Library and Archive

PAPA WESTRAY

LOCATION: 59.3494°N 2.9020°W

GRID REFERENCE: HY488518

POPULATION: 90

SIZE: 9.2km²

Take-off and Landing

Aircraft enthusiasts come here from every continent to take a seat on one of the most unusual passenger services in the world. Those making the journey from Westray to Papa Westray aren't up in the air for long – at less than two minutes, this is the shortest scheduled flight anywhere on the planet. If you include an overnight stay on these northern islands, you'll be in line for a sizable discount on the fare. Be sure to book it in advance because the quirky journey tends to fill up – demand often outstrips supply because there are only ten seats on board, and one of those is taken by the pilot!

Papay Bird Life

The island of Papa Westray, known to locals simply as Papay, is one of the smallest inhabited islands of the Orkney group. In such a remote location, life can be challenging but investment and broadband has helped the population to stabilise in recent years and increase from a low in the 1990s. One of the highlights of a visit to Papay is the bird population that also calls this island home. The nature reserve around North Hill is a good place to see what's on offer. Although it's rightly called a hill, it's not all that tall at just 48m (157ft) above the nearby sea. It's the moorland surrounding it that makes this such a fascinating place to spend an afternoon. The former coastguard hut now houses the Hyndgreenie Hide and is an ideal place from which to spot lapwings, oystercatchers and great skuas – known locally as Bonxies.

GETTING THERE: Ferry services leave Kirkwall for Papa Westray and flights are also available to the island from Orkney Mainland. Flights and ferry services also operate between Papa Westray and Westray. For more information contact Orkney Ferries (**T:** 01856 872044, **W:** www. orkneyferries.co.uk) or Loganair (**T:** 0344 8002855, **W:** www.loganair. co.uk).

WHERE TO STAY: Papa Westray Hostel, Beltane House, Papa Westray, KW17 2BU, **T:** 01857 644321, **W:** www.papawestray.co.uk/beltane-house.

Why I love...
Papa Westray

'Papa Westray, Papay to the locals, is a small island caught between two oceans. Clinging to the edge of the Atlantic and backed by the North Sea, it is a beautiful location. Linked by ferry and light aircraft to so-called "civilisation", life can be tough but always rewarding for the islanders. Boasting the oldest constructed house in Europe, a community has existed here, perhaps unbroken, for 6,500 years.'

Jim Hewitson,
a Papay resident
for 40 years

This Old House...

Even for islands rooted in history, the Knap of Howar on Papa Westray is something special. These two Neolithic houses date back to around 3800 BC and were excavated in the early 20th century. They are – and let this sink in – the oldest standing dwellings in the whole of northern Europe.

ROUSAY

Egypt of the North

There may not be any pyramids and the weather certainly won't be comparable, but there is good reason why Rousay has earned the nickname 'Egypt of the North'. Well over 150 ancient archaeological wonders can be found on this small island, dating back to the time when the Egyptian civilisation was thriving. It may be less romantic to study the ancient history of Rousay when compared to the pharaohs and it may not make for such a wonderful primary school topic, but the historic finds on this amazing island are no less remarkable. You could spend weeks exploring them, but if time is limited here are a few highlights.

- **Midhowe Cairn**. This site has been known as the Great Ship of Death since excavations in the 1930s found the remains of 25 people in crouched positions. It is the largest of all the burial cairns on Orkney.

LOCATION: 59.1606°N 3.0387°W

GRID REFERENCE: HY407309

POPULATION: 216

SIZE: 48.6km²

GETTING THERE: Ferries leave Tingwall and arrive at Rousay 25 minutes later. For more information contact Orkney Ferries (**T:** 01856 872044, **W:** www.orkneyferries.co.uk).

WHERE TO STAY: The Taversoe, Gripps, Rousay, KW17 2PT, **T:** 01856 821325, **W:** www.taversoehotel.co.uk.

- **Midhowe Broch**. Fireplaces, stairways and alcoves are all visible in this well-preserved fortification that dates back to around 200 BC.

Rousay is home to a wonderful array of burial cairns.

Rousay is served by a regular ferry, making day trips from Orkney Mainland a great option.

Climb any hill in Orkney and you will be rewarded with views of several other islands.

- **Knowe of Swandro**. Although it's covered up in the winter months, visit in the summer to get a first-hand encounter with modern archaeology. Students come from all over the world to take part in excavations here and free tours are available.

- **Westness**. Important Viking discoveries have been made here, including two Norse brooches and a Viking grave. All the finds are on display in Edinburgh, but you can still explore the site.

- **Taversoe Tuick**. At the end of the 19th century, an unusual discovery was made on Rousay – one of only two tombs in the Orkney Islands placed one on top of the other. Experts determined this was a burial place for farmers around 4,500 years ago and several skeletons were excavated here in the 1930s.

Wacky Races

One of the most colourful times to experience Rousay is during the Regatta held every summer to raise cash for the RNLI. The programme starts with a sailing event that sees yachts arriving from far and wide. But it's the raft race that demands the most attention from the locals and pulls in the biggest crowds. Local teams are challenged to build their own rafts and they come in all shapes and sizes with some incredibly creative designs. Expect to see the likes of Shrek and vehicles from the Wacky Races heading off from Rousay Pier on the way to Wyre Pier and back. Onlookers can either watch the fun from the piers or on one of the boat trips that follow the rafts to the finish line.

SANDAY

LOCATION: 59.2552°N 2.5681°W

GRID REFERENCE: HY677411

POPULATION: 494

SIZE: 50km²

Life's a Beach

Of all the Orkney Islands, many people point to Sanday as being home to the finest beaches. Large bays pierce rocky points and the expanses of white sand are ideal for strolling along and, in good weather, relaxing. Sanday's coastline is a joy to explore and miles and miles of stunning walks make a few days on Sanday a real joy. On a tidal island accessible only at low tide, Start Point Lighthouse is one of the most unusual you'll see. Keeping ships safe since 1870, its distinctive black and white striped appearance makes it look like a seaside humbug towering above the shoreline. The arrival of lighthouses here – the first came in the early 19th century – helped to reduce the number of shipwrecks, but they weren't always welcome – there's a lack of peat on Sanday, and the driftwood coming ashore from wrecks was a good source of fuel.

GETTING THERE: Sanday is linked to Orkney Mainland by a ferry and plane service. For more information contact Orkney Ferries (**T:** 01856 872044, **W:** www.orkneyferries.co.uk) or Loganair (**T:** 0344 800 2855, **W:** www.loganair.co.uk).

WHERE TO STAY: Braeswick B&B, Braeswick, Sanday, KW17 2BA, **T:** 01857 600708, **W:** www.braeswick.co.uk. Ayres Rock Hostel & Campsite, Coo Road, Sanday, KW17 2AY, **T:** 01857 600410, **W:** www.ayres-rock-hostel-orkney.com.

WHERE TO EAT: The Belsair, Sanday, **T:** 01857 600206. Backaskaill B&B and Restaurant, Backaskaill, Sanday, KW17 2BA, **T:** 01857 600305.

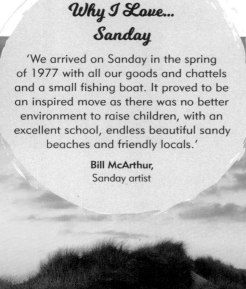

Why I Love...
Sanday

'We arrived on Sanday in the spring of 1977 with all our goods and chattels and a small fishing boat. It proved to be an inspired move as there was no better environment to raise children, with an excellent school, endless beautiful sandy beaches and friendly locals.'

Bill McArthur,
Sanday artist

The sun sets on another day on Sanday, home to many great beaches.

Why I Love...
Sanday

'Sanday has been described as "the Eldorado of the North Isles". I don't know about that but it is certainly a bonny place to live. It is an island rich in history and tradition, from Neolithic cairns to our unique lighthouse. But most of all, the people are friendly, compassionate and kind and the landscape is wild, untamed and has a stunning beach at every turn.'

Tracey Ranger,
Orkney Angora

▲ *The lovely stretch of sand at Whitemill Bay.*

▶ *The island is home to a thriving Angora wool industry.*

Cairn You Dig It?

Hundreds of archaeological riches lie beneath the ground on Sanday and most have not been excavated. Of all the brochs and cairns here, Quoyness Chambered Cairn is the one not to miss. The tomb, which is 4,000 years old, is partially reconstructed to give visitors more of a sense of what it was like when local people were buried here.

Bunny Business

One of the more unusual cottage industries on all our islands is to be found on Sanday. Orkney Angora cuts the long fur of the fluffy Angora rabbit and turns it into hand-dyed yarns that are shipped all over the UK and abroad. Dealing exclusively online at orkneyangora. co.uk, Orkney Angora also sells a range of thermal clothing made on the island.

Waves of Inspiration

The sandy bays and ever-changing seascapes around Sanday have prompted many artists to capture what they see. Bill McArthur specialises in seascape art and has been based on the island since the 1970s. Originally earning a living as a fisherman in the waters off north Scotland, he gradually turned his attention to art and now works in his studio on the island. Some of his wave-inspired work can be seen at his website, www.seascape-art-orkney.co.uk.

SHAPINSAY

LOCATION: 59.0452°N 2.8644°W

GRID REFERENCE: HY505179

POPULATION: 307

SIZE: 29.5km²

Balfour

Shapinsay is accessible to reach as a day trip from Orkney Mainland; it's just a short journey north across the water from Kirkwall to Balfour. Despite its proximity to the Mainland and being clearly visible from Kirkwall, Balfour has a unique feel. Much of this comes from the island's history and architecture. The village – the only one on Shapinsay – is named after the family who owned the island and invested in rebuilding the settlement, which was originally named Shoreside. Some of their additions can still be seen including the harbour's fortifications and an ornate gatehouse. The Balfour family died out in the 1960s, but until then they lived in the island's castle. You get a good view of this baronial home, which remains a private house, from the ferry as you arrive.

Heritage centre

There's a thriving arts and crafts scene on Shapinsay. The best way to get to grips with the range of products – and to take a piece home with you – is to venture to the Heritage Centre in Balfour. The diverse nature of what's designed and made on the island then becomes clearer, be it jewellery, ceramics, clothing or glass. The Heritage Centre also has a section on the island's history and a café at which you can rest before the boat returns. If you've time to explore the wildlife, Shapinsay is popular among birders, not least because there are large numbers of gulls, terns, geese and swans.

GETTING THERE: Shapinsay is within easy reach of Orkney Mainland by both ferry and plane. For more information about boats leaving from Kirkwall, contact Orkney Ferries (**T:** 01856 872044, **W:** www. orkneyferries.co.uk) and for plane journeys it's Loganair (**T:** 0344 800 2855, **W:** www.loganair.co.uk).

WHERE TO STAY: Kirkwall Hotel, Harbour Street, Kirkwall, KW15 1LE, **T:** 01856 872232, **W:** www. kirkwallhotel.com. St Ola, Harbour St, Kirkwall, KW15 1LE, **T:** 01856 875090, **W:** www.stolahotel.co.uk.

WHERE TO EAT: The Smithy Café, Balfour, Shapinsay, KW17 2DX.

SOUTH RONALDSAY

LOCATION: 59.0452°N 2.8644°W

GRID REFERENCE: ND449899

POPULATION: 909

SIZE: 49.8km²

GETTING THERE: Easily accessible from Kirkwall, South Ronaldsay is reached via a series of causeways linking it to the Orkney Mainland.

WHERE TO STAY: The Murray Arms Hotel, Back Road, St Margaret's Hope, South Ronaldsay, KW17 2SP, **T:** 01856 831205, **W:** www. themurrayarmshotel.com. The Creel B&B, Front Road, St Margaret's Hope, South Ronaldsay, KW17 2SL, **T:** 01856 831311, **W:** www.thecreel.co.uk.

WHERE TO EAT: Skerries Bistro, St Margaret's Hope, South Ronaldsay, KW17 2RW, **T:** 01856 831605, **W:** www.skerriesbistro.co.uk.

▲ *Gazing out from South Ronaldsay, an island of such strategic importance that heavy wartime defences were built along the coast.*

What's in a Name?

Head across the Churchill Barriers and you'll eventually arrive at South Ronaldsay, a lovely island stretching south and coming within 11km (7 miles) of mainland Scotland. Just the short strip of the Pentland Firth separates John O'Groats from South Ronaldsay, but there is still very much an island feel here. The main settlement is the gloriously named St Margaret's Hope, or 'The Hope' to locals. The origins of the unusual name are thought to be the Maid of Norway, who died here at the end of the 13th century, shortly after being proclaimed the Queen of Scotland. Margaret, daughter of the King of Norway, was said to be on her way to marry the future King Edward II of England in a union that would have brought the two countries together. Keep your eyes peeled for seals as you walk along the coast. The Churchill Barriers are also a good place to look for otters at dusk and dawn.

A journey to South Ronaldsay won't be complete until you've been to what is one of the most spectacular ancient burial sites in the world. In the south-eastern extremes of the island, the Tomb of the Eagles lay undiscovered until the 1950s, when a local farmer came across it. There's a visitor centre and a Bronze Age burnt mound to whet your appetite for the local history, but the truly remarkable experience is found along a well-marked path through a mile of stunning scenery. The chambered cairn is almost on the edge of the cliff. The entrance is so small that to head inside you need to lie down on a trolley and pull yourself along on a rope. The more hardy have the option of crawling on their hands and knees.

Inside the Tomb...

Farmer Ronnie Simison found a cache of artefacts the same summer's evening he discovered the tomb. They included axe heads and a knife. A few days later he returned to the site and discovered an even more important chamber with 30 human skulls. After initially thinking the site had been a dwelling, this new discovery confirmed it to be a 5,000-year-old burial site. Alongside the bodies were the bones and talons of 14 sea eagles. Having animals in such numbers buried alongside humans is unusual, leaving archaeologists to conclude there was a strong link between the ancient islanders and sea eagles.

STRONSAY

Thriving Economies

At the end of the pier, the café in the old fish mart provides the ideal place to call at before and after ferry crossings. There's a fresh bakery here and the opportunity to snack on treats, full meals and takeaway food. This historic building – also home to a hostel – used to be the hub of the island's fishing industry, the place where herring was bought and sold during the boom years of the 19th century. It's hard to imagine the scale of the fishing trade here; in the 1840s, 400 boats were based at Whitehall, the main settlement on Stronsay. Around 5,000 lived and worked here during the fishing heyday, and hundreds of female workers on the island earned a living from gutting the fish. And that wasn't the first economic golden age to provide employment on Stronsay. In the 18th century, 3,000 people collected seaweed around this coast and sold the kelp to various chemical industries. Whitehall is a relatively sleepy village today, welcoming tourists as each ferry arrives. The rows of fishing cottages are still home to a handful of people making a living from the sea.

Sandstone, Seabirds and Cycling

The peaceful, gentle landscape and the stunning coastline of Stronsay make it a popular place for nature lovers. The low-lying topography of the island means it's a perfect place to explore on two feet or two wheels. Gorgeous beaches are to be found in several bays, where the clear waters of the sea and fine sands implore you to take off your shoes and socks. For many, the appeal is in the drama-strewn sandstone cliffs that are home to thousands of seabirds. Make sure you include a stroll to the Vat of Kirbister – a stunning natural arch and one of Orkney's top film locations.

▲ *The spectacular Vat of Kirbister – formed when the roof of a large sea cave collapsed.*

LOCATION: 59.1006°N 2.5795°W

GRID REFERENCE: HY669239

POPULATION: 349

SIZE: 32.8km²

GETTING THERE: You can reach Stronsay via ferry or plane from Orkney Mainland. For more information contact Orkney Ferries (**T:** 01856 872044, **W:** www.orkneyferries.co.uk) or Loganair (**T:** 0344 8002855, **W:** www.loganair.co.uk).

WHERE TO STAY: Stronsay Hotel, Whitehall, Stronsay, KW17 2AR, **T:** 01857 616213. Storehouse B&B, Whitehall, Stronsay, KW17 2AR, **T:** 01857 616263, **W:** www.stronsaystorehousebedandbreakfast.co.uk.

WHERE TO EAT: Stronsay Fish Mart Café, Whitehall, Stronsay, KW17 2AR, **T:** 01857 616401, **W:** www.stronsaycafehostel.weebly.com.

WESTRAY

LOCATION: 59.2978°N 2.9481°W

GRID REFERENCE: HY461461

POPULATION: 588

SIZE: 47.1km²

GETTING THERE: Ferry services leave Kirkwall for Westray and flights are also available to the island from Orkney Mainland. Flights and ferry services also operate between Papa Westray and Westray. For more information contact Orkney Ferries (**T:** 01856 872044, **W:** www.orkney ferries.co.uk) or Loganair (**T:** 0344 8002855, **W:** www.loganair.co.uk).

WHERE TO STAY: Pierowall Hotel, Westray, KW17 2BZ, **T:** 01857 677472, **W:** www.pierowallhotel.co.uk. Cleaton House Hotel, Westray, KW17 2DB, **T:** 01857 677540, **W:** www. cleatonhousehotel.business.site.

WHERE TO EAT: Richans Retreat, Rapness, Westray, KW17 2DE, **T:** 01857 677877, **W:** www.aakwork. co.uk.

Plot Development

The standout building on Westray is the huge 16th-century sandstone Noltland Castle. It's found in the north of the island just outside Pierowall, Westray's main settlement. The Bishop of Orkney gave Noltland to Gilbert Balfour and he set to work on the castle straight away. Balfour was a key supporter of Mary, Queen of Scots, and when she was deposed he joined a failed uprising to return her to power. The result of the struggle saw him fleeing to Sweden, where he ran into more trouble and was executed for plotting to kill the king.

Walk This Way

There are plenty of walks to indulge in when you visit Westray, but perhaps the best is found on the western coast. Noup Head is way out at the north-western tip, where dramatic seascapes and an incredible array of 100,000 birds await in the summer months. It's a real bombardment of the senses. From here, a coastal path heads south to the Bay of Kirbist. Nearby you'll see the highest point of the Westray, Fitty Hill, and from the 170m (557ft) peak you can gain a good vantage point of the northern islands. The best place for birdwatching on the east coast is Castle O'Burrian, just off the main road. Puffins come here in great numbers in June and July.

Rich Heritage

For a taste of what life has been like for those living on Westray down the decades, it's well worth heading to Westray's Heritage Centre. You'll find a collection of photographs of life in the 20th century, from church activities to sports and transport. The two world wars are also covered and the Heritage Trust updates the display with a fresh focus each year.

▼ *Noltland Castle.*

WYRE

LOCATION: 59.1190°N 2.9711°W

GRID REFERENCE: HY445262

POPULATION: 9

SIZE: 3km²

GETTING THERE: Ferries serve the island from Tingwall on the Orkney Mainland and also link to nearby islands Rousay and Egilsay. Contact Orkney Ferries for more information (**T:** 01856 872044, **W:** www.orkney ferries.co.uk).

WHERE TO STAY: Accommodation is available on Rousay, a 5-minute ferry journey away. Try the Taversoe, Gripps, Rousay, KW17 2PT, **T:** 01856 821325, **W:** www.taversoehotel.co.uk.

▲ *Ferry from Rousay to Wyre.*
◄ *Cubbie Roo's Castle, c1145, remains of the oldest medieval castle known to exist in Scotland.*

Muir's Isle

Wyre is a small island you can explore in a day trip either from Rousay or the Orkney Mainland. Look out for bird life as you wander along the paths near the coast, but the real wildlife appeal on Wyre is the seals. There's a chance of seeing them on any stretch of the island's coast, but head to The Taing on the eastern extreme of Wyre. From this cool vantage point you're likely to see both common and grey seals.

For such a tiny and easily navigated area, there's also plenty of human history to explore in the buildings dotted around. Best known is Cubbie Roo's Castle, a 12th-century fort mentioned in the sagas. The nearby St Mary's Chapel was once home to the Bishop of Orkney. On the southern side of the island is the home known as the Bu – the place where Scottish poet Edwin Muir spent some of his childhood years. Muir, who also wrote novels and translated several pieces of work, is one of the subjects covered by the Wyre Heritage Centre.

BALESHARE

Flat, flat, flat!

When you drive onto Baleshare, the first thing you notice is the landscape. This is a flat island. Not just a little bit flat, but incredibly flat. From shore to shore there isn't a great deal of topographic change. If you have an Ordnance Survey 1:50000 map of the area to hand, you'll see just how devoid of hills this island is; there isn't a solitary contour line on the map, and there aren't many islands with such a flat claim to fame. The causeway provided such an important link to the local community when it was built in 1962 and has played a part in maintaining a healthy population on the island ever since.

This is a remote location and the best activity to enjoy is taking a brisk walk around the shoreline. The flat landscape adds a mystery to the views from Baleshare; the sea mixes with the sky, separated by dunes in places to create scenes worthy of a painting at every turn. This is part of a Special Area of Conservation and a joy in the summer, when the endangered great yellow bumblebee visits the machair. The island's name means 'east village' in Gaelic. There was once a 'west village' but it was wiped away in a severe storm in the 16th century.

LOCATION: 57.5327°N 7.3691°W

GRID REFERENCE: NF788619

POPULATION: 58

SIZE: 9.1km²

GETTING THERE: A causeway links the island with the A865 on North Uist, just north of Carinish.

WHERE TO STAY: Bagh Alluin B&B, 21 Baleshare, Western Isles, HS6 5HG, **T:** 01876 580370, **W:** www. jacvol beda.co.uk. An Airigh, Claddach Kirkibost, North Uist, HS6 4EP, **T:** 01224 825509.

The island is well known for an awesome blend of seascapes with skyscapes.

BARRA

LOCATION: 56.9833°N 7.4667°W

GRID REFERENCE: NF687004

POPULATION: 1,174

SIZE: 58.8km²

GETTING THERE: Ferry crossings from Oban on the mainland take just under five hours. A ferry also links Barra with Eriskay, which is a 40-minute journey. See www.calmac.co.uk for more details. Flights leave various destinations in the UK for Barra. Check www.loganair.co.uk for routes.

WHERE TO STAY: Heathbank, Northbay, Isle of Barra, HS9 5YQ, **T:** 01871 890266, **W:** www.barrahotel.co.uk. Craigard Hotel, Castlebay, Isle of Barra, HS9 5XD, **T:** 01871 810200, **W:** www.craigardhotel.co.uk.

WHERE TO EAT: Kisimul Café, Castlebay, Isle of Barra, HS9 5XD, **T:** 01871 810645, **W:** www.cafekisimul.co.uk. Joan's Barra Pizza, Borve, Isle of Barra, HS9 5XR, **T:** 01871 810570, **W:** www.joans-barra-pizza.business.site.

A Runway Success

The best way to arrive on Barra is undoubtedly by air. Landing at the island's airport sees you join a fairly exclusive club of people to have touched down on a beach. Taking off and landing at Barra Airport is an experience you won't get at any other; it's the only airport in the world that uses a stretch of sand for scheduled flights. Walking across the cockleshell beach to your Twin Otter and seeing the clear sea shine in the distance is a moment you won't forget. It's all idyllic and romantic, but there's just one problem – the planes cannot operate when it's high tide because the runway on The Great Beach disappears beneath the sea. Flight times fluctuate from day to day with the tide times, further entwining the island's relationship with the sea.

Elsewhere on the island of Barra, you can explore the island's distillery, which is home to the delicious Atlantic Gin, and take a trip to Kisimul Castle, a fort standing in the waters off Castlebay. This rock is thought to have been fortified as early as the 10th century and it has seen plenty of action down the decades as various Scottish rivals attempted to make a grab for power.

BENBECULA

LOCATION: 57.4500°N 7.3252°W

GRID REFERENCE: NF807525

POPULATION: 1,283

SIZE: 82km²

Ticket to Ride

With long, sandy beaches disappearing into the distance and dramatic skies seeming to change every few minutes, the time you spend in Benbecula almost demands to be spectacular. One of the most breathtaking experiences to be had is on horseback, riding along the glistening sand and splashing in the edge of the sea. The Uist Community Riding School (www.ridehebrides.org) is the place to head for, and you can bet your four-legged companion will enjoy the adventure as much as you!

Rueval

It's not going to win awards for being the toughest climb, but a trek up to the top of 124m (407ft)-high Rueval is a must-do activity here on Benbecula. From the top, you'll get an astounding 360-degree perspective of the low-lying, far-reaching Western Isles and how they are dented with freshwater lakes. Clear days are obviously best to tackle this route, when you may be treated to a view out to the Isle of Skye and might even be able to make out St Kilda. The path to the top sets off close to the council building near the crossroads on the A835.

Isle of Defence

Built in the middle of the 14th century by Amy MacRuairi, the first wife of John, Lord of the Isles, Borve Castle was once the most important castle in the Outer Hebrides. The ruins stand in the village of Torlum. The island is still important for defence today, with a radar station being sited here. In the decades following the Second World War thousands of soldiers were stationed on Benbecula, but the base was downgraded in the late 1990s.

GETTING THERE: Benbecula is well connected to North and South Uist via the A865 on North Uist causeways. The airport on the island has regular flight connections with Glasgow and Stornoway.

WHERE TO STAY: Nunton House Hostel, Benbecula, HS7 5LU, **T:** 01870 602017, **W:** www.nunton househostel.com. Borve Guest House, 5A, Torlum, Benbecula, HS7 5PP, **T:** 01870 602685, **W:** www.borve.scot.

WHERE TO EAT: The Stepping Stone Restaurant, Balivanich, Benbecula, HS7 5LA, **T:** 01870 603377, **W:** www.facebook.com/ TheSteppingStoneRestaurant. Charlie's Bistro, The Old Shop, Balivanich, Benbecula, HS7 5LA, **T:** 01870 603242, **W:** www.charlies-hebridean-bistro.business.site.

Take care on the roads and watch out for the island's wildlife.

BERNERAY

LOCATION: 57.7185°N 7.1881°W

GRID REFERENCE: NF912817

POPULATION: 138

SIZE: 10.1km²

Little Berneray of Sunshine

The road into Berneray from North Uist brings you in on the eastern side of the island, where you can sit and look for seals in the calm bay and maybe call for a lunch of smoked salmon at the bistro. Both are well worth doing – a large population of seals live on the island and the salmon is a local delicacy. But the real family adventures lie on the western side of the island, where a 4.8km (3 mile) long beach with clear seas and white sands might make you think you're in the tropics. The weather will probably bring you back down to earth, but the sandy stretch on Berneray is certainly one of the finest you'll see in the British Isles. Rock pools sit nearby awaiting investigation, and a curious sea otter came to visit us when we were taking a walk. A road signed for the beach twists and turns across fields before reaching a small car park. A short walk through the dunes brings you out at this coastal haven, where the mountains of Harris can be seen to the north. You'll have plenty of this huge beach to yourself even in the height of summer.

Tall Tales

It's not often you come across a monument to a giant, so make sure you visit the one for Giant Macaskill at the southern end of the island. Perhaps Berneray's most famous son, Aonghas Mor MacAsgaill was thought to be the world's tallest person at 2.3m (7ft 9in) tall. He spent most of his life over the Atlantic in Nova Scotia, but is remembered to this day in the Outer Hebrides.

GETTING THERE: Berneray is linked to North Uist by a causeway and so accessible by car. There is a ferry link to Leverburgh on Harris, taking 1 hour 20 minutes. See www.calmac.co.uk for more details.

WHERE TO STAY: Seal View B&B, 16 Backhill, Berneray, HS6 5BD, **T:** 01876 540209, **W:** www.sealview.com. Tir nan Og B&B and Tea Room, North End, Main Road, Berneray, HS6 5BQ, **T:** 01876 540333.

WHERE TO EAT: Berneray Shop and Bistro, Berneray, HS6 5BJ, **T:** 01876 540288, **W:** www.berneray shopandbistro.co.uk.

There are fine beaches and rock pools on Berneray, making it an ideal family destination.

Why I Love... Berneray

'As a young couple we spent an afternoon here, walking on the beach, enjoying the tranquillity of the island, listening to the waves crashing and watching an inquisitive otter. Many years later we returned with our children to discover the rock pools, run along the endless sands and splash in crystal clear water. This is a unique place, a place where time stands still and you can lose yourself in the beauty of the moment with your loved ones.'

Nicola Harper,
teacher

ERISKAY

Whisky Galore!

Eriskay was destined to earn its place in history when the SS *Politician* ran aground just off the island in 1941. Locals could not believe it when they discovered the cargo on board that was bound for the United States – 246,000 bottles of whisky! Some islanders decided to board the ship and remove the spirits, hiding it in various places to keep it secret from customs officials who were taking a keen interest in the incident. The wartime story became legendary when Compton Mackenzie – a resident of Barra at the time – penned the classic story *Whisky Galore* (1947), which was based on the events. The book's fictional account took place on the islands Great Todday and Little Todday, while the boat was renamed the SS *Cabinet Minister*. The Ealing comedy that followed in 1949 brought the tale to a larger audience and saw demand grow for the salvaged bottles in various auctions. The pub on the island, opened as recently as 1988, is named after the SS *Politician* and has various artefacts from the wreckage, including a couple of the original bottles of whisky.

The Beautiful, Bumpy Game

Windswept and rocky, this hilly island doesn't exactly stand out as being a footballing haven. But FIFA has recognised the pitch on Eriskay as being one of the most unique in the game. The location is spellbinding; it's a wonder any goalkeeper can keep focused on the action with the stunning views beyond the playing surface. As for tactics, there are several things players have to keep in mind that don't arise in a game staged at Wembley. For a start, one of the corners is on a little hill. There's also the rabbit holes and the bumps throughout the penalty area. The players in those green and white kits certainly get to know their opponents well – the league has only six teams. And yes, Eriskay FC have won it a few times in their history.

Make time to walk around Eriskay. It's a beautiful island, with sandy beaches leading to unique stretches of machair. You'll no doubt see some Eriskay ponies, with their easily recognisable grey coat.

LOCATION: 57.0726°N 7.2907°W

GRID REFERENCE: NF795104

POPULATION: 40

SIZE: 7km²

GETTING THERE: A causeway connects Eriskay with South Uist. The ferry service to Barra takes 40min. See www.calmac.co.uk for more details.

WHERE TO STAY: An Taigh Mor, Eriskay, HS8 5JL, **T:** 01878 720717, **W:** www.antaighmor.com. Taigh Mo Sheanair, Rudha Ban House, Eriskay, HS8 5JJ, **T:** 07801 547107, **W:** www.eriskayholidayhome.co.uk.

WHERE TO EAT: Am Politician, 3 Balla, Eriskay, HS8 5JL, **T:** 01878 720246.

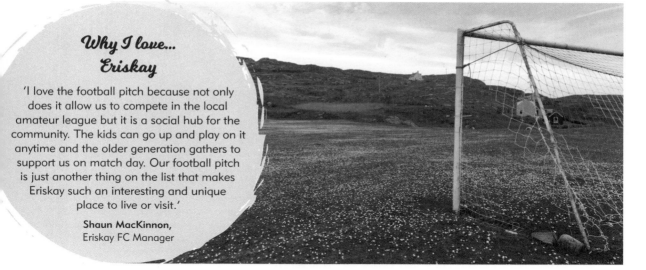

FLODAIGH

Seal Life Centre

This small tidal island is connected to Benbecula by a causeway that makes it easier for the local population to stay in situ. It's also one of the best places in the Outer Hebrides to go for a secluded walk and spend time watching this quiet, remote part of the world go by. At the end of the public road, paths take you down to the coast, where seals haul onto the rocks at low tide. One of the most popular spots for the seals is the small island sitting out in the bay. It's a special place that makes you feel at one with nature.

LOCATION: 57.4778°N 7.2641°W

GRID REFERENCE: NF846553

POPULATION: 7

SIZE: 1.5km²

GETTING THERE: Turn off the A865 on Benbecula and head east towards Flodaigh, with a causeway connecting the two islands.

WHERE TO STAY: Isle of Benbecula House Hotel, Benbecula, HS7 5PG, **T:** 01870 603046, **W:** www.isleshotel group.co.uk. Dark Island Hotel, Linaclate, Benbecula, HS7 5PJ, **T:** 01870 603030, **W:** www.isleshotel group.co.uk.

GREAT BERNERA

I Predict a Riot

As you cross over the bridge from Lewis to Great Bernera, an incredible megalithic structure looms high on the hill above. Although the huge Callanish Stones on the west coast of Lewis are the most famous in the region, there are several other similar examples – including the semi-circular stones known as Callanish VIII on Great Bernera. Four large stones create the semi-circle and although it may not look like it from the bridge, the largest of the stones reaches nearly 3m (10ft) in height. It's a humbling greeting to what is a beautiful and remote island on the western edges of the Outer Hebrides. Spending time here allows you to enjoy walks around the coast and explore the freshwater lochs in the centre of Great Bernera.

Despite the resident population of over 250, you don't have to travel far to experience solitude here. It's perhaps surprising, then, that this calm and peaceful island is known for a so-called riot that took place in 1874. When the bailiffs arrived on the island during the infamous Highland Clearances, they were pelted with clods of earth in what turned out to be an important and historic protest against oppression. The standoff between landlords and tenants here on Great Bernera resulted in the first recorded legal victory for the small-tenants, who refused to accept their grazing land being reduced into smaller and smaller areas.

LOCATION: 58.2066°N 6.8332°W

GRID REFERENCE: NB162344

POPULATION: 252

SIZE: 21km²

GETTING THERE: A bridge links Great Bernera to the west coast of Lewis.

WHERE TO STAY: Threeways Bed & Breakfast, 25 Kirkibost, Great Bernera, HS2 9LX, **T:** 01851 612360, **W:** www.isleoflewisbandb.co.uk. Creagan Bed & Breakfast, Creagan, Callanish, Isle of Lewis, HS2 9DY, **T:** 01851 621200, **W:** www.creagan-bedandbreakfast.co.uk.

GRIMSAY

LOCATION: 57.4954°N 7.2516°W	
GRID REFERENCE: NF855572	
POPULATION: 169	
SIZE: 8.3km²	

Grimsay Causeway

Getting to Grimsay today is a relatively easy task compared to the 1950s, when the causeway opened. Back then, you had to take a ferry from North Uist but because of local rocks it only operated at high tide. The harbour at Kallin was an even more recent transport addition to Grimsay, having been built in 1985 to support the growing shellfish industry.

Hebridean Catch

NAMARA Seafood is based near the harbour at Kallin on Grimsay and has given this small island a reputation for fine cuisine through its 'Hebridean Catch'. Boats head out into the clean Scottish seas daily and return with a cache

GETTING THERE: Grimsay is connected to Benbecula and North Uist via a causeway.

WHERE TO STAY: Moorcroft Holidays campsite, Carinish, North Uist, HS6 5HN, **T:** 01876 580305, **W:** www. moorcroft holidays.co.uk.

WHERE TO EAT: NAMARA Marine Supplies & Seafood Café, Kallin Harbour, Grimsay, HS6 5HY, **T:** 01870 602812, **W:** www.namaraseafoods.co.uk.

of fresh seafood, some of which is destined for eateries around the world and some for serving in the café. Products on offer in the shop include locally sourced scallops shucked on site and ready for consumption within hours of being landed. Brown crabs from the eastern and western shores of the Hebrides are caught in creels using traditional methods throughout the year, and Hebridean lobsters are a particular favourite, sent live to locations all over the globe. Another popular Scottish export from Grimsay is the langoustine, caught on the eastern coast. Often langoustine live in burrowed holes on the bottom of the sea in waters as deep as 100 fathoms and bait is used to get them out and into the creels. Tuck into a langoustine when you're out of the country and there's a fair chance it came from these Scottish waters. The café offers plenty of tasty seafood morsels for you to sample, and many of the dishes are something to write home about. A well-stocked shop allows you to take Scottish seafood produce home with you as well.

Mysterious Grimsay

One of the best examples of an ancient Iron Age wheelhouse is found on Grimsay, between Loch Hornary and the north coast. It's a marvellous site and archaeologists have found evidence of metal smelting here. The wild, desolate horizon of the Western Isles adds to the mystery of the location. It can be tricky to find as it's not on the OS map of the island, but it is worth the effort.

LEWIS AND HARRIS

Although physically not separate from each other and occupying the one island, Lewis and Harris have their own distinctive identities, landscapes and history, so I've made the decision to treat them as their own place rather than lumping them together. The cultural rift between Lewis and Harris can be traced back to a divide in the MacLeod clan aeons ago, the reasons for which have been forgotten over the generations. The two communities were also sitting in different counties until a border change in 1975. Lewis was part of Ross and Cromarty, with the more southerly Harris being aligned with Inverness-shire. The official border between the two is just 9.7km (6 miles) long, running from Loch Reasort in the west to Loch Shiphoirt in the east.

ISLE OF LEWIS

LOCATION: 58.2193°N 6.3849°W

GRID REFERENCE: NB426340

POPULATION: 18,500

SIZE: 1,770km²

GETTING THERE: The ferry to Stornoway on Lewis takes 2 hours 45 minutes, leaving from Ullapool. See www.calmac.co.uk for more details.

WHERE TO STAY: Stornoway Bed and Breakfast, 29 & 32 Kenneth Street, Stornoway, HS1 2DR, **T:** 07917 035295, **W:** www.stornoway bedandbreakfast.co.uk. The Crown Inn, Castle Street, Stornoway, HS1 2BD, **T:** 01851 703734, **W:** www.crownhotelstornoway.com.

WHERE TO EAT: Loch Croistean Coffee Shop & Restaurant, Loch Croistean Old School, Loch Croistean, Isle of Lewis, HS2 9EP, **T:** 01851 672772. Digby Chick, Bank Street, Stornoway, HS1 2XG, **T:** 01851 700026, **W:** www.digbychick.co.uk.

Stones of Great Standing

Before planning a trip to Lewis, you'll more than likely see pictures of the great Callanish Standing Stones, but no image I have seen has ever done the place justice. There are nearly 50 gneiss monoliths here, carefully arranged in a position we still don't fully understand the meaning of. The huge stones – some towering 4.6m (15ft) tall – draw obvious comparisons with Stonehenge but the Callanish monoliths are on a grander scale and in a much more sublime setting. You'll also be able to wander around them and snap photographs without the throngs of tourists that would be here were the stones in a more populous location. The Callanish Visitor Centre nearby has a shop, café and small museum, but perhaps most importantly it offers shelter from the frequently harsh elements.

A Beautiful Butt

Head to the northern outposts of the island and you'll pass through small Presbyterian villages with plain churches and strict rules about keeping the noise down on Sundays – some children's playgrounds have signs up politely asking for respect on the Sabbath. The most northerly tip is the Butt of Lewis, where cliffs around the lighthouse are home to skuas, gannets, kittiwakes and fulmars. The coastline up on this northern extreme of the Outer Hebrides is stunning. The Butt of Lewis was actually once listed in the *Guinness Book of Records* as being the windiest place in the country. And if you come when it's blowing a gale you'll soon see why!

Blackhouses

A visit to a traditional blackhouse – and there are several open to the public, dotted along the island's west coast – offers an insightful glance into what living here was like decades ago. At Geranin, there is not one but a whole hamlet of blackhouses. You can wander inside many of them, with their dark interiors and peat fires providing heat and generating smoke that drifts up through thatched chimneys. Others have been converted into holiday cottages and offer the chance to stay in a truly historic environment.

The Bright Lights of Stornoway

If you've been travelling around the Outer Hebrides for some time and visiting tiny, remote islands, the urban centre of Stornoway can come as a bit of a shock. Bustling from its ferry links with Ullapool and providing jobs, entertainment, schooling and accommodation for its 8,000 residents, this busy town can seem out of place and in contrast with the rest of the island. You do not have to venture far out of Stornoway until you are back into the boggy, peaty landscapes for which Lewis is famous. Those visitors looking for peace and quiet tend to stay away from Stornoway, or perhaps only venture in when they need to restock provisions. I enjoyed paying a visit to Stornoway because as a child, it was one of the mysteriously remote places to feature in our family favourite board game, The Great Game of Britain.

Get up close to historic blackhouses at Geranin.

ISLE OF HARRIS

River Deep, Mountain High

Whether you're arriving to Harris from the flatter, boggier Lewis or the rolling beaches of Berneray, the first thing to grab your attention is the landscape. Harris is divided in two by a thin stretch of land at Tarbert, the north notable for its towering mountains and the south for its phenomenal beaches. The Calmac ferry takes around an hour to negotiate the rocky waters that divide Harris from Berneray, but the slow-moving journey gives a great opportunity to watch for wildlife. After landing at Leverburgh, the A859 takes you north along the west coast, where the waves of the Atlantic crash onto famously picturesque beaches like Luskentyre. But it's the mountains in the north of Harris that are the real scenic pull here. The main road running from north to south takes you through some incredible landscapes, strewn with boulders, shaped by glaciers and dotted with lofty peaks. If you fancy a diversion to a picture-perfect coastal scene, take the narrow B887, which winds a steady way right to the front of Abhainnsuidhe Castle and the nearby river. Time it right and you'll see salmon leaping in an attempt to get upstream beyond the waterfall.

After a quick look at the castle, it's off to see the salmon leaping.

LOCATION: 57.9028°N 6.8041°W

GRID REFERENCE: NB155005

POPULATION: 1,916

SIZE: 409km²

GETTING THERE: The ferry leaves Berneray and takes around an hour to reach Leverburgh on Harris. See www.calmac.co.uk for more details.

WHERE TO STAY: Harris Hotel, Scott Road, Tarbert, Isle of Harris, HS3 3DL, **T:** 01859 502154, **W:** www.harrishotel.com. Hotel Hebrides, Pier Road, Tarbert, HS3 3DG, **T:** 01859 502364, **W:** www.hotel-hebrides.com.

WHERE TO EAT: The Machair Kitchen, Tall ana Mara Community Enterprise Centre, Isle of Harris, HS3 3AE, **T:** 01859 550333, **W:** www.hotel-hebrides.com/the-machair-kitchen. Butty Bus, Pier Rd, Leverburgh, Isle of Harris, HS5 3UF, **T:** 07899 786574.

Harris Tweed

The souvenir of choice to take home is, of course, some Harris Tweed. The distinctive woollen fabric is instantly recognisable, but look for the sign confirming it has been crafted locally. There are Harris Tweed items to suit all budgets, from bookmarks, teddy bears and flat caps at the cheaper end right through to tailor-made suits that can run into hundreds – or thousands – of pounds. Harris Tweed has been made here for over 2,000 years, although methods have moved on from the times it was dipped in stale urine to soften it up.

NORTH UIST

Unmatched Flora and Fauna

North Uist is a stunning island when it comes to watching wildlife. Set an afternoon aside and some unforgettable encounters are pretty much guaranteed. Seals are often spotted off the shore, not surprising when you learn this is the UK's largest colony – an incredible 9,000 seal pups are born on North Uist each year. The island is also home to otters, an animal I was lucky enough to encounter more than once on different shores. There's a nature reserve at Balranald with an interesting visitor centre and a chance to spot oystercatchers, lapwings and redshanks. Many tourists visit to listen to the elusive corncrake, a bird often heard but rarely seen.

One of the rarest landscapes in Europe is also best discovered on a trip to North Uist – the machair. A Gaelic word meaning fertile low-lying grassy plain, machair is only found in certain places on the west coast of Scotland and Ireland. Formed when fine shell-based sand is blown in by Atlantic winds, it's led to a rich landscape that is farmed on rotation. Fallow areas of the machair produce an abundance of wildflowers – dozens of species in every square metre – which is an unforgettable sight.

Salmon, Stacks and Single Tracks

Don't leave North Uist without sampling the local delicacy, smoked salmon. The Hebridean Smokehouse has been producing delicious peat-smoked produce for 30 years and has developed a global reputation. North Uist smoked salmon has appeared in lists of the best foods in the world.

In the south of the island, a short stroll from the main road, the 5,000-year-old burial chamber at Barpa Langass is worth exploring. It's remarkable how little hype there is for something this historic, likely the burial place of a local chieftain. You'll most likely be the only people here, making this a spiritual place to visit.

As you drive around North Uist, look out for large peat stacks cut by local people on the island's crofts and stored as a fuel source. Stacked in a traditional way, the idea is the outer cuts of peat keep the middle ones dry and ready to burn.

Driving is notably different up here on North Uist. Many roads are single track and have 'passing places', which leads to a friendly courtesy few other places have. You'll find yourself waiting at these regularly, and always remember to raise a hand to say 'hi' when you pass your fellow islanders.

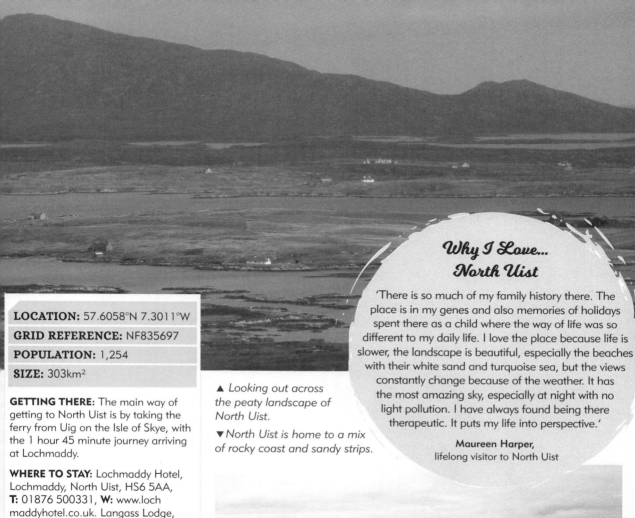

LOCATION: 57.6058°N 7.3011°W

GRID REFERENCE: NF835697

POPULATION: 1,254

SIZE: 303km²

GETTING THERE: The main way of getting to North Uist is by taking the ferry from Uig on the Isle of Skye, with the 1 hour 45 minute journey arriving at Lochmaddy.

WHERE TO STAY: Lochmaddy Hotel, Lochmaddy, North Uist, HS6 5AA, **T:** 01876 500331, **W:** www.loch maddyhotel.co.uk. Langass Lodge, Locheport, North Uist, HS6 5HA, **T:** 01876 580285, **W:** www.langass lodge.co.uk.

WHERE TO EAT: Langass Lodge, Locheport, North Uist, HS6 5HA, **T:** 01876 580285, **W:** www.langass lodge.co.uk. Westford Inn, Claddach Kirkibost, North Uist, HS6 5EP, **T:** 01876 580653, **W:** www.westford inn.com.

▲ *Looking out across the peaty landscape of North Uist.*

▼ *North Uist is home to a mix of rocky coast and sandy strips.*

Why I Love... North Uist

'There is so much of my family history there. The place is in my genes and also memories of holidays spent there as a child where the way of life was so different to my daily life. I love the place because life is slower, the landscape is beautiful, especially the beaches with their white sand and turquoise sea, but the views constantly change because of the weather. It has the most amazing sky, especially at night with no light pollution. I have always found being there therapeutic. It puts my life into perspective.'

Maureen Harper,
lifelong visitor to North Uist

SCALPAY

First Light

Crossing over the bridge from Harris to Scalpay, there's a real sense of an increasing remoteness with every metre travelled. Nowhere on the island is as intriguing and wild as the eastern tip, where the road gives way to a path heading to the peninsula of Eilean Glas. It's here, above treacherous rocks, where the first lighthouse in the Outer Hebrides – and one of the first in Scotland – was established. The original light was switched on in 1789, although it was replaced by the current Robert Stevenson light in 1824. Painted with two red bands so it could also serve as a daymarker, the lighthouse is now automated and continues to protect ships from the dangerous rocks on and around the island.

LOCATION: 57.8707°N 6.7002°W

GRID REFERENCE: NG214965

POPULATION: 291

SIZE: 6.5km²

GETTING THERE: A bridge links Scalpay to the Isle of Harris.

WHERE TO STAY: Hirta House, Scalpay, HS4 3XZ, **T:** 01859 540394, **W:** www.hirtahouse.co.uk. Highcroft Bed & Breakfast, Isle of Scalpay, HS4 3YB, **T:** 01859 540305, **W:** www.scalpayharris.com.

WHERE TO EAT: North Harbour Bistro, North Harbour, Isle of Scalpay, HS4 3XU, **T:** 01859 540218.

Scalpay was the unintentional temporary home of Bonnie Prince Charlie as he fled north following defeat at Culloden in 1746. After setting sail for Eriskay from Skye, his boat was blown off course and he arrived at Eilean Glas. He spent time here unsuccessfully trying to secure a boat that would take him to France.

Scalpay comes from the Norse *skalp-ray*, or 'the island shaped like a boat'. You might need to use your imagination to see this when you look at a map, but the origin of the name reflects Scalpay's strong relationship with the sea.

The bridge from Harris to Scalpay.

SOUTH UIST

LOCATION: 57.2858°N 7.3363°W

GRID REFERENCE: NF786343

POPULATION: 1,818

SIZE: 320km²

Stepping Back in Time

Of all the islands that lead south from Lewis and Harris, South Uist is the longest and it's also the most diverse. Whether you've arrived directly from the Scottish mainland, taken the ferry from Barra or travelled down from North Uist through Benbecula, there is a temptation to simply and quickly gain lots of ground on South Uist by pressing on along the A865. This would cut out many of the island's most scenic and historic haunts, so try to plan time to explore this varied and wonderful island.

The roadside, though, is one place to start on your journey into the culture of South Uist; you'll no doubt see plenty of shrines as you drive along. This is because the island remains traditionally Roman Catholic, simply because the Reformation never reached these shores. Another feature here that you rarely spot in North Uist are the hills. There are several prominent climbs as you enter the island from Benbecula, including Rueval close to the roadside and Beinn Mhor about halfway down the island. It's possible to ramble around this hilly region of the island, but you'll need a detailed OS map, not only to negotiate the climb but also to find your starting point on the smaller roads that twist and turn off the A865. If the north is for the hill walkers, the entire western stretch

is for the beach lovers. There are many white sandy beaches to seek out and explore, with one of the best loved being accessed from Howmore. The scene couldn't be any more typical of South Uist if it tried – the plain church, the crofting settlements and the gorgeous flowering machair all have to be passed before you hear the waves lapping on the beach.

The main population centre on South Uist is Lochboisdale, where the ferries arrive. It's a functional place with several facilities in and around it. To learn more about the island's history, you need to travel north from Lochboisdale until you reach the Kildonan Museum. This small collection of exhibitions and old photographs is renowned and thoroughly worth exploring, taking you on a journey into Hebridean kitchens through time and a range

GETTING THERE: Ferries to Lochboisdale arrive from Mallaig, which is a 3 hour 30 minute sailing, and Oban, which takes 5 hours 10 minutes.

WHERE TO STAY: Lochboisdale Hotel, Lochboisdale South Uist, HS8 5TH, **T:** 01878 700332, **W:** www.lochbois dale.com. Polochar Inn, West Kilbride, South Uist, HS8 5TT, **T:** 01878 700215, **W:** www.polocharinn.com.

WHERE TO EAT: Try the family-friendly Orasay Inn, Lochcarnan, South Uist, HS8 5PD, **T:** 01870 610298, **W:** www.orasayinn.com. Kilbride Café, West Kilbride, South Uist, HS8 5TT, **T:** 01878 700008, **W:** www.kilbride-cafe-south-uist.business.site.

of aspects of South Uist life. In the same building there is a welcome café and a room that holds ceilidhs.

TARANSAY

Castaway

There used to be as many as 100 people living on Taransay, but the island was abandoned in 1974 and today it is the largest of all the Scottish islands without a permanent population. However, it remains a destination for day-trippers who want to truly get away from everything.

Taransay found fame some 26 years after the last inhabitants moved away when it became the focus of the experimental BBC TV series *Castaway*. The show, which was broadcast around the world, brought together 36 strangers and left them marooned on the island for a year to test their resilience to living in such a remote community. By the end of the experiment, only 29 castaways remained – including Ben Fogle, who went on to become a BBC TV presenter, writer and adventurer. One of the most enjoyable ways to spend time on the island is to stride along the deserted beaches of fine white sand, becoming a castaway in your own right.

LOCATION:	57.9015°N 7.0236°W
GRID REFERENCE:	NB025013
POPULATION:	0
SIZE:	14.8km²

GETTING THERE: With no permanent ferry, visitors need to charter a boat or join a trip. Contact www.borvelodge.com for more information.

WHERE TO STAY: Holiday cottages on Harris are available on the Borve Estate, which owns Taransay, **T:** 01859 550358, **W:** www.borvelodge.com.

VATERSAY

Stormy Weather

Until the early 1990s, visitors to Vatersay arrived on a small ferry from the neighbouring island, Barra. The convenient causeway now linking these two Hebridean outposts makes travel between them a good deal easier.

The long stretches of white sand that make for beautiful coastal walks on Vatersay are its main draw. Plan to spend several hours on these beaches, that is if the blustery weather allows. The Outer Hebrides is no stranger to strong wind and it was during a terrifying storm in 1853 that one of the grimmest moments in the island's history took place. The ship *Annie Gray* was taking migrants from Liverpool to start a new life in North America when she broke up on rocks. Islanders did their best to rescue survivors, but around 350 people died in the sea that night.

The Hebridean Way

A challenge for the adventurous visitor to Vatersay is to set out on the Hebridean Way, a walking and cycling route that journeys north across ten islands and six causeways. It's symbolic that the tour starts here, on the southernmost and westernmost island in the Outer Hebrides.

LOCATION: 57.8139°N 8.5801°W

GRID REFERENCE: NL631944

POPULATION: 90

SIZE: 9.6km²

GETTING THERE: A causeway links Vatersay to the Isle of Barra.

WHERE TO STAY: Tigh Na Mara, Castlebay, Isle of Barra, HS9 5XD, **T:** 01871 810304, **W:** www.tighnamara.co.uk. Castlebay Hotel, The Square, Castlebay, Isle of Barra, HS9 5XD, **T:** 01871 810223, **W:** www.castlebayhotel.com.

Why I Love... Vatersay

'I completed the 297km (185 mile) long Hebridean Way cycling route in September 2019, starting on Vatersay. I'd arrived on the islands by ferry to Barra so had to head south before returning north. From an iron plinth that marked the start, I cycled back onto Barra and five days later the Butt of Lewis marked the end of a wonderful trip.'

Peter Adcock,
cycling instructor

ST KILDA

The Legendary Outpost

When it comes to the ultimate Scottish island trip, they don't come more wild, adventurous or extreme than St Kilda. A visit to this remote island – uninhabited since 1930 – is top of the bucket list for many island explorers. On a clear day you can see St Kilda from the highest point on North Uist, but make no mistake that the most dramatic approach to this phenomenal island is when the base is shrouded in an eerie mist and the 430m (1,140ft) peak of Conochair rises above the clouds.

The Evacuation

The famous evacuation that removed all the inhabitants of St Kilda in 1930 is now the stuff of legend and was caused by a combination of factors that made island life incredibly tough. Early tourists in the 19th century began sailing to St Kilda and although they brought economic opportunities they also brought diseases that claimed many victims. Crop failures in the 1920s made matters worse and towards the end of that decade islanders questioned how much more they could cope with. The final decision to leave and resettle on the mainland was taken collectively and, in August 1930, a ship called the *Harebell* sailed away from St Kilda with the last of the islanders – 36 in total – on board.

The Wildlife

As well as the history of the settlers and the chance to see the collection of buildings in which they lived, a St Kilda trip is a delight for wildlife enthusiasts. Gannets, puffins and fulmars all use the island as a breeding ground, bombarding the senses in the summer. Keep a look out for the rare sub-species – the St Kilda wren and St Kilda field mouse – that are endemic to the island. The island is also well known for its hardy population of Soay sheep, a short-tailed brown breed descended from feral sheep on the nearby island of the same name. With a reputation for surviving on this remote archipelago, it's no wonder that Soay sheep have been introduced to other island environments, including Lundy and Holy Island off the coast of Arran.

LOCATION: 57.8139°N 8.5801°W

GRID REFERENCE: NF095995

POPULATION: 0

SIZE: 8.5km²

GETTING THERE: Several companies organise trips to St Kilda from the mainland and various Hebridean islands, including Kilda Cruises, **T:** 01859 502060, **W:** www.kilda cruises.co.uk.

WHERE TO STAY: It is possible to camp on St Kilda. Booking is essential and there is a limit on the number of nights you can stay (**T:** 01463 732645, **W:** www.gotostkilda.co.uk).

▼ *St Kilda's abandoned Main Street.*

The Thrill of It

But don't go into this iconic visit thinking it's going to be a walk in the park. The most remarkable fact about St Kilda is not that it has been uninhabited since 1930 but that it was inhabited at all! When you're here it's almost impossible to imagine how a community could survive on a rock out in the middle of nowhere. St Kilda has the reputation of being an extreme day out for a reason – getting there can be a slog and the voyage over the waves is often stomach wrenching. It's a 12-hour round-trip visit to the end of the Earth from the Western Isles and you'll be left thrilled and tired out by the incredible experience.

Gannets swooping around the misty summit of Boreray.

Featherstore with island of Dun in the background.

Why I Love... St Kilda

'St Kilda is an awe-inspiring place. The remoteness and wildness amplifies the wonder at how past communities used to inhabit the islands. The wildlife, in particular the bird colonies, are both spectacular and mesmerising to observe. The magnificent Boreray, Stac Lee and Stac Armin make for a truly memorable visit. Once seen, never forgotten. A cultural, geographic, natural and historical wonder.'

Seumas Morrison,
Sea Harris

FAIR ISLE

| LOCATION: 59.5307°N 1.6322°W |
| GRID REFERENCE: HZ209717 |
| POPULATION: 55 |
| SIZE: 7.7km² |

Bird Life

One of the main reasons for making a trip to Fair Isle is to marvel at the incredible number of birds living here. Without doubt, this is one of the best places in Europe to spot rare species, and in the past they've included the likes of the lanceolated warbler, calandra lark and Pechora pipit. It's not surprising, then, that a bird observatory was established on the island in 1948. The observatory also has a sterling reputation as a provider of accommodation and food for those wanting to spend time in solitude with a pair of binoculars and a recording pad. A new observatory was built in 2010 – a two-storey construction that housed as many as 30 guests. But tragedy struck in 2019 when it was destroyed by fire, which had a huge impact on the island's economy. A new building is due to open in late 2021, which will increase the number of visitors arriving at this beautiful island sandwiched between Orkney and Shetland.

Fair Isle Knitting

Known around the world, the fabulous knitted jumpers created on Fair Isle have become quite the fashion item. Popular with those calling in on passing ships for hundreds of years, the style began trending when protagonist Sarah Lund wore one on the popular Danish TV series *The Killing*. The products made on Fair Isle by talented knitters are both warm and durable thanks to the unique yarns stranded into a double layer. Fair Isle knitted crafts, including a wide range of jumpers and hats in traditional patterns, are available from the small number of artisans operating on the island. See www.mativentrillon.co.uk for an idea of what's on offer.

Power to the People!

Electricity is available around the clock on Fair Isle, but this is only relatively recently the case. The island is not connected to the national grid and so has to produce its own power. In the 1980s this was achieved with two diesel generators and a couple of wind turbines, but since late 2018, when new turbines, solar panels and batteries were installed, green energy has been abundant.

GETTING THERE: Passenger ferries leave Grutness Pier in south Shetland during the summer months, with the journey taking 2 hours 30 minutes. (**T:** 01595 760363, **W:** www.shetland. gov.uk). Flying is also possible with Airtask (**T:** 01595 840246, **W:** www. airtask.com).

WHERE TO STAY: South Lighthouse, Fair Isle, ZE2 9JU, **T:** 07919 156827, **W:** www.southlightfairisle.scot. The Auld Haa Guest House, Fair Isle, ZE2 9JU, **T:** 01595 760349.

WHERE TO EAT: Several of the island's accommodation providers also have meal options.

Traditional crofts dot the landscape across Fair Isle.

◀ The stunning north cliffs of Fair Isle are a birder's paradise.

BRESSAY

LOCATION: 60.1467°N 1.0888°W

GRID REFERENCE: HU507406

POPULATION: 368

SIZE: 28.1km²

A Rich History

The western coast of Bressay wraps a caring arm around Lerwick on Shetland Mainland, providing shelter in the Bressay Sound between the two islands. Bressay is the fifth largest island in Shetland and people have called this place home for over 6,000 years. Neolithic remains found across the island have been the focus of archaeological digs and there's sure to be more important historic information discovered here in the future. One of the most significant sites is found at Cullingsburgh, where a well-preserved Pictish cross was unearthed in an abandoned 12th-century church. The ornate cross is decorated with animals and symbols, including a horse and a boar. Norse names feature next to Gaelic words, prompting some historians to suggest the Viking invasion of Scotland was more peaceful than is often portrayed. More recently, in the 18th and 19th centuries, Bressay's population peaked, as the island became a popular location for crofters. Many of the old crofts are now empty, dotted around the island as reminders of the more recent population decline. But crofting is not the only industry to have provided employment here down the centuries. Spoil heaps remain from a once vibrant slate quarrying operation and the remains of herring stations can also be seen. One of Bressay's two fish processing centres is still open, maintaining strong links between the inhabitants and surrounding seas. All is explored in more detail at the Bressay Heritage Centre, located close to the ferry terminal and open during the summer months.

GETTING THERE: Ferries leave the harbour at Lerwick hourly for Bressay and the journey takes just 5 minutes (**T:** 01595 693535, **W:** www.shetland. gov.uk for more information). Trips to Bressay are also available with www. seabirds-and-seals.com.

WHERE TO STAY: Maryfield House, Maryfield, Bressay, ZE2 9EL, **T:** 01595 820203, **W:** www.maryfieldhousehotel. co.uk. Bressay Lighthouse Cottages, Bressay Lighthouse, ZE2 9ER, **T:** 01595 694688, **W:** www.shetland lighthouse.com.

WHERE TO EAT: Speldiburn Café, Gunnista Road, Bressay, ZE2 9EN, **T:** 01595 820706, **W:** www.bressay. org.

Light the Way

Four Shetland lighthouses were constructed in the 1850s by the Stevenson brothers, who were prolific designers of the iconic buildings (see also Eilean Bàn, page 51). The lighthouse on Bressay is especially beautiful, hugging the coastline with extensive grounds and keeping an eye on ships heading along Bressay Sound to and from Lerwick. At first the Stevensons didn't want to take on the project, though – it was thought the seas up here were too rough and the islands too dangerous to attract much traffic.

Another building of note to be seen on the west coast of Bressay is Gardie House, a fantastic example of a laird home dating back to the 18th century. Scottish novelist Sir Walter Scott was among the many to be entertained here on a visit to Shetland. The house has passed through different families over the decades and is still privately owned.

▶ *The impressive rocks of Bressay are an important home to thousands of seabirds.*

Why I Love...
Bressay

'Bressay's inspiring coastal landscape, rocks and landforms make it a real adventure playground. The coastline is perfect for historic and dramatic sites like the cliffs of the Ord, the striking natural arch known as "Giant's Leg" and sea caves. Our ROV showing on screens can discover rocky reefs and kelp beds that house starfish, crabs, sea urchins, soft corals and jellyfish.'

Marie Leasky,
Bressay Tour Guide for
www.seabirds-and-seals.com

FETLAR

LOCATION: 60.6057°N 0.8695°W

GRID REFERENCE: HU620919

POPULATION: 52

SIZE: 40.8km²

GETTING THERE: Getting to Fetlar from Lerwick involves a 72km (45-mile) drive and two ferry crossings, the first heading to Yell and then on to Fetlar. For more information on boat services, call 01595 745804 or visit www.shetland.gov.uk.

WHERE TO STAY: Fetlar Lodge, Fetlar, ZE2 9DJ, **T:** 07855 451619, **W:** www.fetlarlodge.com.

Hide Away

There aren't many places in Britain where you can spend the afternoon in a hide and watch the red-necked phalarope, but Fetlar is one of them. Take a packed lunch and binoculars to the best spot – on the eastern side of the Loch of Funzie, overlooking marshland. An important RSPB reserve on Fetlar is also home to colonies of Arctic skua and whimbrel. The rich bird life on the island is explored further – along with Fetlar's archaeological finds – at the Fetlar Interpretive Centre in Houbie.

Blooms and Beaches

With a reputation for meadows blooming into a carpet of flowers during the summer, Fetlar has been labelled the 'Garden of Shetland'. As well as housing the best blooms, Fetlar is also home to the finest beach in the island group; Tresta is an idyllic stretch of sand that has won award after award.

Island Life...

A well-stocked shop and café is found in Gord, but you'll need to time your visit well to get the supplies you want. Bread cakes and pies arrive fresh from Yell on Tuesdays and Fridays, while meat and dairy arrive with fruit and veg at the end of each week. You are advised to order in advance and let the café know if you're visiting with a group.

▶ *Beach lovers will love their time on Fetlar, wandering along the beautiful stretches of sand.*

Why I Love... Fetlar

'Fetlar, or "fat land" in Norse, might be small but it is one of the prettiest islands in the Shetland archipelago. This "Garden of Shetland" is by far the greenest of all the islands. Walking the coastline of Fetlar is an unforgettable experience with magnificent views, wildflowers, orchids, otters and, of course, birds. Fetlar is especially famous for the red-necked phalarope, an enchanting little wader that can be found on its moorland pools and mires.'

Bridget Cheyne,
Fetlar resident

We're Gonna Build a Wall

Thousands of years before the Berlin Wall was built and Donald Trump wanted to construct a barrier between the United States and Mexico, a divide was being dreamt up on this far-flung island in north Shetland. Here on Fetlar, the island was divided into 'east' and 'west' by a wall that ran for over 4km (2.5 miles). As with many historical features dating back millennia, nobody is precisely sure when the wall, known as Funzie Girt, was built and what its purpose was. But it did the job of splitting up Fetlar into two sections of similar size, perhaps keeping two tribes apart. This Bronze Age wall is still visible in the north of the island. There are other examples of dividing walls in Shetland, but Funzie Girt is the best preserved and the sheer size of the structure – all of it made from local stone – emphasises what a huge achievement it was.

Not so Funzie

Don't make a blunder with the way you say Funzie! On Fetlar, you pronounce it 'Finny'.

FOULA

LOCATION: 60.1373°N 2.0738°W

GRID REFERENCE: HT960392

POPULATION: 33

SIZE: 12.6km²

Bird Island

Welcome to the edge of the world! There are few places like Foula, a small island that is home to the UK's most remote and isolated community. Around 22.5km (14 miles) from the Shetland Mainland, it's a mountainous island with some fabulously scenic cliffs – all best seen from the approach by ferry or plane.

To say that Foula is important as a bird habitat is an understatement. The bird population can reach 250,000 and species such as guillemots, puffins and gannets can be seen perching on seemingly impossibly narrow ledges in the cliffs. There's also an incredible 3,000 pairs of great skuas on Foula, breeding and attacking unsuspecting tourists getting too close during nesting season. Unsurprisingly, the name of the island comes from the Old Norse for 'bird island'.

Cool Yule!

Christmas is done differently in these parts and if you plan to visit for the festive period you need to make sure you've checked the Julian calendar. The big day is celebrated as Auld Yule on 6 January, with the Old New Year kicking in a week later. The island-wide celebration sees all the residents gathering in one house.

GETTING THERE: Ferries to Foula take 2 hours 15 minutes, leaving from the Pier at Walls on the west Mainland. Booking is essential and cars are not carried. For more information on boat services, call 01595 745804 or visit www.shetland.gov.uk. Flights to the island leave from Lerwick (www.airtask.com).

WHERE TO STAY: The Burns self-catering cottage, Foula, ZE2 9PN, **T:** 01595 753273, **W:** www.selfcateringfoula.co.uk.

The Edge of the World

The story of Scotland's islands struggling to keep their young residents and failing to attract people from the mainland is a familiar one. Dozens of communities have seen their island hit by depopulation over a long period of time. In 1937, Michael Powell directed *The Edge of the World*, loosely based on the evacuation of inhabitants from St Kilda. It was filmed on Foula over four months because Powell couldn't get permission to film on St Kilda itself.

Ripping Yarns

If you fancy wearing your own piece of Foula, explore the island's range of wool, which is made exclusively from the sheep living here. The well-maintained stock of Shetland sheep bred in this remote, isolated environment has a distinctive range of natural colours, available online at www.foulawool.co.uk. The crofters who tend the sheep on the island's steep slopes are the same people despatching the soft, strong Foula wool to keen knitters around the world.

ISLE OF NOSS

Natural Haven

This small nature reserve on the eastern coast of Bressay was once home to a tiny fishing and farming community, but nobody has permanently lived here since 1939. Some wildlife wardens stay over here during the summer, but most folk come to Noss as day-tripping nature tourists. Around 2,000 people a year take the inflatable boat service from Bressay when the weather allows, spending a day on this wildlife haven that was once connected to its larger neighbour. Access to the Isle of Noss is available between May and August, when the island's visitor centre is open and the breeding bird population reaches its peak. Good trails allow for a complete walk around the island in just three hours, which gives you ample chance to observe many different species and the often intriguing rituals they have for raising their young. Look out for skuas, puffins and gannets in the spring, and keep an eye on the water for signs of porpoises or perhaps even orcas.

LOCATION: 60.1453°N 1.0222°W

GRID REFERENCE: HU544405

POPULATION: 0

SIZE: 3.4km²

GETTING THERE: A small boat takes visitors to the Isle of Noss from Bressay, crossing the narrow Noss Sound. Telephone the visitor centre on 01463 667600 for more information between May and August. Trips to Noss are also available with www. seabirds-and-seals.com.

WHERE TO STAY: Maryfield House, Maryfield, Bressay, ZE2 9EL, **T:** 01595 820203, **W:** www.maryfieldhousehotel. co.uk. Bressay Lighthouse Cottages, Bressay Lighthouse, ZE2 9ER, **T:** 01595 694688, **W:** www.shetland lighthouse.com.

MAINLAND

Shetland Pride

For Shetlanders this island, the largest and most populous in the group, is the mainland – not the larger island further south that contains Edinburgh. Calling this the 'Mainland' and referring to the outlying communities as the islands reveals a lot about what it means to be a Shetlander. They are proud people and many look at Scotland as a completely different nation. On the map, the island appears as a long, pointy finger edging down to the most southerly point of Shetland from a bony hand that dominates the group of islands. The hub is Lerwick, where ferries from Aberdeen and Orkney arrive and a third of the population lives, and where the quayside is frequently home to cruise ships and smaller boats working in the fishing and oil industries. The oil boom of the 1970s saw development extend Lerwick substantially, but as well as the modern side to the town there are parts that date back centuries. Look out for the closses – former slum areas, which the wealthy escaped from in the 19th century and that now have street signs featuring all their rebranded names. And don't miss Fort Charlotte, built for Charles II in 1665, repaired by George III and named to honour his wife.

LOCATION: 60.2797°N 1.2532°W

GRID REFERENCE: HU414553

POPULATION: 18,765

SIZE: 968.8km²

GETTING THERE: The ferry to Lerwick leaves Aberdeen seven times a week and takes at least 12 hours 30 minutes, depending on if it calls at Orkney. For more information, call Northlink Ferries on 0845 6000 449 or visit www.northlinkferries.co.uk.

WHERE TO STAY: Aald Harbour Bed and Breakfast, 7 Church Road, Lerwick, Shetland, ZE1 0AE, **T:** 01595 840689, **W:** www.aaldharbourbedandbreakfast.com. Fairview, Gulberwick, Shetland, ZE2 9JX, **T:** 07809 439370, **W:** www.fairviewshetland.co.uk.

WHERE TO EAT: Fjarå Coffee, Sea Road, Lerwick, Shetland, ZE1 0ZJ, **T:** 01595 697388, **W:** www.fjaracoffee.com. The Dowry, 98 Commercial Street, Lerwick, Shetland, ZE1 0EX, **T:** 01595 692373.

◄ Cannon at 17th century Fort Charlotte in the centre of Lerwick and cruise ship in the Bressay Sound, Shetland Islands.

The Secret Shetland Bus

Shetland saw remarkable secret operations carried out during the Second World War, which to this day create a strong link between the islands and neighbouring Norway. Dodging the threat of attack by Germany's aircraft and naval might, small Norwegian fishing boats ran the gauntlet across the North Sea to move people and weapons between the nations. Setting out from the fjords, the boats brought Norwegians at risk of being arrested and returned during a 24-hour journey stockpiled with guns and ammunition. Islanders kept the operations under their hats and instructions were issued in coded radio broadcasts during three years of clandestine trips. By the end of the war, 350 Norwegians had left the country on what became known as the Shetland Bus and an incredible 400 tons of weaponry was sent to fight German troops in Scandinavia.

Shetland Ponies

The small ponies are synonymous with Shetland and you'll see many as you travel around the Mainland. Originally used as pack animals, they were sold to English mines during the 19th century because their size made them ideal to cope with the cramped underground spaces. Some of the island's ponies even travelled across the Atlantic to work in US mines. Fishermen also used their tail hair to make fishing nets, and today the ponies are an iconic symbol of Shetland and the breed has its own category at the Horse of the Year Show.

Up Helly-Aa

If you're wondering when to make the trip to Shetland, consider the colder end of the year rather than the summer if you want to catch one of the world's most memorable festivals. On the last Tuesday in January, the island hosts a wave of jaw-dropping events at the largest in a series of fire festivals that attract visitors from across the world. Up Helly-Aa features local men dressed in lavish Viking costumes, sporting polished silver axes and elaborate shields. Other groups join the parade in a selection of costumes, bringing the number of participants close to a thousand. At the end of the parade, the flaming torches are thrown onto the longship built for that year. There are many parties in 'halls' following the parade, but these are mainly for the local community and are invitation only. To get anywhere near a ticket you'll have to be well organised and plan in advance, checking listings in the local paper and getting on a waiting list at the tourist office. If you head to Shetland in the summer, you can see the longship and a range of costumes in the Galley Shed.

MUCKLE ROE

Lovely Slice of Ham

The highlight of a visit to this quiet island is a stunning clifftop walk. You'll be wanting to stop and use your camera every few steps to capture images of stacks, arches, caves and the way the rocks twist and bend into fascinating shapes around the coastline. Large bays on the island

are known as 'The Hams' and the delightful coastal path leads up to North Ham and South Ham, both of which are stunning places to spend time. The circular walk, which also passes the island's lighthouse, is well signed and starts from the car park at Little Ayre, where the main road comes to an end. Take OS Explorer Map 469 with you.

Muckle Roe (Big Red Island) is famous for the red, unspoilt granite cliffs and beaches.

LOCATION: 60.3677°N 1.4271°W

GRID REFERENCE: HU317650

POPULATION: 130

SIZE: 17.8km²

GETTING THERE: Muckle Roe is connected to Shetland Mainland by a road bridge.

WHERE TO STAY: Orwick Lodge Self Catering, Muckle Roe, ZE2 9QW, **T:** 01806 522777, **W:** www.orwicklodge.co.uk. Busta House Hotel, Busta, Shetland, ZE2 9QN, **T:** 01806 522506, **W:** www.bustahouse.com.

PAPA STOUR

A Geologist's Paradise

The ferry to Papa Stour can take a vehicle across, but there's not much on the island in terms of roads so the best thing to do is explore on foot. And there's plenty to explore here on this island of volcanic rock. Papa Stour is one of the least visited of our British islands but it has some of the most dramatic scenery. There is a range of natural features – including stacks, arches, skerries and some fabulous caves – on its Atlantic coast, created over thousands of years by the powerful waves crashing against the rocks. The most well known cave is a subterranean labyrinth called Kirstan Hol, or Christie's Hole. Divers and small boats can explore the caves and the marine life found on the rocks inside. Offshore, reefs are teeming with life and the island has been designated a Special Area of Conservation. Papa Stour is also a hot location

LOCATION: 60.3300°N 1.6957°W

GRID REFERENCE: HU169607

POPULATION: 15

SIZE: 8.3km²

GETTING THERE: The ferry leaves Weat Burrafirth for the 45-minute journey to Papa Stour, operating five days a week. Booking is essential. For more information on boat services, call 01595 693535 or visit www.shetland.gov.uk.

WHERE TO STAY: Wild camping is possible. For more information contact the Shetland Tourist Information Office on 01595 693434.

for archaeological riches, with more than its fair share of Neolithic burial chambers.

Visit on a windswept day and you may not see many of the handful of residents who still call this island home. It's hard to imagine that 400 people lived here in the 1840s, earning a living from a once thriving fishing station. Earlier, in the 18th century, people suspected of having leprosy were sent to live here, though it now appears they weren't lepers after all and probably had a vitamin deficiency.

The population crashed during the second half of the 19th century, though, and by the Second World War there were fewer than 100 inhabitants left. Things became desperate in the 1970s – as the population plummeted to below 20 and the local school closed its doors – and an advert was placed in a newspaper offering a free croft. It received a massive amount of interest and there was a slight surge in residents as people wanting to escape the rat race made the move to the Shetland paradise. But most didn't stick it out and today Papa Stour's numbers once again teeter on the brink.

A visit to Papa Stour has the potential to deliver a sense of solitude and inner peace difficult to find at many places on our shores. If you get a chance to go, grab it and cherish it.

UNST

The Most Northerly...

When the boat arrives on this most extreme of islands, you are well and truly at the northern end of Britain. Unst is at a higher latitude than any other inhabited British island and, as a result, you can expect to see the words 'most northerly' in several places here. Victoria's Vintage Tea Rooms is a great spot to enjoy a cuppa, and it prides itself on being the most northerly tea rooms in the country. Skaw, in the north-east of the island, is the most northerly settlement. Haroldswick is the proud home of the most northerly church and there isn't a British lighthouse further north than the beautifully named Muckle Flugga, sited on a small island visible from the north of Unst.

Another choice destination on Unst is the most northerly brewery in Britain, which taps Viking and Shetland heritage through its name, Valhalla Brewery. The innovative brewing operation rose from the ashes of despair in 1996 when the airport on Unst closed down and the island became that little bit more remote. Sonny Priest was one of many made redundant that year and he decided to set up the brewery. A year later, the first pint of Auld Rock was poured, and another popular Shetland brand was born. And if you happen to enjoy a sample of the local brew, it will taste all the better up here, knowing that you're closer to Oslo than London.

LOCATION: 60.7604°N 0.9007°W	
GRID REFERENCE: HU600091	
POPULATION: 632	
SIZE: 120.7km²	

GETTING THERE: From Lerwick, you first need to get the ferry to Yell and then head north to catch a second ferry bound for Unst. For more information on boat services, call 01595 745804 or visit www.shetland.gov.uk.

WHERE TO STAY: Baltasound Hotel, Unst, ZE2 9DS, **T:** 01957 711334, **W:** www.baltasoundhotel.co.uk. Mailersta Bed and Breakfast, Unst, ZE2 9DL, **T:** 01957 755344.

WHERE TO EAT: Victoria's Vintage Tea Rooms, Haroldswick, Unst, Shetland, ZE2 9DU, **T:** 01957 711885, **W:** www.victoriasvintagetearooms.co.uk. Balta Light, Baltasound, Unst, ZE2 9TW, **T:** 01957 711545.

Bobby's Bus Shelter

Waiting for a bus on Unst could be a thoroughly unpleasant experience if the wind and rain are sweeping across the island. But you're unlikely to see a bus shelter as pleasant and inviting as the one just outside Baltasound. When the council demolished the old shelter, Bobby, a young boy who used the shelter on his way to school, started a campaign to get a new one. When the replacement shelter was built, it soon began to attract mysterious objects, including a sofa, a TV, a microwave, a carpet and curtains. But this isn't fly-tipping! The items are carefully placed, and local residents take pride in protecting the shelter and its treasures from the inclement weather.

WHALSAY

Fisherman's Friend

This is an island still dominated by fishing. You'll notice the activity of both large and small fishing boats in the harbour at Symister, the largest settlement on the island. It's a multi-million pound industry here on Whalsay and is crucial for employment. To really get to grips with the importance of the island's fishing heritage, make a trip to the Pier House Museum. By the time you leave you'll have discovered plenty about trade on the islands down the centuries. As well as hosting displays about the fishing industry, the building itself has a rich history linked to the boats in the harbour.

LOCATION: 60.3543°N 0.9869°W

GRID REFERENCE: HU560638

POPULATION: 1,061

SIZE: 19.7km²

GETTING THERE: Ferries leave for Whalsay from Laxo on the Shetland Mainland, with the journey taking around 30 minutes. For more information on boat services, call 01595 745804 or visit www.shetland.gov.uk.

WHERE TO STAY: Moorfield Hotel, Moorfield Ring Road, Brae, Shetland, ZE2 9UX, **T:** 01806 520010, **W:** www.themoorfieldhotelshetland.co.uk.

WHERE TO EAT: Aairvhous Café, Huxter Loch, Whalsay, Shetland, ZE2 9AQ. **T:** 01806 566768.

Dried and salted fish were exported to the Hanseatic League from here until 1707. Germans would arrive with their iron tools, salt and cloth, bartering with the people of Whalsay for their fish products.

Golfers should pack their clubs when they pay a visit here. Whalsay's 18-hole golf course is the most northerly course in Britain so teeing off at 60 degrees north provides the chance to tick off a sporting extremity.

YELL

An Island to Shout About

There's a temptation to see Yell as a 'connecting island' – somewhere you pass through when moving between Unst and the Shetland Mainland. Plenty of travellers disembark at one end and don't stop until they've reached the boat departure point at the other. But those who do whizz through Yell are missing plenty and it's worth spending time on the minor roads to explore the island's coastline. This is without doubt one of the best places in Europe to spot otters. They love the low-lying coastal land, the natural bays and the peaty shoreline. It all combines to make a des res for otters, who can freely dig extensive holts and have good access to fresh water supplies. Perhaps surprisingly, the otters of Yell are European river otters, not sea otters. They do catch most of their fish in salty water, but this means they have to give themselves a thorough wash in fresh water after the hunt so their fur continues to work as a good insulator. One place to keep an eye out is along the gorgeous voes that penetrate the interior of Yell. These natural harbours provide calmer waters today, but during the Second World War they provided an opportunistic hiding place for German U-boats.

LOCATION: 60.6218°N 1.1028°W

GRID REFERENCE: HU492935

POPULATION: 966

SIZE: 212.1km²

GETTING THERE: The car ferry leaves Toft on the Mainland and arrives at Ulsta on Yell 20 minutes later. Booking is advised. This route and the short service from Yell to Unst have frequent departures. For more information on boat services, call 01595 745804 or visit www.shetland.gov.uk.

WHERE TO STAY: Quam B&B, West Sandwick, Yell, ZE2 9BH, **T:** 01957 766256, **W:** www.quambandbyell shetland.co.uk. The Old Post Office, Gutcher Ferry Terminal, A968, Yell, ZE2 9DF, **T:** 01957 744293, **E:** pdobbing@gmail.com.

WHERE TO EAT: LJ's Diner, Mid Yell, Yell, ZE2 9BN, **T:** 01957 702349. Geoffreys of Shetland, A968, Yell, ZE2 9DF.

Boats in harbour, Burravoe, Yell.

Textile Tours

If you're interested in the rich relationship these islands have with textiles and clothing, make sure Global Yell is on your radar (www.globalyell.org). The organisation runs a series of four- and five-day tours that visit factories, galleries, studios and museums and explore the role textiles play in Shetland's different regions.

Art in Heaven

With an undoubted beauty and constantly changing light, Shetland has been loved by artists for centuries. In 2012, the Shetland Gallery was established on Yell to put the work of some island artists into the spotlight. You'll find it at Sellafirth and seeing the range of Shetland painters and their work on local scenes is a delight. This is the most northerly art gallery in the country and the remote surroundings somehow add to the painted scenes on display.

Lost in Translation...

Shetland is well known for having its own very distinct dialect and hearing the locals speak is like unlocking an audible treasure trove. No matter how accustomed you are to the different regional dialects of Britain, speaking to somebody on Shetland could well leave you stumped because there are many words that just don't exist in English. Hence the reason why some shops around these islands stock a small Shetland-English dictionary! Each of the islands has its own distinct accent, and those from Yell are noted for having among the strongest there is.

A Gem of a Beach

Head north of Gutcher to find one of the loveliest beaches Shetland has to offer. Crushed seashells make up the Sands of Brekken, which is a great place for a picnic if the weather is kind. A cove to the north of Cullivoe provides shelter and scenery in equal measure.

BRURAY

The Out Skerries

Three rocky landmasses make up the Out Skerries, or just 'Skerries' for short – the most easterly group of islands in Shetland. Grunay is currently uninhabited, but there is a small community on both Housay and Bruray. These two islands are joined by a bridge and sometimes referred to collectively. The majority of islanders in the Out Skerries depend on the sea for a living; fishing provides a major source of employment. However, it's sometimes a case of 'water, water everywhere and not a drop to drink' out here. Water shortages have been known to occur because of the small landmass that can gather rain and the impermeable rocks that help it run off into the sea. A water catchment drain has been installed atop the highest point – Bruray Wart – to collect more when it falls.

Exploring on foot is the best method in the Out Skerries – there's less than a mile of road on all three islands!

Go West!

Everybody else in Scotland lives west of Bruray. This Shetland outpost houses the easternmost settlement in Scotland, making it the geographic opposite to the people living in Vatersay, way out west in the Outer Hebrides. The extreme easterly location is part of the appeal to wildlife enthusiasts wanting to see a strong bird population. For several species migrating from the east, the Out Skerries is the first land they see and an ideal place to stop.

School's Out

Bruray used to have the country's smallest schools – educating three young people in a secondary and just one at a primary. The island hit the news in 2014 when the secondary school closed down and again two years later when the lone child at the primary school saw the classroom door close for the last time. Now all children of school age need to get the boat over to Lerwick to attend lessons. There has been genuine concern over the decision and whether it will lead to young families moving elsewhere in Shetland.

LOCATION: 60.4259°N 0.7504°W

GRID REFERENCE: HU689720

POPULATION: 24

SIZE: >1km²

GETTING THERE: Ferry services from Vidlin and Lerwick leave for the Out Skerries. Bruray is linked to Housay by a bridge. For more information on boat services, call 01595 693535 or visit www.shetland.gov.uk.

WHERE TO STAY: Hillside Self-catering Cottage, Bruray, ZE2 9AS, **T:** 01806 515252. Rocklea Crofthouse B&B, Bruray, **T:** 01806 515228, **W:** www.rockleaok.co.uk.

The North Mouth of Skerries separating the islands of Housay and Bruray.

HOUSAY

House Island

The largest of the Out Skerries, Housay is home to most of the island group's population – appropriate, as the name comes from the Norse for 'house island'. A good time to find yourself here is August, not only because you're likely to catch the better weather but also because you'll see the annual yacht race that heads in from Lerwick. Celebrations reach a peak in the evening with a ceilidh in the community hall.

Housay is home to the smallest cinema in Scotland – a 20-seat movie theatre that acquired old seats from the Odeon in Manchester and was opened to provide islanders with more entertainment options.

LOCATION: 60.4234°N 0.7666°W

GRID REFERENCE: HU680717

POPULATION: 50

SIZE: 1.6km²

GETTING THERE: Ferry services from Vidlin and Lerwick leave for the Out Skerries. Housay and Bruray are linked by a bridge. For more information on boat services, call 01595 693535 or visit www.shetland.gov.uk.

WHERE TO STAY: Vaarheim Guest House, Housay, Shetland, ZE2 9AS, **T:** 01806 515253.

Why I Love... Housay

'Our home is a special island filled with and run by our community spirit and love. To live on such a peaceful island is a real pleasure, with its pure-clean air, each breath you take makes you feel more alive. Having no light pollution means the evening sky lights up our island in a magical way and once in a while the Northern Lights can be seen shining down upon us. I wouldn't live anywhere else.'

Christopher Harris,
local resident

EAST BURRA

The Scalloway Islands

East Burra is one of the Scalloway Islands, a subgroup in Shetland that also includes West Burra and Trondra, along with uninhabited islands like Oxna and St Ninian's Isle. This small archipelago is found on the west of the mainland of Shetland, opposite the little village that gives them their name.

The Bear Necessities

If you go down to the woods today, you'd better call in and get one of the famous Burra Bears to go with you! East Burra has become famous for making unique and sought-after teddies after a business idea was born from a second-hand Fair Isle jumper. Craft-lover Pauline McGinty decided to cut up an old jumper to make a bear for a present and hasn't looked back. Once word got out, so many people wanted a Burra Bear that the spare Fair Isle material ran out and now special designs are made using Shetland wool at a local college. Other bear designs feature local lace and tweed, each one bearing a name influenced by places in Shetland. You can even have a Burra Bear made with a piece of clothing that's special to you, stuffed with spare scraps of recycled Shetland wool to give it a generous tummy!

LOCATION:	60.0879°N 1.3043°W
GRID REFERENCE:	HU388339
POPULATION:	76
SIZE:	5.2km²

GETTING THERE: East Burra is linked to West Burra by a bridge and so is accessible by road from Lerwick.

WHERE TO STAY: Holmfield Self Catering, East Burra, **T:** 01595 859445, **W:** www.holmfieldshetland. co.uk. Braeview Self Catering, West Burra, ZE2 9UY, **T:** 01595 694006, **W:** www.braeviewshetland.co.uk.

Why I Love... East Burra

'I was born and brought up in Shetland and feel privileged to live and work in a place I love. The natural beauty and uniqueness of Shetland and its people draws you in and keeps you coming back for more. East Burra is just one of our many amazing islands.'

Wendy Inkster,
Burra Bears

Hard at work creating special Burra Bears to be shipped far and wide.

TRONDRA

LOCATION: 60.1165°N 1.2857°W

GRID REFERENCE: HU398371

POPULATION: 135

SIZE: 2.8km²

Burland Croft

Like other islands, Trondra was hit by chronic depopulation in the 19th and early 20th centuries. At one point in the early 1960s the number of people living here dropped to a mere 20. The road linking this string of islands to the Mainland reversed the trend. Follow it from Scalloway and you can use Trondra as a stepping stone to reach East Burra and West Burra. But press on too fast across this island and you'll skip one of the most popular tourist attractions in Shetland. The Burland Croft Trail is an enjoyable day out for visitors to Shetland but also enjoyed by the locals. School trips come here regularly. The working croft aims to maintain native Shetland breeds of animals and grow crops using traditional methods. Free-range ducks wander around, along with sheep and Shetland ponies, Shetland cows and pigs.

GETTING THERE: Trondra is accessed by road, with a bridge linking it to the West Mainland just to the south of Scalloway.

WHERE TO STAY: Midshore Guest House, 1 New Rd, Scalloway, Shetland, ZE1 0TS, **T:** 01595 880765. The Cornerstone, Main Street, Scalloway, Shetland, ZE1 0TR, **T:** 01595 880346, **W:** www.thecornerstonebandb.com.

WEST BURRA

LOCATION: 60.0746°N 1.3405°W

GRID REFERENCE: HU368324

POPULATION: 776

SIZE: 7.4km²

GETTING THERE: West Burra is connected to the Shetland mainland via bridges that link to Trondra.

WHERE TO STAY: Glen B&B, Bay Cottage, Glen, Hamnavoe, ZE2 9JY, **T:** 01595 859419, **W:** www.glenbb shetland.co.uk. Fishers Croft Self Catering, Branchiclett, Hamnavoe, West Burra, ZE2 9LA, **T:** 01223 208437, **W:** www.shetland coastalcottages.co.uk.

WHERE TO EAT: There is an occasional café in the village hall at Hamnavoe.

▲ *Easthouse Croft, restored traditional white crofter's house with thatch roof.*

Another Lovely Beach

If beaches are your thing, you'll be in your element in Shetland, where the islands clock up an unbelievable 2,736km (1,700 miles) of coastline. There are many options with varied features, from different kinds of sand and rock to shorelines strewn with boulders. One of the prize picks has to be Meal Sands, a popular place to set up camp for the day, play games, go for a swim, have a barbecue or wander along the fine sandy landscape. Out of season, you may find yourself alone here or sharing the beautiful beach with just a handful of people. During the summer months, this can be one of the busier coastal places on Shetland, but we're not talking Benidorm proportions of crowding so you're still likely to have plenty of space.

Go West Burra!

Fishing plays a key role in sustaining the population of nearly 800 people living on West Burra. None of the larger Shetland fishing vessels comes into Hamnavoe – the largest settlement here – but smaller boats leave the island in search of shellfish. Mussel and salmon farms also provide jobs for islanders.

Turn to Stone

Just to the north of the beach at Meal, an ancient stone from pre-Viking days gave clues about the island's history when it was discovered in the churchyard at Papil. The Papil Stone is still somewhat of a mystery, but it is thought to date back 1,300 years, to when the islands were occupied by the Picts, a century before the Vikings arrived. The stone features images of monks, an animal many think is a lion and creatures with long beaks, all positioned beneath a cross. Experts cannot confirm why it was carved. Some think it was a preaching stone for local religious leaders, while others suggest it was a marker for the grave of an important person. Either way, a replica can be seen on the spot where the original was found – to see the real thing you'll have to go to the National Museum of Scotland in Edinburgh.

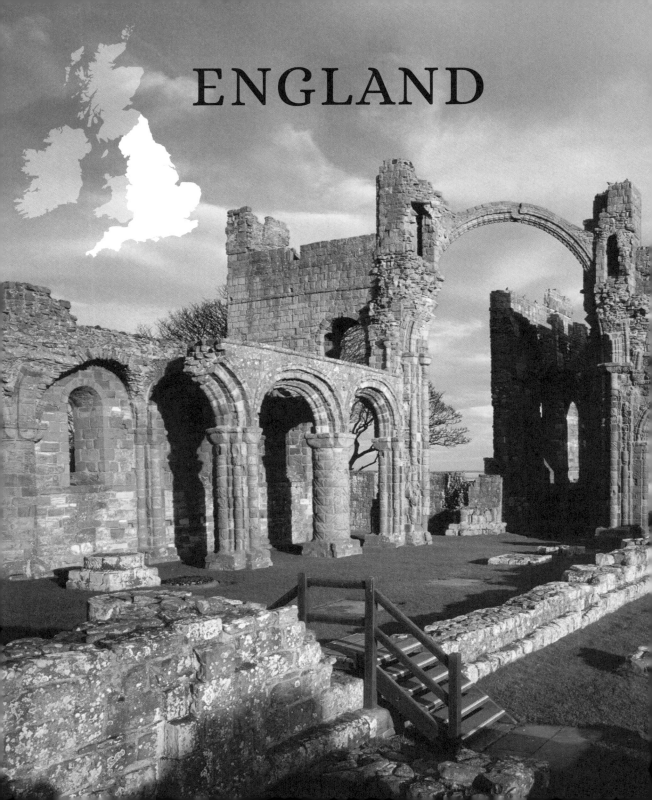

ENGLAND

It may not be the first place to spring to mind when you're thinking about offshore settlements, but England has some wonderful islands to explore. Indeed, the most populous of Britain's islands sits off the south coast, the Isle of Wight being just a short boat trip from Portsmouth. Boasting a large enough population to deserve its own MP, the Isle of Wight has the facilities and natural attractions to make it a holiday dream for kids mesmerised by wide beaches, dinosaurs, fossils and different-coloured sands.

Elsewhere in England, many smaller islands have a charm and eccentricity that make them irresistible. Browse the artistic wares on Eel Pie Island, lie lazily in the sun on one of the oases of calm in the River Thames, visit a remote pub off the Cumbrian coast, sample wine made on Essex's Mersea Island and discover how islands in the Lake District inspired literary greats. Nature and history can also be found on England's islands. Lindisfarne was the location of the first Viking invasion, while an invasion of migratory birds takes place each year on the Farne Islands, a little further south.

DON'T MISS

- Staying on Lindisfarne when high tide arrives and the tourists depart
- Taking a canoe to the islands of Derwentwater that meant so much to children's author Beatrix Potter
- Discovering dinosaur fossils on the vibrant Isle of Wight
- Getting away from the stresses of the city by exploring one of the many calm islands on the Thames
- Eating and drinking on Kelham Island, one of the coolest places in the country

◄ The 'Rainbow Arch', one of Lindisfarne Priory's most dramatic features.

DESBOROUGH ISLAND

A Sporting Island

Desborough is a man-made island less than 100 years old. It was created in 1930 when a channel was cut so boats could avoid a series of meanders that lengthened their journey. The resulting Desborough Cut and Desborough Island were named after Lord Desborough, an Olympic silver medallist fencer who also rowed in the university Boat Race and was chairman of the Thames Conservancy. Sport thrives on the island today, as it's the home of the curiously named Weybridge Vandals rugby club. With a senior team and a range of junior squads, rugby weekends are always busy on Desborough Island during the season. In the spring, the rugby club is home to the Weybridge Beer Festival, which transforms the island into a haven for those who love sampling a wide range of ales and ciders.

Good Karma

Fans of 1980s pop may recognise Desborough Island as the video location for Culture Club's massive hit 'Karma Chameleon'. The banks of the Thames stood in for the Mississippi in this musical story of gambling, theft and steamboats, set in the American Deep South.

LOCATION: 51.3861°N 0.4446°W

GRID REFERENCE: TQ083663

POPULATION: 0

SIZE: <1km²

GETTING THERE: Two bridges connect Desborough Island with Walton Lane, just north of Weybridge.

WHERE TO STAY: The Innkeeper's Lodge, Oatlands Chase, Weybridge, KT13 9RW, **T:** 01932 253277, **W:** www.innkeeperslodge.com. Ship Hotel, Monument Green, High Street, Weybridge, KT13 8BQ, **T:** 01932 848364, **W:** www.bestwestern.co.uk.

EEL PIE ISLAND

Artist Community

A 'Private Property' sign warns casual visitors to keep away from the community of artists working on this iconic mudflat in the middle of the Thames. But twice a year, the painters, sculptors and potters of Eel Pie Island throw open their doors to the public. These are very popular weekend events when you can browse to your heart's content and pick up an exclusive artwork to take home. The studios are built around an old boatyard and are reached via a footpath that twists and turns past a range of arty knick-knacks. Space is limited in many of the studios, so expect to queue among the Bohemian hubbub on what should be an unforgettable island exploration.

Back in the 1960s, Eel Pie was one of the coolest music venues in the country, thanks to the dated 19th-century hotel that shared the island's name. The Rolling Stones played regular gigs here, as did The Who and Pink Floyd. The hotel burnt down in the early 1970s, bringing an end to an iconic music venue. But Eel Pie retains an artistic individuality – plan ahead by checking online listings.

LOCATION: 51.4452°N 0.3246°W

GRID REFERENCE: TQ516173

POPULATION: 120

SIZE: <1km²

GETTING THERE: A footbridge takes visitors over to Eel Pie Island from the Embankment at Twickenham.

WHERE TO STAY: Alexander Pope Hotel, Cross Deep, Twickenham, TW1 4RB, **T:** 020 8892 3050, **W:** www. alexanderpope.co.uk. Twickenham Travelodge, London Road, Twickenham, TW1 3QS, **T:** 0871 984 6503, **W:** www.travelodge.co.uk.

FORMOSA

A Walk in the Woods

Formosa is a long, thin island that snakes its way along the Thames, with the river's channels running to the north and south. This island, one of the largest non-tidal islands in the Thames and dominated by a large wood,

is a lovely place to escape for a walk, which can be combined with longer routes alongside on the Thames Path National Trail. Visitors to Formosa cross over the channel via the footbridge at Cookham. The channel used to be a mill stream, the source of power for a paper mill at Cookham.

LOCATION: 51.5612°N 0.6960°W

GRID REFERENCE: SU904855

POPULATION: 0

SIZE: <1km²

GETTING THERE: A footbridge gives access to Formosa from Cookham.

WHERE TO STAY: Bel & the Dragon, High Street, Cookham, SL6 9SQ, **T:** 01628 521263, **W:** www.belandthedragon-cookham.co.uk. The Crown, The Moor, Cookham, SL6 9SB, **T:** 01628 520163, **W:** www.barrelandstone.co.uk

HURLEY LOCK

Hurley Lock

At Hurley, the River Thames splits up into several small channels and the resulting series of islands is collectively known as Hurley Lock. The easy access to the river makes Hurley Lock best during the summer and weekends, especially when conditions are just right for getting out on the water. The islands are hugely popular with kayakers hoping to catch the waves when the various gates are opened. If you want to see the waters around Hurley Lock in full swing, head here for the rodeo weekend, held every March. At quieter times, you'll be able to park up in Hurley and take the short walk across the footbridge.

LOCATION: 51.5513°N 0.8089°W

GRID REFERENCE: SU826842

POPULATION: 0

SIZE: <1km²

GETTING THERE: A footbridge joins the island to the centre of Hurley, which is south-west of Marlow.

WHERE TO STAY: Hurley Riverside Park, Hurley, SL6 5NE, **T:** 01628 824493, **W:** www.hurleyriversidepark.co.uk. Crazy Fox, High Street, Hurley, SL6 5NB, **T:** 01628 825086, **W:** www.crazyfoxhurley.com.

WHERE TO EAT: A tea shop is open on the island over the summer.

NAG'S HEAD ISLAND

LOCATION: 51.6685°N 1.2789°W

GRID REFERENCE: SU499968

POPULATION: 0

SIZE: <1km²

GETTING THERE: To the south of Abingdon, visitors to the island are able to walk across the island on the A415 (Bridge Street).

WHERE TO STAY: Crown and Thistle, Bridge Street, Abingdon, OX14 3HS, **T:** 01235 522556, **W:** www.crown andthistleabingdon.co.uk. St Ethelwold's House, East St Helen St, Abingdon, **T:** 01235 555486, **W:** www.ethelwoldhouse.com.

WHERE TO EAT: The Nag's Head, The Bridge, Abingdon, OX14 3HX, **T:** 01235 524516, **W:** www.thenags headonthethames.co.uk.

The Nag's Head

This island retreat in the middle of the River Thames is all about the pub after which it is named. The Nag's Head is an iconic venue in the locality and is directly accessed from the bridge heading out of Abingdon. But there's much more to the experience of visiting this island pub than simply sitting at the bar and enjoying a pint. Save your visit for a warm summer day and you can take advantage of the pub's extensive grounds at the side of the river. Grab a drink, order food and watch the boats sail by. As visits to British islands go, this one could certainly be the easiest and the most merry!

OSNEY ISLAND

LOCATION: 51.7518°N 1.2726°E

GRID REFERENCE: SP503061

POPULATION: 400

SIZE: <1km²

City Solitude

Osney Island is now part of Oxford – just west of the city centre – and the area known as Osney also extends away from the island. Osney Island has a rich history, with an abbey being established here and thriving until the dissolution of the monasteries. The island is also referred to in one of the most famous pieces of English literature, Geoffrey Chaucer's *Canterbury Tales*, written between 1387 and 1400. In 'The Miller's Tale', the carpenter, John, works on 'Osneye', on land belonging to the abbey.

It's easy to reach Osney Island, which is just a stone's throw away from the train station. A main road cuts through the centre of the island and there are three footbridges for pedestrians. But despite its proximity to the popular tourist destination that is Oxford, Osney has a quiet feel to it in places. With just the one road linking Osney to the city, as soon as you move away from the traffic you can discover a more peaceful place. Residential streets contain Victorian terraces and there are parks to take a rest and watch the world go by. Stretch out by strolling along the towpath hugging the rivers that surround this body of land and make it an unusual inland island. And, of course, when you have finished exploring the tranquil nature of this urban island, the historic and cosmopolitan centre of Oxford is just a short walk away.

GETTING THERE: Osney Island is on the A420 Botley Road, west of Oxford. The city's train station is just across the river to the east.

WHERE TO STAY: The Osney Arms, Botley Road, Oxford, OX2 0BP, **T:** 01865 243498, **W:** www.theosney arms.co.uk. River Hotel, Botley Road, Oxford, OX2 0AA, **T:** 01865 243475, **W:** www.riverhotel.co.uk.

WHERE TO EAT: The Punter, South Street, Oxford, OX2 0BE, **T:** 01865 248832, **W:** www.thepunteroxford.co.uk.

Why I Love... Osney

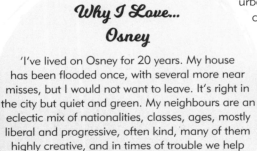

'I've lived on Osney for 20 years. My house has been flooded once, with several more near misses, but I would not want to leave. It's right in the city but quiet and green. My neighbours are an eclectic mix of nationalities, classes, ages, mostly liberal and progressive, often kind, many of them highly creative, and in times of trouble we help each other out.'

Jane Buekett,
Editorial Manager

▲ *Osney Bridge, where the water sometimes runs high.*

◄ *Osney is a quiet island, away from the hustle and bustle of the city centre.*

PIPERS ISLAND

Island Bar

This popular island on the Thames between Caversham and Reading is devoted to quenching your thirst and satisfying your taste buds. Although originally home to a boathouse, extensions over the years made it big enough to host hundreds of people and it was converted into a pub. In 2004, the old building was demolished and the new Island Bar developed, with huge windows and terrace areas to take full advantage of its unique position on the River Thames, with boats coming and going all day. The Island Bar has an area where you can enjoy drinks and a restaurant serving meals. Its location makes it a popular place for business meetings and weddings.

LOCATION: 51.4657°N 0.9765°W

GRID REFERENCE: SU471174

POPULATION: 0

SIZE: <1km²

GETTING THERE: A walkway connects the island to the bridge taking the A4155 into Reading.

WHERE TO STAY: Crowne Plaza, Caversham Bridge, Reading, RG1 8BD, **T:** 0118 925 9900, **W:** www.cp-reading.co.uk. Premier Inn, Richfield Avenue, Reading, RG1 8EQ, **T:** 0333 321 8344, **W:** www.premierinn.com.

WHERE TO EAT: Island Bar, Pipers Island, Caversham Bridge, Reading, RG4 8AH, **T:** 947 9530, **W:** island-bar.edan.io.

RIVERMEAD ISLAND

LOCATION: 51.4042°N 0.4084°W

GRID REFERENCE: TQ107684

POPULATION: 0

SIZE: <1km²

Regattas and Relaxation

Throughout the year, this small, grassy island in the middle of the Thames in Surrey is an important retreat for those wanting to take time to reflect, stretch their legs, walk the dog or even enjoy a wild swim. During one weekend in summer, though, the island is transformed into a carnival, during which time the local community celebrates the river by holding a series of races. The Sunbury Amateur Regatta, whose aim is to raise money for charities encouraging the use of the Thames for sporting purposes, is held in early August. There are over 60 events, so whether you enjoy skiffing, rowing, punting, or land-based fun like face painting and tug o' war, there is plenty to get excited about.

GETTING THERE: A footbridge provides a link to the island on the south shore.

WHERE TO STAY: Weir Hotel, Waterside Drive, Walton-on-Thames, KT12 2JB, **T:** 01932 784530, **W:** www.weirhotel.co.uk. The Flower Pot, Thames Street, Sunbury-on-Thames, TW16 6AA, **T:** 01932 780741, **W:** www.theflowerpotsunbury. co.uk.

SASHES

Roman Around the Thames

Now mainly used as farmland, Sashes is the larger island found immediately next to Formosa (see page 154). It's a popular place for taking a stroll and getting out on the water, but this understated island also has a rich history. It is thought the lengthy Roman road known as the Camlet Way crossed the Thames at this point en route from St Albans to Silchester, a village in Hampshire. Wooden stakes were discovered here in the 19th century and again in the 1960s, prompting some to believe there was once a substantial wooden bridge here. Roman vases have also been discovered on the riverbed nearby.

The route on to the island involves crossing to Formosa first, and then over the river once more to Sashes. A lovely path runs from one side of the island to the other. When you arrive at Cookham Lock on the island's eastern edge, make sure to stop and take in the idyllic view across to the National Trust's Cliveden. The first pound lock was built here in 1830. In the decades before there had been issues with barges getting in trouble, not least because of the narrow channels and rocks falling from Cliveden Cliff.

Sashes is also one of the quirkiest places to camp in England, an island experience that is car-free and a true way to escape mainland worries. In the summer, the chances are you'll probably see a few adventurers enjoying time with a canoe or kayak. The island is also an ideal stopover for those who are midway through a longer journey along the route of the Thames.

LOCATION: 51.5611°N 0.6947°W

GRID REFERENCE: SU905855

POPULATION: 0

SIZE: <1km²

GETTING THERE: Take the footbridge to Formosa island from Cookham and another footbridge bridges the gap to Sashes.

WHERE TO STAY: Cookham Lock Campsite, Odney Lane, Cookham, SL6 9SR, **T:** 01628 520752.

WHERE TO EAT: A tea room is available on the island during the summer.

SONNING EYE

LOCATION: 51.4779°N 0.9214°W

GRID REFERENCE: SU474176

POPULATION: 107

SIZE: <1km²

Drinks by the River

The River Thames diverges for a short stretch after passing through Reading, with water flowing either side of the island known as Sonning Eye. It's a recreational dream for urbanites wanting to pass a lovely Sunday afternoon. There are pubs where you can sit by the riverbank, the Thames Riverside Path goes by here, boats are launched from the marina and there's the chance to go fishing.

Sonning Eye is also an architecturally significant conservation area, containing 12 Grade II listed buildings, including one owned by Hollywood star George Clooney. It's also an important cultural centre, thanks to the converted watermill that now houses a theatre. There's been a mill on Sonning Eye since the 11th century, although much of the present building dates from the late Victorian era. Operating until the 1960s, it was one of the last flour mills on the Thames to be powered by waterwheel. Wheat was brought to the door from London by a number of barges. On its closure, the building stood empty until the theatre was opened in 1982. Today, you'll find a wide range of productions staged throughout the year and a musical on offer over Christmas.

GETTING THERE: North-east of Reading, the B478 bridges the gap to Sonning Eye.

WHERE TO STAY: The Great House, Thames Street, Sonning, RG4 6UT, **T:** 0118 969 2277, **W:** www.great houseatsonning.co.uk. The Bull Inn, High Street, Sonning, RG4 6UP, **T:** 0118 969 3901, **W:** www. bullinnsonning.co.uk.

WHERE TO EAT: The Mill at Sonning, Sonning Eye, RG4 6TY, **T:** 0118 969 8000, **W:** www.millatsonning.com.

TEMPLE MILL ISLAND

LOCATION: 51.5527°N 0.7886°W

GRID REFERENCE: SU840844

POPULATION: 61

SIZE: <1km²

Aqua Marina

The Knights Templar once owned this island on the Thames and the mill that operated on it, giving the local area its name. Three watermills have operated on the island, providing the power to produce flour and later to beat copper and brass. Temple Mill Island once boasted the largest millwheel on the length of the River Thames. From the mid-19th century, millworkers switched to making brown paper, an industry that continued here until 1969. The mill and wheels are no longer here, cleared in the 1970s to make way for houses and a marina. However, a wander around this small island still provides an insight into how it was possible to live on a relatively secluded island in the middle of such a heavily populated area.

GETTING THERE: To the south-west of Marlow, the road link to this island is called Temple Lane.

WHERE TO STAY: The Olde Bell, High Street, Hurley, SL6 5LX, **T:** 01628 825881, **W:** www.theoldebell.co.uk. Crazy Fox, High Street, Hurley, SL6 5NB, **T:** 01628 825086, **W:** www.crazy foxhurley.com.

BROWNSMAN

Seal Haven

Brownsman was used by the monks who lived on the Farne Islands in the 7th century, but the two buildings you can see on the island tell a more recent historical story. The remains of the tower show where an old lighthouse stood. The first Brownsman Island lighthouse was built in 1800 but quickly fell victim to the adverse weather. It was replaced in 1811 and became the early home of Grace Darling. When Grace was just three weeks old, the family came to live at the Brownsman Lighthouse and her father, William, worked here until they all transferred to the new lighthouse on Longstone during 1826 (see Longstone, page 166). The stump of the tower remains, alongside the original lighthouse. Both are now Grade II listed buildings.

Today, the National Trust looks after the island and bird wardens stay here during the summer months. But it's not just birds that thrive on the Farne Islands. As many as 7,000 grey seals make up the colony here and all the boat trips leaving Seahouses get up close enough for you to take stunning photographs of them basking on the rocks and bobbing about in the sea. The seals have pups between October and December, which is a great time to take the trip.

▼ *A boat trip around the Farne Islands will bring you up close with a large seal colony.*

▶ *Remnants of the past can be seen in the buildings of Brownsman.*

LOCATION: 55.6333°N 1.6237°W

GRID REFERENCE: NU237378

POPULATION: 0

SIZE: <1km²

GETTING THERE: Landing is not permitted on Brownsman, but several boat companies take you to within a very good viewing distance, including Golden Gate (**T:** 07904 800590, **W:** www.discoverthefarneislands.co.uk).

WHERE TO STAY: There are many places to stay in Seahouses, where the boat trips depart. Bamburgh Castle Inn, Seahouses, NE68 7SQ, **T:** 01665 720283, **W:** www.bamburghcastlehotel.co.uk. The Olde Ship Inn, Main Street, Seahouses, NE68 7RD, **T:** 01665 720200, **W:** www.seahouses.co.uk.

INNER FARNE

View From a Farne

National Trust rangers live and work on Inner Farne between March and December. For those looking to make a career in conservation, it's a dream job and is hard to come by but it's by no means glamorous. Those employed on the island during this time enjoy basic conditions. The male dorm is at the lighthouse and female staff members live in the tower. After working for five days, they have two days off and usually head over to the mainland to stock up on supplies and take advantage of the shower that's supplied for them. There's no running water on the island, as you'll find out if you need to use the loo during your stay. Large bottles of water are lined up outside the toilet block so you can flush. Of course, the chance to get off the island and grab a pint is dependent on the weather, which means rangers can be holed up here for lengthy periods.

When you climb the small hill from the jetty and get up to St Cuthbert's Chapel, the vantage point gives you a great overview of the Farne Islands. There are 28 of them at low water, half being covered up at high tide. The low-level, sprawling nature of the islands is best appreciated from the top of Inner Farne. Viewed together, the small collection of islands looks like the stepping stones a giant could use to travel from one side to the other.

St Cuthbert's Chapel

The real gem that sets Inner Farne apart from nearby islands is the 14th-century chapel, which is open for people to explore. It was once part of a larger monastic site, which covered what is now the visitor centre and courtyard. The monastery was used until dissolved by King Henry VIII and had extensive renovations carried out in the 19th century. Monks living here from around 1370 grew crops on this and surrounding islands, keeping livestock on them as well. Seals were also valuable to the monks – because they were from the sea they could be eaten on a Friday. Today, the National Trust looks after the island, including the chapel, and maintenance is carried out each year. In 2016, a badly eroded cross of St Cuthbert from the Victorian era was replaced by the new one carved by a local stonemason.

▶ *St Cuthbert's Chapel, beautiful on the inside and out.*

Thousands of birds visit the spectacular cliffs of Inner Farne every year.

Inset: Boats leave for the Farne Islands from Seahouses.

LOCATION: 55.6153°N 1.6557°W

GRID REFERENCE: NU245390

POPULATION: 0

SIZE: <1km²

GETTING THERE: The harbour at Seahouses is bustling in summer months, with people choosing their trip and queuing to begin their Farne Island adventure. Several different boat companies operate out of the harbour, including Billy Shiel's Boat Trip (**T:** 01665 720308, **W:** www.farne-islands.com). A landing fee is payable to the National Trust at the harbour, members go free.

WHERE TO STAY: See Brownsman, page 163.

LONGSTONE

LOCATION: 55.6438°N 1.6108°W

GRID REFERENCE: NU245389

POPULATION: 0

SIZE: <1km²

Grace Darling's Lighthouse

The distinctive red and white lighthouse on Longstone dates back to 1826 and is famed as the home of Grace Darling. During a violent storm in the early hours of 7 September 1838, Darling's brave actions resulted in one of the most famous rescues in British history and secured the place of this lighthouse keeper's daughter as a Victorian celebrity.

Looking out of her window halfway up the lighthouse, Grace saw the wreck of the *Forfarshire* and some surviving crew members stranded on Big Harcar, a nearby rocky island. With the weather far too rough for the lifeboat to leave Seahouses on the mainland, Grace and her father set out in a rowing boat, taking a mile-long route to avoid dangerous rocks. They managed to bring nine people back to safety in the stormy conditions. Nine others survived by launching a lifeboat from the *Forfarshire*, but the rest of the 62-strong crew died in the tragic incident. Grace Darling became a hero for her part in the rescue. The story appeared in newspapers and she was presented with a silver medal for bravery. Many artists travelled to Longstone to paint her and she received hundreds of gifts and letters. Sadly, just four years later and at the age of 26, Darling died of tuberculosis.

The visit to Longstone from Seahouses allows you to get a first-hand experience of this famous story by enjoying a tour around the country's only offshore rock lighthouse open to the public. You can visit the delightfully informative Grace Darling Museum in Bamburgh for more information, though nothing is really as poignant as standing at the window where Grace Darling looked out on that stormy night. On a clear day from the top of the lighthouse you can also see Scotland. The tours are given by the current lighthouse attendant and also provide an opportunity to learn about the work of Trinity House, an organisation dedicated to maritime safety since it was granted a Royal Charter in 1514 by King Henry VIII. When the tour of the lighthouse is over, the boat follows the route Grace Darling and her father took in 1838, via Big Harcar to see where the ship was wrecked and the rocks they rescued the crew from on that fateful night.

GETTING THERE: Visits to Longstone can be made with the Golden Gate boat company, the only one with a licence to land there (**T:** 07904 800590, **W:** www.discoverthefarneislands.co.uk). A landing fee is payable to the National Trust at the harbour, members go free.

WHERE TO STAY: See Brownsman, page 163.

▶ *Standing proud and home to a legend, Grace Darling's Lighthouse.*

STAPLE ISLAND

LOCATION:	55.6322°N 1.6241°W
GRID REFERENCE:	NU237375
POPULATION:	0
SIZE:	<1km²

GETTING THERE: Billy Shiel's boat company runs a trip that lands on Staple Island during May, June and July. Excursions at other times allow views of the island from the boat, (**T:** 01665 720308, **W:** www.farne-islands.com). A landing fee is payable to the National Trust at the harbour, members go free.

WHERE TO STAY: See Brownsman, page 163.

Rock on Tommy Noddy

The Farne Islands make up the largest offshore bird sanctuary in Europe and Staple Island is one of the best places to appreciate the sanctuary's importance. During the peak summer months, 20,000 pairs of breeding birds descend on these rocky Farne Islands, including terns, razorbills, kittiwakes and cormorants. But half the birds are puffins – the colourful favourite known locally as Tommy Noddy. Boat trips get you to within a few feet of the nesting birds, and summer landings are allowed on Staple Island, where puffins are the most prevalent bird. Over 10,000 pairs make their home on this small rocky island each year. And the walkway that crosses Staple Island is incredible, taking you straight through the area where they are nesting on the ground. You're unlikely to need your binoculars, as you'll be so close to the action, but make sure you bring your camera because there are impressive nature shots to be had at every step.

Just off Staple Island are the Pinnacles, a group of rock stacks that provide a perfect viewing stage for the birds. It's remarkable to see how they pack so tightly into such small spaces, fly off and then know the exact spot to return to. The sounds, smells and sights will stay with you forever.

The island is managed by the National Trust and bird wardens are here during the months boat trips are permitted to land. The difficult terrain on Staple Island means landing may be inappropriate for disabled visitors and choppy conditions at sea may mean the skipper decides not to go ahead with the visit ashore.

ISLANDS OF THE LAKE DISTRICT

BELLE ISLE

LOCATION: 54.3624°N 2.0338°W

GRID REFERENCE: SD393496

POPULATION: 0

SIZE: <1km²

Paddling Adventure

The largest of all 18 islands on Windermere, Belle Isle is also the only one to have had permanent inhabitants. The isle is privately owned so you're asked not to land on it. Hiring a canoe or kayak, though, allows you to paddle around the shoreline and get a good look at the historic Island House (see below) while having plenty of fun along the way. The well-kept island is also framed by one of the finest panoramas in the country, with stunning views greeting your every turn.

Use of this lovely little island dates back to Roman times, when a governor at Ambleside chose to site a villa here. Roman designs were also the influence for the Pantheon-style three-storey Island House, built in 1774 and still standing today. When the house and the island were sold to the Curwen family in 1781, they renamed it Isabella, after their daughter. Descendants of the family continued to live on the island until the 1990s.

GETTING THERE: The best views of Belle Isle are from out on the water, either on one of the cruises that launch from Bowness-on-Windermere or by hiring a canoe or kayak (**P:** LA23 3JH, **T:** 015394 44451, **W:** www.windermerecanoekayak.com).

WHERE TO STAY: Burnside Hotel & Spa, Lake Road, Bowness-on-Windermere, LA23 3HH, **T:** 015394 42211, **W:** www.burnsidehotel.com. The Angel Inn, Helm Road, Bowness-on-Windermere, LA23 3BU, **T:** 015394 44080, **W:** www.angelbowness.com.

Belle Isle cuts across England's biggest stretch of inland water, Windermere.

DERWENT ISLAND

LOCATION: 54.5912°N 3.1449°W

GRID REFERENCE: NY261223

POPULATION: 2

SIZE: <1km²

GETTING THERE: Derwent Island is best viewed from Derwentwater. Canoes and kayaks can be hired from Platty+ (**P:** CA12 5UX, **T:** 016973 71069, **W:** www.plattyplus.co.uk), a short drive from Keswick. The island is open for visitors on five days of the year. For information on which days are planned and how to book, visit www.nationaltrust.org.uk/borrowdale-and-derwent-water.

WHERE TO STAY: Keswick View, Lake Road, Keswick, CA12 5BX, **T:** 017687 85130, **W:** www.keswickview.co.uk. The Royal Oak, Main Street, Keswick, CA12 5HZ, **T:** 017687 73135, **W:** royaloakkeswick.co.uk.

A National Treasure

On days set by the National Trust, people can be ferried to and from Derwent Island via a canoe from Keswick. The voyage only carries 18 people at a time so it's important to book a timed ticket for your trip. It's a short crossing and you'll be met by a guide, who will take you on a 45-minute tour of the house's main rooms. You then have an extra hour or so on the island before making the return journey.

Many people have lived on Derwent Island down the centuries, including monks and those with royal links. In the 16th century it housed a camp for German miners working in the area. They settled in well, farming the land and brewing their own beer. The current house was built by 18th-century eccentric Joseph Pocklington, who also constructed a small fort he used for mock battles during regattas on the lake. If you opt to get out onto the lake on a day when the house is closed, you are still allowed to paddle around the island and take an admiring look at the impressive house.

LORD'S ISLAND

Gaze Upon the Geese

Close to the shore of Derwentwater, Lord's Island is an idyllic place to spend some time. Sitting in a boat, drifting gently along with the Lake District fells in the background, is a wonderfully peaceful experience. This serene location used to be the home of the Earls of Derwentwater. A large house once stood here, dating back to the 15th century, with a drawbridge connecting it to the mainland. The foundations of the house can still be made out, but they are all that remain from that period.

This quiet corner of the lake attracts plenty of wildlife and there are nesting geese and other birds on the island. This is the reason why the National Trust restricts access here; people on Derwentwater are asked not to land on Lord's Island or paddle between it and the shore.

LOCATION: 54.5869°N 3.1369°W	
GRID REFERENCE: NY265219	
POPULATION: 0	
SIZE: <1km²	

GETTING THERE: Lord's Island is best viewed from Derwentwater. Canoes and kayaks can be hired from Platty+ (**P:** CA12 5UX, **T:** 016973 71069, **W:** www.plattyplus.co.uk), a short drive from Keswick.

WHERE TO STAY: Inn on the Square, Market Square, Keswick, CA12 5JF, **T:** 0800 840 1247, **W:** www.innon thesquare.co.uk. The Beeches, Penrith Road, Keswick, CA12 4LJ, **T:** 017687 72266, **W:** www.thebeechesatkeswick. co.uk.

PEEL ISLAND

LOCATION: 54.3177°N 3.0852°W

GRID REFERENCE: SD295919

POPULATION: 0

SIZE: <1km²

GETTING THERE: Peel Island can be reached by hiring a vessel from Coniston Boat Hire and setting out onto the water (**P:** LA21 8AN, **T:** 015394 41366, **W:** www.conistonboatingcentre.co.uk). Confident wild swimmers are able to reach the island from the eastern shoreline of Coniston Water.

WHERE TO STAY: The Sun, Sun Hill, Coniston, LA21 8HQ, **T:** 015394 41248, **W:** www.thesunconiston.com. Black Bull, Yewdale Road, Coniston, LA21 8DU, **T:** 015394 41335, **W:** www.blackbullconiston.co.uk.

Swallows and Amazons

An afternoon boating on Coniston Water can be so rewarding in all seasons, especially in calm waters when the magnificent mountains reflect in the mirror-like water. There's so much water to explore here that it's worth intending to be out for a few hours, so take lunch with you – just like author Arthur Ransome, who enjoyed a family picnic as the seed was being sewn for *Swallows and Amazons*. In the 1930s, Ransome's books captured the hearts of readers and introduced them to two adventuring families of children in the Lake District. The Walker children come to the area on holiday and are allowed to sail to the island and camp. When they discover a rival group of local youths, battle ensues for who has control over the small piece of land.

Since then, the children's adventures on the water in their dinghies *Swallow* and *Amazon* have been made into several films and a TV series. In 2016, a cinematic remake of the tale was filmed on St Herbert's Island and Derwentwater, and the premier was screened close by at Keswick's Theatre on the Lake. Today, some refer to Peel Island as 'Wild Cat Island', giving it the moniker from Ransome's famous book. It was close to Peel Island that disaster struck for Donald Campbell as he tried to break the world water speed record in 1967 in his famous *Bluebird* boat. The vessel broke up and cartwheeled across the water as he tried to reach speeds of more than 480kmh (300mph). His body was finally recovered from the bottom of Coniston Water in 2001 and it now rests in nearby Coniston.

ST HERBERT'S ISLAND

LOCATION: 54.5812°N 3.1475°W

GRID REFERENCE: NY259212

POPULATION: 0

SIZE: <1km²

Owl Island

Beatrix Potter loved the Lake District and set many of her animal stories in this part of the world. As a child, she and her family would holiday in Cumbria, and her love for the region followed her into adulthood, when she made Hilltop Farm in Near Sawrey her home. As her books became more popular, she started to buy land in the hills surrounding the farmhouse, donating much of it to the National Trust to ensure the beauty of the area was preserved. St Herbert's Island was one of her special places and she based the story of Squirrel Nutkin here, changing its name to 'Owl Island'. Like all of her books, Squirrel Nutkin has become a much-loved classic to thousands of families since it was first published in 1903. It tells the tale of the titular squirrel and his cousins who make rafts from twigs and sail over to the island, giving the resident owl, Old Brown, a gift in exchange for harvesting nuts there. Squirrel Nutkin, however, does not pay Old Brown the respect he deserves, and the owl makes a grab for him. In the following furore, Nutkin loses his tail. If you go out on the water, keep your eyes peeled for dozens of furry squirrels sailing over to the island!

GETTING THERE: Derwent Island is best viewed from Derwentwater. Canoes and kayaks can be hired from Platty+ (**P:** CA12 5UX, **T:** 016973 71069, **W:** www.plattyplus.co.uk), a short drive from Keswick.

WHERE TO STAY: Keswick Park Hotel, Station Road, Keswick, CA12 4NA, **T:** 017687 72072, **W:** www.keswickparkhotel.co.uk. Lakeside House, Lake Road, Keswick, CA12 5ES, .**T:** 017687 72868, **W:** www.lakesidehouse.co.uk.

Herbert the Recluse

Long before Beatrix Potter brought literary fame to this tiny Lake District island, it was home to the Anglo-Saxon priest after which it is named. Herbert was a religious recluse who took up residency of the island in the 7th century, living on fish from the lake and the vegetables he grew. Herbert is known as being a good friend of Cuthbert, the revered monk who was another island dweller off the north-east coast at Lindisfarne (see page 175). The pair would meet once a year until their death on the same day – 20 March AD 687. Although Herbert is not as widely remembered as Cuthbert, there is an annual mass held on the island to remember him and people make their own pilgrimages here throughout the year. After visiting the island, you might want to lace up your walking books and stroll around Derwentwater to Friar's Crag. With stunning views of the lake and surrounding fells, this promontory that juts out into the water was named after the monks sailing from here on a pilgrimage to visit St Herbert's Island.

Canoe dig it? A paddle out to St Herbert's Island is a groovy trip.

KELHAM ISLAND

Urban Cool

Widely acknowledged as one of the coolest, hippest urban neighbourhoods to live in, Kelham Island has seen an incredible transformation since the 1990s. Back then, the island itself and the surrounding area – which also goes by the Kelham Island name – had plenty of empty industrial buildings and became a seedy red light district at night. Sheffield band Arctic Monkeys had this less than glamorous side of the neighbourhood in mind when they wrote 'When the Sun Goes Down'. However, the last 20 years has seen a remarkable change, with urban living now sitting hand in hand with a range of popular places to eat and drink. The diverse mix of people hanging out on the island has helped put Kelham on the bohemian map, drawing parallels with hotspots in London, Edinburgh and Berlin.

Industrial Beginnings

Sheffield's industrial history is entwined with Kelham Island. This is a man-made island, formed in the 12th century when a goit was created to divert water from the River Don so it could power a corn mill. Grinding workshops and mills thrived in the area and as technology developed, so did the industry on Kelham. In the early 19th century, an iron foundry was built here and continued to operate until the 1890s. At the turn of the century, it was replaced by a power station designed to power the city's electric trams. This building still survives and now houses the Kelham Island Museum (www.simt.co.uk), where you can see a demonstration of a huge steam engine dating back to 1905.

Twice a year, real ale lovers descend on Kelham Island to enjoy the beer festival held at the museum. It features many of the microbreweries established in Sheffield as well as others from further afield. The ever popular Kelham Island Brewery is sure to be there. Check out the dates at www.sheffield.camra.org.uk.

Kelham Island is a favourite of this boy, who loves to admire the weirs of the River Don.

LOCATION: 53.3888°N 1.4710°W

GRID REFERENCE: SK352881

POPULATION: 915

SIZE: <1km²

GETTING THERE: Kelham Island is easily accessed from the centre of Sheffield, with signs guiding pedestrians to the quarter. The A61 passes by Kelham Island and parking is available on local streets.

WHERE TO STAY: Houseboat Hotels, Victoria Quays, Sheffield, S2 5SY, **T:** 07776 144693, **W:** www.houseboat hotels.com. Premier Inn, Angel Street, Sheffield, S3 8LN, **T:** 0333 321 8468, **W:** www.premierinn.com.

WHERE TO EAT: Craft & Dough, Kelham Square, Sheffield, S3 8SD, **T:** 0114 276 2803, **W:** www.craftand dough.co.uk. Stew and Oyster, Kelham Square, Sheffield, S3 8SE, **T:** 0114 34 5888, **W:** www.stewandoyster.com.

Why I Love... Kelham

'What I love about Kelham Island is that it's a melting pot of Sheffield's past and present. I like the fact that the buildings and surroundings still bear scars of the city's industrial past, such as heatproof bricks and weirs across the river, but buildings now house some of Sheffield's best bars and restaurants. There is still traditional industry in the area, which makes it feel like you've stumbled on to a fiercely kept secret when you have to walk beyond the cutlery and tool factories to get a brilliantly made margarita or a craft beer.'

Gemma Bott,
Sheffield teacher

LINDISFARNE

Timing is Everything

There's no missing the warnings as you approach the island of Lindisfarne, also known as Holy Island. As you reach the mainland's shore there are several reminders about not crossing when it's unsafe. And it's not just about avoiding the journey when the sea is covering the road, as some seem to think. At some points in the day it may look like it's safe to begin the journey across the causeway, but you'll get caught out by the rapidly encroaching tide and end up in a pickle. Photographs on the warning signs show people who have managed to do just that. Cars almost covered in water, people taking refuge sitting atop their vehicle and a lifeboat dinghy coming to the rescue – the images aren't put up to scare people but to let them know that the threat is very real.

LOCATION: 55.6808°N 1.8009°E

GRID REFERENCE: NU129420

POPULATION: 180

SIZE: 4km²

GETTING THERE: The causeway to Lindisfarne is close to the A1, just south of Haggerston. Study the tide times carefully before you cross, to ensure you have enough time.

WHERE TO STAY: Lindisfarne Hotel, Lindisfarne, TD15 2SQ, **T:** 01289 389273, **W:** www.thelindisfarnehotel.co.uk. Manor House Hotel, Church Lane, Lindisfarne, TD15 2RX, **T:** 01289 389207, **W:** manorhouseholyisland.com.

WHERE TO EAT: Pilgrims Coffee House, Marygate, Lindisfarne, TD15 2SJ, **T:** 01289 389109, **W:** www.pilgrims coffee.com. 1st Class Food, Green Lane, Lindisfarne, TD15 2SQ, **T:** 01289 389271, **W:** www.1stclassfoodholyisland.co.uk.

The recently restored castle occupies the high ground on Lindisfarne.

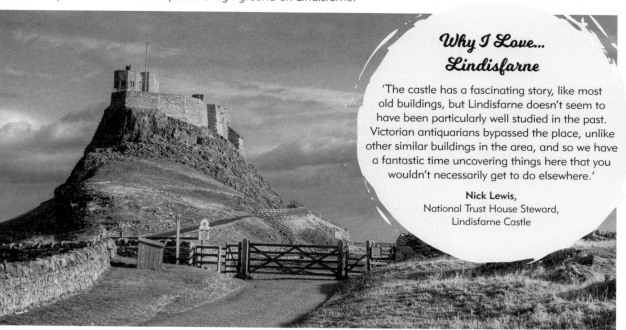

Why I Love... Lindisfarne

'The castle has a fascinating story, like most old buildings, but Lindisfarne doesn't seem to have been particularly well studied in the past. Victorian antiquarians bypassed the place, unlike other similar buildings in the area, and so we have a fantastic time uncovering things here that you wouldn't necessarily get to do elsewhere.'

Nick Lewis,
National Trust House Steward,
Lindisfarne Castle

The tides dominate many things on Lindisfarne, from the time you can grab a coffee to postal deliveries. Many people who work in the island's cafés, shops and pubs are based on the mainland and can only come across when the causeway is clear. Opening times tend to vary each day to match the tides and the point when most of the visitors flood over. When the day's business is complete, tourists and workers alike make sure they're off the island in time, some leaving it until the last minute. The real beauty of a visit to Lindisfarne comes in the hours after the tide flows in and the day-trippers leave. When the sun goes down and you're cut off from the rest of Northumberland, this place becomes a true island idyll.

A Spooky Setting

Anybody who has read Susan Hill's classic, chilling ghost story *The Woman in Black* (1983) will feel a tingle down their spine as they make the causeway crossing. Although Lindisfarne is not expressly mentioned in the novel, it's easy to picture the story taking place here – it is set on a northern tidal island linked to the mainland only at low water, frequently shrouded in mist with dangerous sands lying off the seaweed-strewn link road. I'd urge you to read the book before your visit to Lindisfarne. Or if you've time to stay over on the island, wait until the crowds have gone, grab a stiff drink and start turning the pages. I'd leave the light on.

Pop into St Aidan's Winery in the centre of the village to sample the renowned Lindisfarne Mead. Made on the island using fermented white grapes, honey, herbs and local spring water, it's a sweet alcoholic drink that travellers from around the world take back with them. Drunk for centuries, mead has a reputation as an aphrodisiac that increases fertility.

Going Down in History

• The ruins of Lindisfarne Priory, which are of a remarkable scale, date back to the 12th century and are on the site of even earlier places of worship. Irish monks arrived here in AD 635 and established a monastery celebrating their bishop, St Cuthbert.

• Lindisfarne was the site of the first major Viking raid in June of AD 793. It was a violent attack on the Christian heart of the Northumbrian Kingdom and sent shock waves through the land. This was the place where St Cuthbert had been bishop and was buried. The severity and frequency of the Viking attacks gained pace in the following years. In just a few decades, armies would be spending winter on these shores. The events are well depicted in the TV series *Vikings*.

• Dramatically perched on top of a small hill, the castle on Lindisfarne has had two uses over the years – military fort and luxury holiday home. The fort first appeared in 1550 and housed soldiers on detachment from Berwick. It was later discovered and developed by Edward Hudson in 1901, becoming his Edwardian holiday home.

▶ *The Priory ruins are our window on the past.*

Why I Love... Lindisfarne

'There is nothing quite like staying over on an evening when the tide is high and the visitors have left, especially when there is a beautiful sunset and the sound of the seals echoes all around the island. Lindisfarne is a fascinating historical place, and it's overwhelming to think that while now you can escape to the North Shore for a tranquil walk, years ago the island was being ravaged and pillaged by Viking warriors. I also love being able to cater for all of those who visit the island each year – it's a delight to be able to serve our own roasted coffee and delicious homemade cakes to pilgrims who have walked over the sand to come and visit this beautiful island!'

Becky Riseborough,
Café Manager, Pilgrim's Coffee

Why I Love... Lindisfarne

'We all love the last few miles of our journey to work; there is a timeless quality to the journey as we cross the causeway with the pilgrim poles on our left and the sun glistening on the sea as the tide recedes or advances. In the Priory people often comment on the special atmosphere, perhaps a place still linked to its history as the cradle of Christianity in the North of England, and say that it is the highlight of their trip, an amazing place that they have longed to visit.'

Dania Jordon, Historic Property Steward at Lindisfarne Priory

SPIKE ISLAND

LOCATION: 53.3527°N 2.7314°W

GRID REFERENCE: SJ514842

POPULATION: 0

SIZE: >1km²

A Chemical World

The calm, peaceful park and woodland that makes Spike Island such a pleasant place to spend an afternoon today masks a surprisingly bustling industrial history. With the adjacent River Mersey and St Helens Canal sandwiching Spike Island, it provided the ideal location for heavy industry during the Industrial Revolution. This island is widely acknowledged as being the birthplace of chemical production. However, as local businesses declined and moved to other sites during the 1970s, the island was left as a wasteland of abandoned plants and railway lines, with pollution being a major issue. A major clean-up transformed the former chemical heartland into a pretty place to visit, with lovely canal walks leading away from here and the Trans Pennine Trail passing through. In a fitting location nearby on the mainland, the Catalyst Science Discovery Centre is the only museum in the country focusing entirely on chemistry.

Manchester band The Stone Roses played a historic outdoor gig here in 1990, with 30,000 fans cramming on to the island.

GETTING THERE: Spike Island sits on the banks of the Mersey, south of Widnes, and is connected to the mainland with a footbridge.

WHERE TO STAY: Premier Inn, Venture Fields, Ashley Way, Widnes, WA8 0GY, **T:** 0333 321 9239, **W:** www.premierinn.com. Hillcrest Hotel, Cronton Lane, Widnes, WA8 9AR, **T:** 0330 058 3858, **W:** www.bestwestern.co.uk.

SPURN

Britain's Newest Island

In harrowing gales during December 2013, a storm surge saw the sea level increase by 2m (6.6ft) during what was already a very high tide. The impact on the natural sandy spit that stretches out to Spurn Head was immense. The road to the houses at Spurn was completely washed away, along with tons of sand and rock. The people of this small settlement, which was once permanently linked to the mainland, woke up in the morning to find themselves living on a tidal island. Like St Mary's Island and Holy Island further up the coast, those wanting to pay a visit to Spurn need to keep a keen eye on the tide times.

The shifting sands at Spurn were deposited by the sea and they have been dramatically altered by the forceful waves many times over the centuries. The first defences to try and combat this were installed in Victorian days and have been replaced, improved and updated many times since. A walk from the visitor centre to Spurn Head is worth it for the wildlife you may encounter, but it's the human impact on this landscape that is most fascinating. You'll see coastal defences that have been battered by the sea, concrete broken up and dumped on the beach and the remains of a road that is almost unrecognisable in places. It's a timely reminder that nature is often the victor in encounters with humans.

LOCATION: 53.3433°N 0.0641°E

GRID REFERENCE: TA398105

POPULATION: 50

SIZE: 1.1km²

GETTING THERE: Parking is available at the newly built visitor centre near Kilnsea. From there, you can walk to Spurn Head or take a trip on an all-terrain vehicle. Take note of the tide time on display to make sure you have enough time to return to the mainland.

WHERE TO STAY: Westmere Farm B&B, Kilnsea Road, Kilnsea, HU12 0UB, **T:** 01964 650258, **W:** www.westmerefarm.co.uk. Crown and Anchor, Easington Road, Kilnsea, HU12 0UB, **T:** 01964 650276, **W:** www.crownandanchorkilnsea.co.uk.

To Hull and back: container ships, tanker and cruise ships sail close to our newest island.

▲ *Be sure to book in for a tour of Spurn's iconic black and white lighthouse.*

▶ *A walk to Spurn Head passes the site of a battle between humans and the sea.*

The main reason for the constant battle with the sea has been to allow road access to the lifeboat station at Spurn Head. Dating back to 1810, it's played a vital role and is highly thought of in communities on both sides of the Humber. Because of its remote location, houses were built for the lifeboat crew and their families. This makes it one of just a handful of lifeboat stations in the UK with full-time staff, and the only one that isn't based on the River Thames.

Shine a Light

Standing at Spurn Head looking out across the Humber Estuary, you won't be waiting too long until a ship or two goes by. Following the deep channel out to sea, cruise ships and cargo vessels pass remarkably close to the shore. Unsurprisingly, there is a long history of having lighthouses at this point. The first – consisting of a high light and a low light – was commissioned in 1767 and used until the black and white replacement was built in 1895. This huge beacon still stands on the sands but was decommissioned in 1985. Thankfully the Yorkshire Wildlife Trust opened it up for tours in 2016 and it's now a popular weekend tourist destination. The Trust offer two-and-a-half-hour trips out to the tidal island from its visitor centre (www.ywt.org.uk). These Spurn Safaris are run by experts who are on hand to dish out information and answer questions as you make your way out towards Yorkshire's very own 'Land's End'.

MIND THE CATERPILLARS!

They may look like harmless little creatures, but the caterpillars around Spurn Point are not quite what they seem. They're called the brown-tail moth caterpillar and they're found in among the plants around the lighthouse and on the path over to the island. Stay away from them because they can cause itchy allergic reactions and respiratory issues for those with asthma or hay fever.

ST MARY'S ISLAND, WHITLEY BAY

LOCATION:	55.0717°N 1.4497°W
GRID REFERENCE:	NZ352753
POPULATION:	0
SIZE:	<1km²

GETTING THERE: At low tide you can park up in Whitley Bay and walk across the causeway.

WHERE TO STAY: Premier Inn, Spanish City Plaza, Whitley Bay, NE26 1BG, **T:** 0333 234 6570, **W:** www.premier inn.com. York House Hotel, Park Avenue, Whitley Bay, NE26 1DN, **T:** 0191 252 8313, **W:** www.yorkhousehotel.com.

Beacon View

Sitting just offshore from the popular north-east seaside resort of Whitley Bay, St Mary's is dominated by the tall white lighthouse rising 46m (150ft) into the sky. Built in 1898 to warn shipping crews about the treacherous rocks found on this coastline, it remained operational until 1984. Since then it's been a popular visitor centre run by North Tyneside Council. There's a small entrance charge and then you can climb the 137 steps to the top of the lighthouse, enjoy spectacular views of the north-east and learn about how the famous beacon used to operate. The lighthouse keepers used to live in the adjacent cottages but were by no means the first residents on St Mary's Island; the 750,000 bricks and 650 blocks of stone were used to construct the lighthouse on the site of an 11th-century monastic chapel. Even back then, the monks used to maintain a light on a tower to warn those out to sea of their proximity to land.

Fitness and Film

The North Tyneside 10k Road Race reaches its finale at the island after a scenic route along the mainland coast. It's a bright, colourful day to visit the area as thousands of out-of-breath keep-fit enthusiasts jog across the causeway, cross the finish line and collect their goody bag and T-shirt. Later in the year, the lighthouse is turned into a temporary cinema for screenings during the Whitley Bay Film Festival. There are always inventive screenings in the programme – one of the most memorable saw people watching *Jaws* on the beach!

▶ *Lifesaver and finish line, the lighthouse of St Mary's.*

THE FURNESS ISLANDS

PIEL ISLAND

LOCATION: 54.0641°N 3.1739°W	
GRID REFERENCE: SD232637	
POPULATION: 10	
SIZE: 0.2km²	

Piel Ale

There's no timetable for the ferry to Piel Island, other than it runs between Easter and the end of September. Outside these months, there's a sign featuring a number to ring and check availability. If you are travelling during the summer it's a case of waiting with other hardy folk until the boat comes back across.

Despite being relatively close to a large town, fewer than a dozen people live on Piel Island, a place dominated by its pub and castle. The Ship Inn is thought to be around 300 years old, with records from the 18th century mentioning an innkeeper on the island. Although you can see plenty of civilisation from Piel Island – the chimneys of Barrow loom large, while a clear day reveals Morecambe and Lancaster – it feels like you're in one of the remotest pubs in the country when you enjoy a pint at The Ship. Traffic to the island picked up in the 19th century as pleasure trips became more popular, but there was a problem with some boatowners enjoying too much ale and getting into trouble on their return journey. After one fatal Victorian incident, the local coroner told the landlord not to serve boatmen if they looked the worse for wear.

GETTING THERE: Ferry leaving from the jetty on Roa Island regularly between Easter and 30 September.

WHERE TO STAY: Clarkes Hotel, Rampside, Barrow-in-Furness, LA13 0PX, **T:** 01229 820303, **W:** www.clarkeshotel.co.uk. Ambrose Hotel, Duke Street, Barrow-in-Furness, LA14 1XT, **T:** 01229 826717, **W:** www.theambrosehotel.co.uk.

WHERE TO EAT: Ship Inn, Piel Island, LA13 0QN, **T:** 07516 453784, **W:** www.pielisland.co.uk.

Furness Fortress

Piel Castle is a magnificent ruin, managed by English Heritage these days and free to look around. The Abbot of Furness oversaw the building of the castle in the 14th century. The fortress was intended to keep out pirates and Scots who threatened Barrow. A remarkable amount is still standing, including the keep and the towered curtain walls.

▶ *A trip to Piel Island should include a visit to the castle and the pub.*

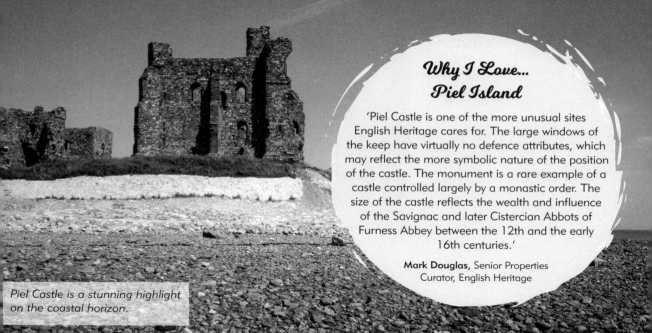

Piel Castle is a stunning highlight on the coastal horizon.

ROA ISLAND

Across the Causeway

Driving across the causeway to Roa Island on a windy autumn day, the surroundings were harsh and beautiful in equal measure. Parking up close to the much-loved Bosuns Locker Café, I got out to feel the chill and appreciate the quiet. Battered by the weather, the island had the feel of the Outer Hebrides – or even Iceland – and not a settlement just to the south of Lakeland. Ominously, on a short walk around Roa, I passed four men painting their windows and doors, giving their family homes a weatherproof coat before the onslaught of winter. This outpost, a kilometre away from the mainland and a short drive from Barrow's bustling industrial heart, is the 16th most populous island in England. The well-maintained road to the mainland certainly makes things easier, but the community here is still very much an island one.

Things used to be much more hectic on Roa Island during the Victorian era. This small island was a major transport centre that linked engines from Furness Railway with steamers that departed for Fleetwood. What started initially as a goods route soon led to a service for passengers as well. Trains rolled onto Roa Island until 1936, and they used the same

LOCATION: 54.0641°N 3.1739°W

GRID REFERENCE: SD232637

POPULATION: 10

SIZE: 0.2km²

GETTING THERE: Ferry leaving from the jetty on Roa Island regularly between Easter and 30 September.

WHERE TO STAY: Clarkes Hotel, Rampside, Barrow-in-Furness, LA13 0PX, **T:** 01229 820303, **W:** www.clarkeshotel.co.uk. Ambrose Hotel, Duke Street, Barrow-in-Furness, LA14 1XT, **T:** 01229 826717, **W:** www.theambrosehotel.co.uk.

WHERE TO EAT: Ship Inn, Piel Island, LA13 0QN, **T:** 07516 453784, **W:** www.pielisland.co.uk.

causeway people drive across today. Although the road that replaced the rail has made Roa Island more accessible than ever before, there is still a sense that much more could be done to tap into the Lakeland tourism market and tempt travellers to visit and take the ferry over to Piel Island. The lifeboat station here looks after the whole of Morecambe Bay and the Irish Sea.

Waiting for the ferryman: the boat leaves Roa Island regularly, but not at set times.

WALNEY ISLAND

Over the Bridge to Walney

Easily the largest of the Furness Islands, Walney is a long, thin island with a curious mix of industrial heritage and natural beauty. Guarding Morecambe Bay to the east and exposed to the Irish Sea in the west, Walney is framed by the mountainscape of the southern Lake District and has some extremely peaceful stretches of coast. You don't have to travel far out of Vickerstown to arrive at a rugged, pebble-strewn beach that has crumbly cliffs stretching into the distance. A haven for wildlife, the nature reserve that occupies the southern part of the island is home to the only seal colony in Cumbria

and has several hides near the lighthouse for birdwatching. Paths criss-cross the nature reserve, but check the tide times before you go; the tidal range of Morecambe Bay can be over 10m (33ft) and a spring tide may see South Walney get cut off from the rest of the island.

Enjoying a beach walk along Walney Island.

LOCATION: 54.1039°N 3.2500°W

GRID REFERENCE: SD183686

POPULATION: 10,651

SIZE: 13km^2

GETTING THERE: A bridge on the A590 links Barrow with Walney Island.

WHERE TO STAY: King Alfred Hotel, Ocean Road, Walney, LA14 3DX, **T:** 01229 471784, **W:** www.kingalfredhotel.com. West Point House, Solway Drive, Walney, LA14 3XN, **T:** 07769 226797, **W:** www.westpointhousewalney.com.

WHERE TO EAT: Andy's Fish and Chips, Hastings Street, Walney, LA14 3LF, **T:** 01229 475908, **W:** https://andys-fish-chips.business.site. The Crown, N Scale, Walney, LA14 3RP, **T:** 01229 475862, **W:** www.thecrownwalney.robinsonbrewery.com.

A Really Useful Island

Fans of Thomas the Tank Engine may have spent their childhood days wondering how to get to the Island of Sodor – and the answer is by heading to Walney Island. The fictional home of Thomas, Henry, Gordon, Percy and all the other colourful engines was situated between Barrow and the Isle of Man, according to the Rev. W Awdry in the famous Railway Series he started in 1945. And he wrote in his 1987 book *The Island of Sodor* that the Fat Controller's homeland is actually a much larger version of Walney, stretching out into the Irish Sea. To reach Sodor, Bertie the Bus or other such vehicles had to cross Jubilee Bridge from Barrow. Although that link to the mainland actually exists, the first settlement reached in the island stories was not Vickerstown but Vicarstown, in a nod to the author's title. Vicarstown was home to the largest station on the loveable fictional Sodor, an island that stretched from Furness to Man.

Why I Love... Walney Island

'I love the fact I can fish for carp in the north Walney ponds in the day and then walk 200m to go bass fishing when it's high tide. The way the sun sets with Black Combe and the fells in the distance is special. The contrast on these islands is unbelievable. You can see a 14th-century castle, the Lake District fells and then huge industrial buildings in the yard. Where else has that mix of industry, natural beauty and geography in one view?'

Local man Matt Burns,
who spent his early years on Barrow
Island before moving to Walney

HAYLING ISLAND

Surf's Up, Dude!

Seeing people windsurfing on the waves around our coast is common these days, but this island off the southern coast of England is where it all started. Inventor and engineer Peter Chilvers came here in 1958 and is credited with being the first person to put a freely rotating mast and sail onto a board – and so the sport of windsurfing was blown into existence. Hayling continues to be a popular place to head out windsurfing, and you're likely to see many people following in Chilvers' footsteps on West Beachlands.

In days gone by, this island was best known for farming, fishing and salt production, but the emphasis is now much more on having a good time. Holiday centres and the Funland amusement park turned Hayling into a popular getaway for people in the towns and cities of southern England. It's still a go-to place for seaside pleasures. Funland offers a mix of rollercoasters, thrills for small children and the much-loved water rides. The emphasis is, of course, on fun. But a visit to Hayling isn't all about the fast rides, fizzy drinks and ice creams we associate with busy seaside destinations. There are many opportunities for solitude and tranquillity along the miles of unspoilt, beautiful beaches awarded European Blue Flag status. Walking and cycling along these stretches is a refreshing way to pass a sunny afternoon. Cyclists will enjoy the 8km (5 mile) easy-going Hayling Billy Coastal Path, which runs from the north of the island to the south and takes in some fine countryside.

LOCATION: 50.7948°N 0.9760°W

GRID REFERENCE: SZ713989

POPULATION: 16,887

SIZE: 30km²

GETTING THERE: Hayling Island is linked to the mainland by a road, which leaves the A27 at Langstone.

WHERE TO STAY: Langstone Quays Resort, Hayling Island, PO11 0NQ, **T:** 023 9246 5011, **W:** www.langstonequays.co.uk. Sinah Warren Hotel, Ferry Road, Hayling Island, PO11 0BZ, **T:** 023 9246 6421, **W:** www.warnerleisurehotels.co.uk.

WHERE TO EAT: Sea View Fish and Chips, Sea Front, Hayling Island, PO11 0AG, **T:** 023 9217 9910. Coastguard Café, Sea Front, Hayling Island, PO11 9HL, **T:** 023 9246 3202.

◀ *Kitesurfers at Hayling Island Beach*

ISLE OF WIGHT

Arriving in Style

The way you travel to the Isle of Wight should be part of your holiday. If you're taking the car, you'll need to book one of the ferries that cross the Solent from Portsmouth, Southampton or Lymington. The journey time varies between 25 minutes and just over an hour depending on the service and route, but there should be opportunity to spend a few minutes on board gazing out to watch the mainland skyline fade away and the Isle of Wight draw closer. If you're travelling on foot or carrying a bicycle across, the most exhilarating way is to take the hovercraft. If you thought these once-pioneering vehicles were a thing of the past, you are nearly correct. There's only one hovercraft still in operation on the entire planet, and it's the one providing a regular link between Ryde and Southsea in Portsmouth. As well as being a hugely fun experience – gliding across the sea on a cushion of air as you sit just 1.5m (5ft) above the water – this is also the fastest way to reach the island. The fabulous journey on such an historically important craft reaches speeds of 45 knots and takes just ten minutes to reach the Isle of Wight.

Slow it Down!

Spending time on the Isle of Wight should enable you to enjoy a change of pace and leave your stresses on the mainland. Even though the Isle of Wight has a large enough population to ensure it has its own MP, it still possesses a traditional island feel that can be a great benefit to those cooped up on the mainland for far too long. Slowing down as soon as you disembark can be a difficult thing to do. Visitors here often notice a more gradual winding down that stops with a sudden jolt when they return over the Solent. To help visitors access the calm that comes with island life, the clever concept of Slow Wight Travel has been introduced. Eight different routes around the island encourage visitors to walk, cycle and catch the bus. They call in at all the highlights the island has to offer, including hidden beaches, food producers and nature reserves, but you'll visit them at a much slower pace than car-based tourists. And at the end of the day you'll feel refreshed for doing it this way.

LOCATION: 50.7321°N 1.1638°W

GRID REFERENCE: SZ591928

POPULATION: 141,000

SIZE: 380km²

GETTING THERE: Ferries cross from Portsmouth and Lymington, with journey times taking from 22 minutes. **W:** www.wightlink.co.uk.

WHERE TO STAY: Hotel Ryde Castle, Esplanade, Ryde, Isle of Wight, PO33 1JA, **T:** 01983 563755, **W:** www.greeneking-pubs.co.uk/pubs/isle-of-wight/ryde-castle-hotel. Haven Hall Hotel, Howard Road, Shanklin, Isle of Wight, PO37 6HD, **T:** 07914 796494, **W:** www.havenhallhotel.com.

WHERE TO EAT: Piano Café, Gate Lane, Freshwater Bay, Isle of Wight, PO40 9PY, **T:** 01983 472874, **W:** www.thepianocafe.co.uk. The Taverner, High Street, Godshill, Isle of Wight, PO38 3HZ, **T:** 01983 840707, **W:** www.thetavernersgodshill.co.uk.

Bembridge Windmill is just one of the stunning sights to visit on the Isle of Wight.

The Mother of All Theme Parks

Long before there was Disneyland and Alton Towers, visitors to the Isle of Wight were queuing up to enter a pioneering theme park that is today the oldest in the UK. Blackgang Chine is just 10km (6 miles) outside Ventnor and contains a handful of themed lands connected to the island's history – Pirate Cove and a dinosaur realm known as Restricted Area 5 are just two of the places worthy of a peek and guaranteed to keep the kids entertained. There are fears, though, the park could end up in an extinction befitting of its prehistoric reptile attractions. Powerful waves battering this section of the coast are leading to dramatic landslides and the loss of land every few decades. The last major event took place in the 1990s when as much of a third of the theme park moved and several features were permanently lost. The owners have taken the decision to move some of the park a little further inland to give it a longer lifespan and maintain what is one of the Isle of Wight's most popular days out. The park is named after a local chine – or coastal ravine – that was a spectacular attraction at the beginning of the 19th century but has since fallen victim to coastal erosion. This is a theme park entwined in all things Isle of Wight, both history and geology.

The Dinosaur Island

The Isle of Wight is a veritable Jurassic Park for fossil hunters wanting to seek out their own piece of dinosaur history. Renowned as one of the richest areas in Europe for digging up dino bones, the rocky shoreline has already earned its 'Dinosaur Island' nickname many times over. A new Dinosaur Map of Britain created by the Natural History Museum's Dr Paul Barrett named the Isle of Wight as the nation's Dinosaur Capital. Anybody who has an interest in history, a soft spot for geology or a fascination with dinosaurs should spend time here on a guided fossil hunt. The level of expertise on offer and the chance of coming across something remarkable make these fascinating strolls some of the best guided activities in the country. A good place to start is the Dinosaur Isle museum, where you can book your place on regular guided tours in advance and

Step back in time and take a fossil walk along the beach.

learn plenty about the island's natural history thanks to the many fossils on display. From early discoveries made in Victorian times through to recent finds on nearby shores, it's a fascinating journey. Look out for the finger bones of a meat-eater discovered by young fossil hunter Gavin Leng on the island's south-west coast in 1995. It turned out to be a completely new species – now named *Eotyrannus lengi* after its finder.

Taste the Wight Stuff

Relax after a busy day of activities by sampling some of the spirits distilled here. The Isle of Wight distillery was set up in 2014 by two friends with a background in brewing and winemaking. They use local spring water to create batches of whisky, vodka, gin and rum that are slow-distilled and have a smooth taste. You can visit the distillery's visitor centre and bar at the old Wishing Well pub in Pondwell.

Isle of Wight produce is flagged up on the menu at Freshwater Bay's Piano Café, where you can tuck into a hearty meal or simply enjoy a drink and small snack. The Isle of Wight blue cheese and locally grown tomatoes are particular favourites. If you're looking for produce to make your own delicious meal, head to Farmer Jack's in Newport to find the best from local producers. Lamb and beef from Isle of Wight farmers is available here, along with plenty of vegetables to go with them and even some locally made pickles for extra flavour.

Rocket Launches

Pay a visit to the National Trust's Old Battery and New Battery, a fascinating set of attractions where you can learn about historic military activity and rocket launches that took place here. And there's a tea room for the obligatory coffee and cake.

This Sand is Your Sand

The ultimate Isle of Wight experience comes at Alum Bay, discovering the different coloured sands found around the unusual cliffs and beach. Sand and clays deposited millions of years ago became part of the bedrock that was pushed up into an almost vertical position to reveal the different shades we see today. The sands – made up of quartz, feldspar and mica – are naturally white but are tinted by other minerals. Right from the early days of Victorian tourism on the island, Alum Bay became a key place to visit and the sand has always been at the heart of the appeal. Thousands of people from around the world have taken home a glass container filled with the multi-coloured grains.

Needle in a Sea Stack

The headland next to Alum is the most iconic location on the island and one of the most photographed natural features in the world. The Needles rocks are a series of three chalk stacks that remain standing in the sea despite years of coastal erosion. Until the 18th century there were four stacks here – a ferocious storm in 1764 saw one topple over. When looking at The Needles, it's obvious where the fourth rock stood; there's a clear gap in the middle of the rocks, like a set of teeth with one missing. This stack was the highest of them all and the one most shaped like a needle, giving the rocks their name. The stump of this once tall needle rock is still visible at low tide.

▼ *The Needles are perhaps the most iconic of all the island's attractions.*

▶ *Rock around the clock: there are plenty of pools to explore at Freshwater Bay.*

Why I Love...
The Isle of Wight

'The Isle of Wight is one of the best places in the world for dinosaurs and so many different types of fossils, with exciting new discoveries being made all the time. You can take a walk around our coastline and find the remains of past life that are thousands or millions of years old. It is fantastic that on the island anyone can come to our beaches, explore for fossils, and immerse themselves in our prehistoric world.'

Alex Peaker,
geologist, Dinosaur Isle

VISIT QUEEN VICTORIA'S FAMILY HOME, OSBORNE HOUSE AT EAST COWES

- www.visitisleofwight.co.uk/things-to-do/osborne-p142751

GO TO THE BEACH

- From the sands of the East Wight at Sandown, Shanklin and Yaverland to the cove at Steephill and right around the West Wight to Compton Bay and Freshwater, you'll be amazed at just how different the landscape becomes (www.visitisleofwight.co.uk/things-to-do/attractions/beaches).

LUNDY

LOCATION: 51.1827°N 4.6698°W

GRID REFERENCE: SS135460

POPULATION: 28

SIZE: 4.5km²

GETTING THERE: The island is linked to the mainland by the supply ship MS *Oldenburg*. Day trips are available from both Bideford and Ilfracombe. In winter months, a helicopter operates instead.

WHERE TO STAY: A range of accommodation is available on the island, all managed by the Landmark Trust (www.landmarktrust.org.uk).

WHERE TO EAT: Marisco Tavern, Lundy, EX39 2EY, **T:** 01237 431831, **W:** www.landmarktrust.org.uk.

Lundy Times

Sitting in the Bristol Channel and visible from both north Devon and South Wales, Lundy is one of the most visited of our small, remote islands – 18,000 people a year take the passenger ship here. Located in the middle of such an important shipping lane, it comes as no surprise to find Lundy's history has been on the front line, and it has changed hands many times down the centuries. One of the most notorious historical figures on Lundy was William de Marisco, who fled here when he was implicated in a 13th-century plot to kill King Henry III. The king captured Marisco and took control of Lundy, building a fort known today as Marisco Castle.

Visits to Lundy are made both by day-trippers and those staying overnight in one of the 23 holiday properties. Either way, you can find some real peace out here in the middle of the Bristol Channel. When the MS *Oldenburg* arrives during the day, bringing up to 267 passengers and supplies to the island, things get a little busier. But there are always corners of Lundy in which you'll be able to bask in isolation should you wish to. The island-hoppers coming for the day stay a few hours and are then taken back to the mainland, leaving Lundy to the lucky few overnighters, including staff employed by the Landmark Trust – the organisation managing Lundy on behalf of the National Trust.

Why I Love... Lundy

'The island offers a rare experience: large enough to have a life of its own, which visitor can share and enjoy, but small and far awa enough to be a world apart.'

Derek Green, Lundy General Manager

A Pub that Never Shuts

On warm days in the summer, one of the most popular places on Lundy is the Marisco Tavern. Visiting a pub this remote is always a special experience and you'll find a range of dishes available to sample – including burgers and pasties containing lamb from the island. The pub becomes a much quieter affair when the MS *Oldenburg* returns, but don't expect to be booted out at night. Although alcohol is only served within normal hours, this is a pub that doesn't shut. And it's the only place to keep lights on when the electric generators are turned off for the night.

Puffin Stamps

Post a letter on Lundy and you'll need to buy a local 'puffin' stamp that covers the cost of transporting it off the island to Bideford Post Office. These have been in operation since the late 1920s, when the GPO withdrew from the island. The distinctive puffin stamps are a collector's item and a popular souvenir.

ISLE OF PORTLAND

LOCATION: 50.5475°N 2.4343°W

GRID REFERENCE: SY690721

POPULATION: 12,844

SIZE: 12km²

GETTING THERE: Follow the A354 south of Weymouth to cross the causeway that links to Chesil Beach and brings you out on the Isle of Portland.

WHERE TO STAY: Heights Hotel, Isle of Portland, Dorset, DT5 2EN, **T:** 01305 821361, **W:** www.heights hotel.com. The Bunker, Victoria Square, Isle of Portland, DT5 1AL, **T:** 07846 401010, **W:** www.the bunkerportland.com.

WHERE TO EAT: Lobster Pot, Portland Bill Road, Isle of Portland, DT5 2JT, **T:** 01305 820242, **W:** www.lobster potrestaurantportland.co.uk. The Boat That Rocks, Portland Marina, Hamm Beach Road, Isle of Portland, DT5 1DX, **T:** 01305 823000, **W:** www.tbtr. co.uk.

Portland Bill

From the pebble-strewn tombolo Chesil Beach, it's quite a hike up to the famous red and white lighthouse that is the most photographed landmark on the Isle of Portland. If you're driving, there's a car park at the top to save you the climb up to Portland Bill. It's a glorious place to explore and on a sunny day there's likely to be a collection of walkers, cyclists and motorists. Three lighthouses stand on this prominent position jutting out into the English Channel, which, I'm sure you can imagine, are busy shipping waters. Just offshore, a dangerous tidal rapid creates fast-moving, hazardous currents that can be devastating for ships attempting to round the island. The Higher and the Lower lighthouse, once used together to give warnings to ships, are now operating as holiday apartments and a bird observatory. The lighthouse currently in use is the famous red and white building that has graced many a coastal postcard. The light is now controlled remotely, but the visitor centre is open and you can have a guided tour of the tower. This southern tip of the island, of course, gave its name to the classic children's TV show from the 1980s. *The Adventures of Portland Bill* – based on a lighthouse keeper called, funnily enough, Portland Bill – consisted of 25 fun-packed stop-animation episodes at a red and white striped lighthouse.

Leave a light on for me – the two historic beacons of Portland Bill.

The 'R' Word

As soon as you cross over to the Isle of Portland there's one word you're not allowed to say – 'rabbits'. For around 100 years, it's been a superstition on the island not to utter the name of the furry little creatures. Mention them in public and you may well hear a few gasps and see the odd raised eyebrow. It all started with quarry workers. When a rabbit was seen emerging from a burrow it often caused a bit of a panic because the tunnelling activities of the creatures had been linked to rockfalls. A rabbit spotted in the quarry sometimes led to workers downing tools for the day and heading off home until safety checks had been carried out. When the 2005 Wallace and Gromit film was released, islanders didn't refer to it as *The Curse of the Were-Rabbit* – instead, special posters were made with the title 'Something Bunny is Going On'. You have been warrened.

Rocky History

An abandoned quarry with superb views over Chesil Beach has been transformed into a 40-acre sculpture park and is well worth taking time to explore. Tout Quarry has provided tons of rock for buildings in London and other cities around the world. The idea became to turn the leftover rock into something special. Established in the 1980s, there are

▲ *Huge chalk cliffs dominate the horizon beyond the island's famous huts.*

over 60 hidden sculptures for you to explore, along with thriving wildlife. Miles of dramatic coastline can be explored in the area, which is part of the Jurassic Coast UNESCO World Heritage Site.

PORTSEA ISLAND

LOCATION: 50.8095°N 1.0759°W

GRID REFERENCE: SU653009

POPULATION: 207,100

SIZE: 24.5km²

Portsmouth – a Maritime Gem

Portsea is a big hitter among the islands of the British Isles. For a start, it houses almost all of one of our greatest cities – Portsmouth. It's also home to well over 200,000 people. This makes it the third most populous island in the British Isles, with only the large landmasses of Great Britain and Ireland having more inhabitants. It contains four railway stations, has three significant road bridges, important links with the Royal Navy and ferry links to the Channel Islands, France and Spain. It's also seen a huge boost to the local economy from tourism, with a handful of globally important maritime exhibitions based here. Portsea is an island with a lot of clout.

Portsea's Top Attractions

1 HARBOUR TOUR

Look at a map of Portsmouth Harbour and you won't be surprised to learn how important the sheltered natural inlet is in the maritime history books of Britain. The best way to appreciate the significance of the historic harbour is to take a guided boat tour. You'll get fabulous views of Portsmouth's skyline on the island, along with modern frigates, helicopter carriers and destroyers on the water. The geography of the river mouth and the harbour made it an attractive base for Roman and Anglo-Saxon armies and Portsea was later used as a mustering station for those fighting France. It was to service the soldiers and boat workers that a town first started to develop on the island. King Richard I granted a Royal Charter to build a harbour in 1194 and Portsmouth started to grow in stature.

2 HMS *VICTORY*

Few ships in Britain's seafaring history evoke so much wonder and intrigue as HMS *Victory*. Anybody who learned about Admiral Nelson and the Battle of Trafalgar at school will adore the audio tour that guides you around this remarkably intact 1759 vessel, which once supported a crew of 821. There

A room with a view atop the Spinnaker Tower.

GETTING THERE: Drivers should follow the M275 onto the island of Portsea and into the centre of Portsmouth. Portsmouth Harbour train station provides access to the city for those arriving by rail.

WHERE TO STAY: The George Hotel, Queen Street, Portsmouth, PO1 3HU, **T:** 023 9275 3885, **W:** www.thegeorgehotel.org.uk. Holiday Inn, Gunwharf Quays, Portsmouth, PO1 3FD, **T:** 03333 209 360, **W:** www.hiexportsmouth.co.uk.

WHERE TO EAT: Midships Cookhouse, Victory Gate, Historic Dockyard, Main Road, Portsmouth, PO1 3LJ, **T:** 023 9282 6077, **W:** www.boathouse4.org. Ship Anson, The Hard, Portsmouth, PO1 3DT, **T:** 023 9282 4152, **W:** www.greeneking-pubs.co.uk/pubs/hampshire/ship-anson.

are plenty of high points on the hour-long visit, including the different conditions on board for the officers and the ordinary crew members. And you'll be able to find the spot where Nelson was shot, surely one of the most well-known incidents in our naval history. A lengthy project to preserve the famous ship is underway so future generations arriving in Portsmouth will be able to continue enjoying the experience.

3 HMS *WARRIOR*

The largest and fastest of all the Royal Navy's ships during the Victorian Age of Steam, HMS *Warrior* became a seagoing celebrity in the years following her 1860 launch. With the Navy embracing new engineering methods and creating formidable ships of a kind never seen before, the national pride in HMS *Warrior* was celebrated across the land. During a Tour of Britain, the ship was opened up to the public like none that had been built before. Tourists loved to see the might of what was the pride of Queen Victoria's fleet and spoke of how it reflected the power of the British Empire. An immersive and impressive experience to this day, make the most of the costumed characters from Victorian England who can tell stories from the ship's past.

4 SPINNAKER TOWER

Since it opened in 2005, the newest addition to Portsmouth's coastal skyline has been a big reason for people arriving on Portsea Island. The Spinnaker Tower can be seen from over 37km (23 miles) away and provides incredible views of Gunwharf Quays, the Historic Dockyard, Whale Island and the coast beyond. Millions of people have taken a trip up to the View Decks using the fast elevator that powers up at 4 metres per second (9 miles per hour). Weighing more than 30,000 tons, the foundations of the tower delve 50m (164ft) into the ground and the building is formed from enough concrete to fill five and a half Olympic-sized swimming pools. It's an unforgettable experience and on a clear day the views of the south coast and out to the Isle of Wight are fabulous.

5 COULD YOU BE A ROYAL MARINES COMMANDO?

There are many different attractions inside Portsmouth's Historic Dockyard, but one will have you breaking out in a sweat. Highly regarded as an elite amphibious fighting force, Royal Marines Commandos, and the process to become one, are as tough as it gets. The display in the dockyard takes you through all the different processes and what it means to get to this level. If you feel you're up to the challenge there is even an assault course and a rotating climbing wall to test your physical abilities. It's not for the faint-hearted!

6 *MARY ROSE*

Broadcast live on TV in October 1982, the raising of the *Mary Rose* from the seabed of the Solent was a national event. After years of careful preservation and the ship being on display in various places, the interactive experience now on offer to visitors is world class. Housed in a huge museum, technology helps to bring the story of King Henry VIII's flagship to life. But there is something to be said for leaving the interactive displays and the information boards aside for a moment and simply staring out at the wooden wreckage that sank during a battle in 1545. After sitting at the bottom of the sea for over 400 years, seeing the *Mary Rose* and the wealth of artefacts recovered from her is a jaw-dropping event.

Portsmouth's famous tower has pointed skyward since 2005.

ST MICHAEL'S MOUNT

Picture Perfect

There's something slightly surreal about seeing St Michael's Mount for the first time. Somewhere between a European bastion and a home for a Disney princess, the small island in the middle of Mount's Bay, with the castle proudly perching on top, is one of the most visually stunning of all the British islands. The approach to St Michael's Mount is even more stunning if you hit the tides at the right time. It's a short, beautiful walk across seaweed-strewn cobbles with sea water lapping at either side, all under the formidable gaze of the impressive castle.

On arrival, the village and picturesque harbour should be explored and there's an opportunity to buy a snack. But the climb to the castle provides the greatest charm, twisting past surprise views as you head up to discover the history of this fascinating place. As soon as you step through the magnificent entrance hall, you'll make jaw-dropping discoveries at every turn, from the 18th-century library used for relaxation, possessions dating back to the English Civil War, a 12th-century chapel and stained glass created in the early 1500s.

LOCATION: 50.1160°N 5.4772°W

GRID REFERENCE: SW514298

POPULATION: 30

SIZE: <1km²

GETTING THERE: A causeway allows you to walk across to the island at low tide, with information notices advising when the water is too high. Boat companies make the journey to the island from Marazion on the mainland.

WHERE TO STAY: Godolphin Arms, West End, Marazion, TR17 0EN, **T:** 01736 888510, **W:** www.the godolphin.com. Marazion Hotel, The Square, Marazion, TR17 0AP, **T:** 01736 710334, **W:** www.marazionhotel.co.uk.

WHERE TO EAT: Sail Loft, St Michael's Mount, TR17 0HT, **T:** 01736 710748, **W:** www.stmichaelsmount.co.uk.

▶ *Rising majestically from the bay, St Michael's Mount sits at the end of a tidal causeway.*

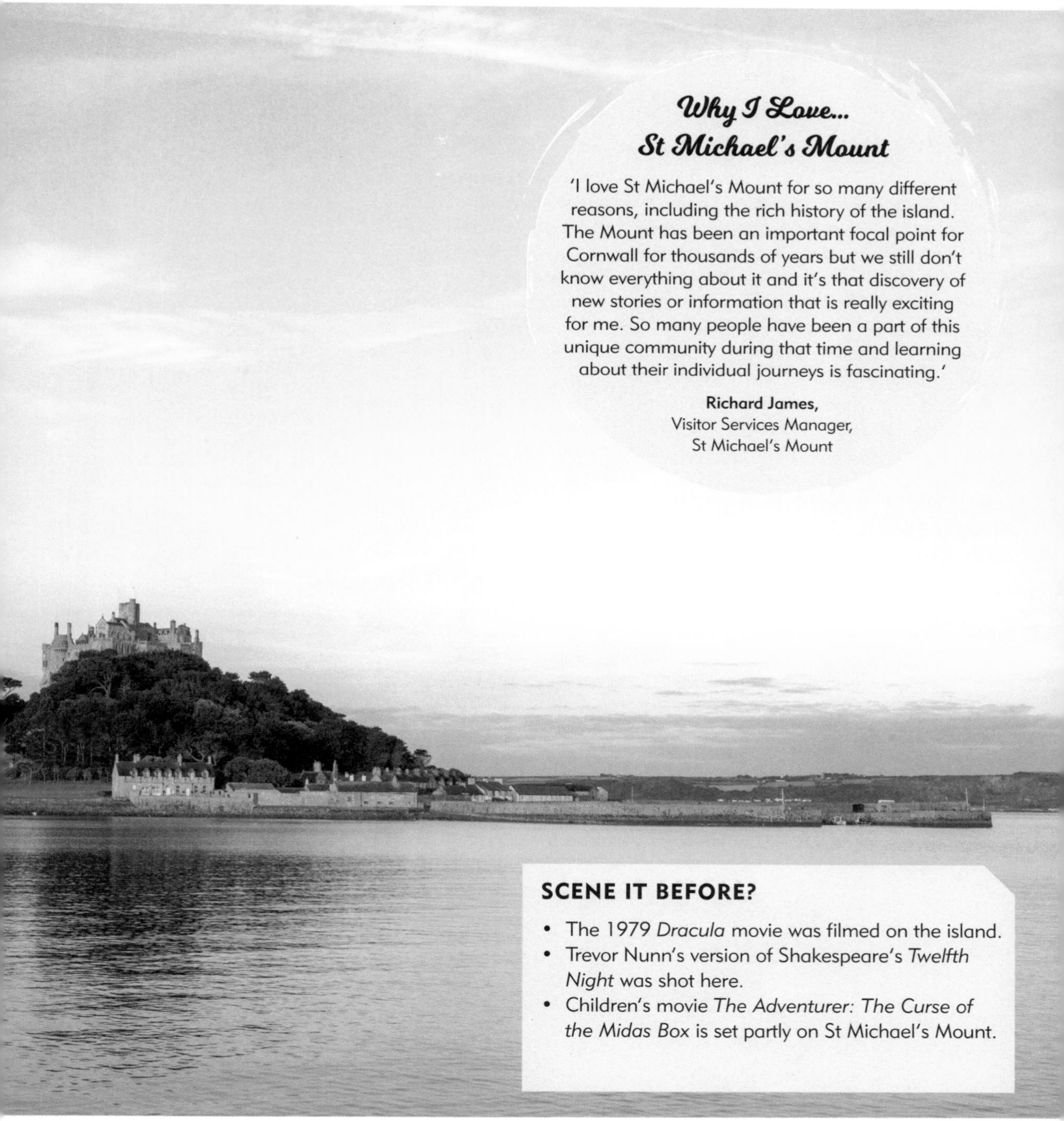

Why I Love...
St Michael's Mount

'I love St Michael's Mount for so many different reasons, including the rich history of the island. The Mount has been an important focal point for Cornwall for thousands of years but we still don't know everything about it and it's that discovery of new stories or information that is really exciting for me. So many people have been a part of this unique community during that time and learning about their individual journeys is fascinating.'

Richard James,
Visitor Services Manager,
St Michael's Mount

SCENE IT BEFORE?

- The 1979 *Dracula* movie was filmed on the island.
- Trevor Nunn's version of Shakespeare's *Twelfth Night* was shot here.
- Children's movie *The Adventurer: The Curse of the Midas Box* is set partly on St Michael's Mount.

THORNEY ISLAND

LOCATION: 50.8160°N 0.9184°W

GRID REFERENCE: GR766051

POPULATION: 1,079

SIZE: 28km²

Missiles and Nature

Thorney Island is a fascinating place, where military activity sits hand in hand with a thriving wildlife population. On paper these two key features of the island do not lie comfortably with each other, but a lovely walk around the perimeter of this low-lying piece of land suggests otherwise. There has been a military interest in Thorney Island since the 1930s when the Royal Air Force moved in, before handing it over to the Coastal Command in the Second World War and the Army from the 1980s. The circular walk that follows the shore attracts plenty of visitors and forms part of the Sussex Border Path – but given the military nature of parts of the island you must make sure you stick to the path. The appeal to wildlife enthusiasts comes primarily from the range of ecosystems found on Thorney Island. Tidal mudflats sit next to grasslands, meadow and reed beds, attracting a diverse range of species. Bring your binoculars and look out for brent geese, oystercatchers, lapwings, skylarks and shelduck. Pilsey Island sits just off Thorney Island and is home to a large number of roosting birds, spiders, insects and plants. There is no access to Pilsey, which is owned by the Ministry of Defence and maintained by the RSPB, but you can find a vantage point and use your binoculars.

GETTING THERE: From Emsworth, turn off the A259 onto Thorney Road and follow it over the Great Deep.

WHERE TO STAY: Langstone Quays Resort, Hayling Island, PO11 0NQ, **T:** 023 9246 5011, **W:** www. langstonequays.co.uk. The Millstream Hotel, Bosham Lane, Bosham, Chichester, PO18 8HL, **T:** 01243 573234, **W:** www.millstreamhotel.com.

WHERE TO EAT: The Deck, Emsworth Yacht Harbour, Thorney Road, PO10 8BP, **T:** 01243 376161, **W:** www.thedeckcafe.co.uk.

WHALE ISLAND

An Unusual Island

A man-made landmass constructed by convicts, Whale Island is now home to the Royal Navy training facility, HMS *Excellent*. The doors of the barricades are occasionally opened to welcome the public on Heritage Days, when tours run every hour. The guided sessions are fascinating and need to be booked in advance when they are available. You'll see an impressive range of Victorian buildings still in use – the Church of St Barbara, an on-site museum and the grounds of what became the first Naval Gunnery School. There's also the chance to learn about the state gun carriage, which is used for state funerals and maintained on Whale Island. One of the most unusual features of the island's history is that there was a zoo here until the Second World War, housing animals from around the globe that were presented as gifts to British representatives.

LOCATION: 50.8158°N 1.0981°W	
GRID REFERENCE: SU639022	
POPULATION: Unknown	
SIZE: <1km²	

GETTING THERE: Road access is via Whale Island Way, close to the ferry terminal on Portsmouth's Portsea Island.

WHERE TO STAY: Hotels close to the island include Portsmouth Travelodge, Kingston Crescent, Portsmouth, PO2 8AB, **T:** 0871 984 6208, **W:** www.travelodge.co.uk and Ferry House Lodge, Mile End Road, Portsmouth PO2 7BX, **T:** 023 9281 1428, **W:** www.ferryhouselodge.com.

CANVEY ISLAND

Canvey

Canvey is a reclaimed island, low-lying and separated from the mainland by a series of rivers and creeks. Many people driving onto Canvey won't be aware they've been brought onto an island at all; it's a subtle transition from the mainland. Well connected by road and with a train station at nearby Benfleet, Canvey is a thriving community where thousands live and work.

Although people have called this island home since Roman times, living on a largely flat piece of land at sea level has not been without its problems. Flooding is a regular issue down the years, with the worst coming in a dreadful storm surge that flooded all the countries lining the North Sea in 1953. The impact on the island was catastrophic, with 58 people losing their lives and 13,000 forced to flee their homes.

LOCATION: 51.5171°N 0.5784°E

GRID REFERENCE: TQ799833

POPULATION: 38,170

SIZE: 18.4km²

GETTING THERE: The A130 and B1040 roads cross over to Canvey Island from Benfleet.

WHERE TO STAY: Endeavour Hotel, Thisselt Road, Canvey Island, SS8 9BQ, **T:** 01268 683243, **W:** www.canveyhotel.co.uk. The Oysterfleet Hotel, Knightswick Road, Canvey Island, SS8 9PA, **T:** 01268 510111, **W:** www.oysterfleethotel.com.

WHERE TO EAT: The Labworth Restaurant, Furtherwick Road, Canvey Island, SS8 7DW, **T:** 01268 683209, **W:** www.thelabworth.com. Jilly Beans Café, Furtherwick Road, Canvey Island, SS8 7AT, **T:** 01268 511393.

The Lobster Smack

Tucked in next to the coastal defences and serving pints below sea level, this is an atmospheric inn that has packed a punch for centuries. It's thought to be the location featured in Charles Dickens' *Great Expectations* (1861), providing a place to stop off for Pip on his journey down the Thames. Legendary tales also abound of the Lobster Smack being a key Victorian venue for bare-knuckle boxing. Family feuds and championship bouts have taken place here, with some lasting several hours and going over 60 rounds. Today the pub is more relaxed, a top destination for people wanting a drink and meal after a walk along the seafront.

A Victorian Getaway

In the late 1890s, Canvey Island began to develop a reputation as a must-visit coastal resort among the people of East London. It was promoted as being a healthy retreat with beneficial sea air. Dream holiday homes were sold to well-to-do folk, and attractions were built to pull in the visitors, including a pier, promenade and winter garden. New tourist developments were added in the 20th century and Canvey Island remained one of the south-east's top holiday spots until the package holidays of the 1970s and 1980s drew families to Spain. There is still a feeling of being in a leisurely place when you spend time on Canvey Island, though. There are plenty of places to eat and drink beside the sea on the southern side of the island. Young people in particular are delighted to spend time at Leisure Island Fun Park, which delivers the coastal rides junior school kids desire – Blackbeard's Revenge is a particular favourite among young adrenaline junkies.

On the Buses

The original building that housed Canvey's bus company in the 1930s is now a museum dedicated to the history of transport on the island. With a striking design typical of its time, it was used as a bus depot until 1978 before the running services were replaced by the museum's range of classic models. There are over 30 classic buses telling the story of how people were transported in the 20th century, some with the beautiful wooden frames that once gave standard buses a more luxurious feel.

ISLE OF SHEPPEY

LOCATION: 51.3903°N 0.8300°E

GRID REFERENCE: TQ968169

POPULATION: 40,300

SIZE: 433km²

Blue is the Colour

The largest settlement on the Isle of Sheppey, Sheerness, with its 12,000 residents, is on the north-eastern point of the island. It's a lively town, with a rich maritime history. A Royal Navy dockyard was first established here in the 17th century and warships were still repaired here up until the 1960s. The curiously named Blue Town is a suburb on the western edge of Sheerness. This place developed during the Napoleonic Wars, when residents preserved their wooden houses with blue paint. The Blue Town Heritage Centre is a must-visit while you're here, a great place to learn about the history of the island's relationship with the sea. The Criterion is on the same site, a beautifully restored Victorian music hall that usually has a diary full of cinema, music and theatre (www.thecriterionbluetown.co.uk).

Mellow Marsh

Away from the populated areas, there is a wealth of wildlife to enjoy in the distinctive Isle of Sheppey landscape. Largely flat and bordering the mouth of the river that bears its name, the Swale National Nature Reserve is an internationally recognised coastal marshland, well known for the butterflies and moths that migrate here. Many waders and large numbers of wildfowl can be found on the network of paths that cut across this protected area. Follow the road from Leysdown-on-Sea to reach this delightful coastal reserve.

GETTING THERE: The Isle of Sheppey is connected to the mainland via the A249, which bridges the River Swale. Visitors can also take the train to Sheerness-on-Sea.

WHERE TO STAY: The Shurland Hotel, High Street, Eastchurch, Sheerness, ME12 4EH, **T:** 01795 881100, **W:** www.hotelshurland.co.uk. Queen Phillippa, High Street, Queenborough, ME11 5AQ, **T:** 01795 228756, **W:** www.queenphillippa.com.

WHERE TO EAT: The Bay View, Leysdown Road, Leysdown-on-Sea, ME12 4AQ, **T:** 01795 511519. Arizona Diner, High Street, Sheerness, ME12 1NS, **T:** 07440 197430.

Sheppey Porridge

Of the sizable population on the island, around 2,800 are inmates at the three prisons located here. HMP Elmley, HMP Standford Hill and HMP Swaleside are all located close to the village of Eastchurch.

MERSEA

LOCATION: 51.7879°N 0.9212°W

GRID REFERENCE: TM015139

POPULATION: 6,925

SIZE: 18km²

GETTING THERE: There is good road access over the B1025 causeway, known as The Strood, but this can flood at high tide.

WHERE TO STAY: Victory at Mersea, Coast Road, Mersea, CO5 8LS, **T:** 01206 382907, **W:** www.victoryat mersea.co.uk. Mersea Island Holiday Park, Fen Lane, Mersea, CO5 8UA, **T:** 01442 508850, **W:** www.away resorts.co.uk/mersea-island.

WHERE TO EAT: West Mersea Oyster Bar, Coast Road, West Mersea, CO5 8LT, **T:** 01206 381600, **W:** westmerseaoysterbar.co.uk. The Coast Inn, Coast Road, West Mersea, CO5 8NA, **T:** 01206 383568, **W:** www.thecoastinn.co.uk.

▲ *There's a flavour of continental Europe about Mersea, in more ways than one.*

Time for Wine

It was a sunny day in the summer when I drove onto Mersea, and I was overwhelmed at how it looked like a different country. The fields of crops, the hum of insects, the red-tiled roofs – I'm sure it depends when you make the trip over The Strood to visit East and West Mersea, but on the day I visited it felt like I could have been in France or Belgium. The sense of being abroad was heightened on discovery of a vineyard, right here in Essex. Mersea Island Vineyard is certainly not only about the grapes – there's a tea room, accommodation and it's also a wedding venue. But when you visit you should check out the wine. Try the dry white Mersea Mehala or the pink Island Blush, both made with locally grown grapes.

Shell Out on a Treat

Mersea is famous for its oysters and there are several places to try this local delicacy. They are sustainably fished from traditional oyster beds that sit in the estuary just off the island. The oysters produced here – known as Wild Pacific Oysters – have a distinctive appearance because of their thick, rippled shells. Available all year round, the oyster business on Mersea has a rich history – oyster fishing from the River Blackwater Estuary has provided for local people since Roman times. Each oyster can reach 140g (4.9oz) and is cleaned in sea water after being harvested. When you try one you're sampling a snack that has taken around two years to grow in the nearby waters.

Elsewhere, top chefs and local produce from around Mersea Island and the Blackwater Estuary are the focus of the lessons taking place at the Mersea Island Cookery School. The school bases many of its popular courses on local and seasonal produce and it puts on a range of different sessions for budding chefs to book.

NORTHEY ISLAND

LOCATION: 51.7230°N 0.7180°E

GRID REFERENCE: TL878062

POPULATION: 0

SIZE: <1km²

GETTING THERE: Access is available at low tide via a causeway, but you need to let the National Trust know you are intending to make the trip as you'll need to buy a permit. Call 01621 853142 to make arrangements.

WHERE TO STAY: Le Bouchon Hotel, The Square, Heybridge, CM9 4LT, **T:** 01621 856511, **W:** www.lebouchon. co.uk. The Limes, Market Hill, Maldon, CM9 4PZ, **T:** 01621 856901, **W:** https://luigisalfresco.com.

WHERE TO EAT: Luigi's Al Fresco at The Limes, Market Hill, Maldon, CM9 4PZ, **T:** 01621 856901, **W:** https:// luigisalfresco.com.

Castaway Campers

Northey Island has been called the 'Wuthering Heights of Essex', a testament to the wild, remote nature of this piece of land in the River Blackwater. Linked by a causeway to the mainland on the southern side of the island, a trip to Northey is possible if you time it with low tide. The island is looked after by the National Trust and the organisation encourages you to experience the peace and tranquillity of hearing birdsong as water laps against the shore. Registering for a permit is essential before you make the trip, whether you want to walk across or moor a boat. For the ultimate experience on Northey Island, sign up for the Castaway event, organised by the Trust during the summer. This provides intrepid island explorers with the chance to camp overnight on Northey, after the tide comes in and cuts you off from the mainland. You'll not be alone being a castaway here; the event has live music and a beer tent to help your island night pass memorably.

Battle of Maldon

The causeway over to the island is thought to be the scene of the bloody Battle of Maldon between Anglo-Saxon defenders and Viking invaders in AD 991. The home forces were commanded by Earl Byrthnoth, but he lost the battle and his life to the Danish invaders. The conflict was later told in a famous poem and a statue to Byrthnoth can be seen in the town of Maldon.

TWO TREE ISLAND

LOCATION: 51.5357°N 0.6306°E

GRID REFERENCE: TQ824851

POPULATION: 0

SIZE: 2.6km²

A Reclaimed Sanctuary

Like several other destinations along the Thames Estuary, Two Tree Island was reclaimed from the sea by building a sea wall so the land behind could be used for farming. Bring binoculars when you visit because this small island, which is just off mainland Essex, is now a nature reserve, attracting a huge number of wildfowl and waders. There's plenty to look at all year round, but the bird population is particularly active during winter. Expect to see brent geese, which come to feed on eelgrass, along with hundreds of waders such as dunlin, avocet and curlew. In summer, wildlife lovers bring their cameras and butterfly books in the hope of spotting the marbled white and the Essex skipper. The island may be teeming with wildlife these days, but it has not always been so well looked after. At the beginning of the 20th century a sewage works was built here and the island spent 40 years as a landfill site.

GETTING THERE: The island is accessible by road from Leigh-on-Sea in Essex and there's a free car park for 30 vehicles with a boat storage area. Leigh-on-Sea train station is close by.

WHERE TO STAY: Staying on nearby Canvey Island is a good plan. The Oysterfleet Hotel, Knightswick Road, Canvey Island, SS8 9PA, **T:** 01268 510111, **W:** www.oysterfleethotel.com.

Why I Love... Two Tree Island

'Two Tree Island, with its big open estuary skies, can provide a remarkable wildlife spectacle throughout the year. Whether it's nature or landscape you seek, the island will provide. Throughout spring the scrub and bushes are chattering and churring away with the sound of whitethroats as they breed after spending the winter in Africa.'

Marc Outten,
Essex Wildlife Trust

WALES

Holiday favourite Anglesey is perhaps the best known of all the Welsh islands, but a trip over the Menai Strait could well involve a cluster of additional, tempting destinations. Anglesey may be the best place to base yourself as you discover locally produced sea salt and the country's longest place name. But be prepared to branch out and visit more island locations off the Welsh coast, as this country is blessed with islands of stunning diversity.

Holy Island is home to Holyhead, a bustling town that is often the stopping-off point for those heading further west to Ireland from the nearby port. You'll be able to see the boats coming and going from the many vantage points on the coast. Over the decades, the vessels out to sea have been guided by the stunning lighthouse at South Stack, a small island linked by a bridge in an incredible setting. And other charmingly small islands around Anglesey are worth visiting – look out for the beautiful Church Island beneath Menai Bridge and the awesome, sandy Llanddwyn Island. Off the south coast of Wales, monks and chocolate await discovery on the idyllic retreat of Caldey Island.

DON'T MISS

- Posing for a picture at the train station with the longest name – Llanfairpwllgwyngyllgogerychwyrndrobwllllantysiliogogogoch
- Sampling chocolate and enjoying cliff walks on the peaceful retreat of Caldey Island
- Exploring the tranquil and atmospheric Church Island beneath the monumental Menai Bridge
- Listening to the crashing waves on rocks below the lighthouse on South Stack
- Taking photographs of the Seeks and teeming bird life on a visit to Puffin Island

◀ *A Napoleonic fortress sits atop St Catherine's Island.*

ANGLESEY

LOCATION:	53.2260°N 4.1633°W
GRID REFERENCE:	SH556720
POPULATION:	56,000
SIZE:	714km²

Karma Farmer

Anglesey is a top foodie destination, and if you're hoping to get the best taste out of your trip, try to time it with one of the island's famous farmers' markets – top producers come together on the third Saturday of each month to sell their wares at Princes Pier, Menai Bridge. Local chocolatier Cocoaroma sells flavoured drops of mouth-watering treats, while wild foods foraged from around the island form the ingredients of the Celtic Kitchen's Welsh Dragon Chilli Chutney. There is plenty of locally smoked fish for sale and some of the finest bread you'll taste from the Becws Môn, an island bakery supplying over 70 outlets.

A Pinch of Salt

Surrounded by clean waters, Anglesey has developed a global reputation for producing some of the finest sea salt. One of the island's best-known companies, Halen Môn, has been evaporating sea water since 1997 to produce salt crystals. They started selling the prized salt to a local butcher and things soon grew; the salt was served at the 2012 Olympic Games, features as a key ingredient in Pipers crisps, is sold by food chains throughout the country and is even a favourite of former US President Barack Obama. Behind-the-scenes tours are available to discover first hand the process of producing the seasoning loved by many top chefs.

GETTING THERE: The island is linked to the mainland by two bridges: the Menai Bridge carries the A5 and the Britannia Bridge provides a seamless route for the North Wales Expressway. A regular train service also serves Anglesey, connecting it with mainland Wales and Holyhead.

WHERE TO STAY: Anglesey Arms, Mona Road, Menai Bridge, LL59 5EA, **T:** 01248 712305, **W:** www.anglesey-arms.co.uk. Château Rhianfa, Beaumaris Road, Menai Bridge, LL59 5NS, **T:** 01248 880090, **W:** www.chateaurhianfa.com.

WHERE TO EAT: The Tavern on the Bay, Red Wharf Bay, Anglesey, LL75 8RJ, **T:** 01248 852751, **W:** www. thetavernonthebay.co.uk. Tom's Hamburger House, High Street, Menai Bridge, LL59 5EF, **T:** 01248 712211.

Why I Love... Anglesey

'Despite being born and raised on Anglesey for 18 years and returning each year, I still discover something new every time I go back home, whether it's an ancient site, a white sand beach or abandoned curiosity. It's a pretty mysterious and magical place that feels relatively undiscovered compared to other parts of the UK.'

Donna Lee,
teacher

Coastal Ramble

Some of the finest coastline in the British Isles is found in Anglesey, and islanders are rightly proud of their beaches and cliffs. Most of Anglesey's 201km (125-mile) long coastline is designated an Area of Outstanding Natural Beauty, preserved because of its valuable heath, dunes and saltmarsh. One of the best ways to get up close to this wonderful nature and enjoy the fabulous scenery is to walk the Isle of Anglesey Coastal Path. At 210km (130 miles) long and taking an average of 12 days to complete, it's something you can dip into for the day or commit a longer and more strenuous holiday to.

What's in a Name?

When it comes to hard-to-pronounce Welsh names, one place on Anglesey proves to be more than a mouthful. Visitors can try their best to say Llanfairpwllgwyngyllgogerychwyrndrobwllllantysiliogogogoch but they're unlikely to get it right. Perhaps you're better off sticking to the slightly friendlier, shorter version, Llanfair-pwll. Or maybe have a go at the literal translation – St Mary's Church in the Hollow of the White Hazel near a Rapid Whirlpool and the Church of St Tysilio near the Red Cave.

Why I Love... Anglesey

'The isle of Anglesey has a combination of land and sea that I have yet to find anywhere else. At Halen Môn we look out over the Menai Strait – the stretch of water separating us from the mainland – with the ravishing backdrop of Snowdonia. You can taste the quality of the landscape in our food.'

Jess Lea-Wilson,
Halen Môn
Brand Manager

LLANFAIRPWLLGWYNGYLLGOGERYCHWYRNDROBWLLLLANTYSILIOGOGOGOCH
Llan-vire-pooll-guin-gill-go-ger-u-queern-drob-ooll-llandus-ilio-gogo-goch

CHURCH ISLAND

LOCATION: 53.2224°N 4.1712°W

GRID REFERENCE: SH551716

POPULATION: 0

SIZE: <1km²

Thomas Telford's World-Famous Bridge

The clue is very much in the name of this unusual place of worship in the middle of the Menai Strait; it's an island with a church. And it's a beautiful church at that, dedicated to St Tysilio and dating back to the 15th century. The building and surrounding churchyard dominate the entire island, which can only be reached on foot via a causeway that runs from the popular walkway known as the Belgian Promenade. It's the setting of the island that makes it such an unforgettable place to visit. The swirling waters of the Menai Strait surge close by at high tide and the looming presence of the Menai Bridge cannot be ignored while you are here. Thomas Telford's iconic suspension bridge adds an element of drama to the scene. The importance of that Grade I listed structure cannot be overstated for people living on this side of the Menai Strait – it was the first permanent link with the mainland. Points of interest inside the churchyard include the burial place of Welsh poet Cynan and a memorial to those lost in the two world wars.

GETTING THERE: Access to the island is via the Belgian Promenade footpath that runs next to the Menai Strait, at the bottom of the Menai Bridge. You walk across a causeway to reach Church Island. Car parking is available on Mona Road.

WHERE TO STAY: Bulkeley Arms, Uxbridge Square, Menai Bridge, Anglesey, LL59 5DF, **T:** 01248 717219, **W:** www.robinsonsbrewery. com/pubs/bulkeley-arms-menai-bridge/. Anglesey Arms, Mona Road, Menai Bridge, Anglesey, LL59 5EA, **T:** 01248 712305, **W:** www.anglesey-arms.co.uk.

Telford's iconic structure bridges the gap between Anglesey and the mainland.

CRIBINAU

LOCATION: 53.1847°N 4.4917°W

GRID REFERENCE: SH336682

POPULATION: 0

SIZE: <1km²

GETTING THERE: There is no vehicular access, but a path winds down to the coast from the nearest road. To reach it, take the country road off the A4080 towards Anglesey Circuit.

WHERE TO STAY: The Prince Llewelyn, Aberffraw, Ty Croes, Anglesey, LL63 5YU, **T:** 01407 840090, **W:** www.princellewelynanglesey.co.uk. Cefn Dref, Rhosneigr, LL64 5JH, **T:** 01407 810714, **W:** www.cefndref.co.uk.

A Hidden Gem

As you walk down a country lane towards the tiny tidal island of Cribinau, the anticipation builds. You may have seen a photo of the church, perched atop this small piece of land, but it doesn't really prepare you for the stunning sight when it suddenly comes into view. This island, hidden off the beaten track on the west coast of Anglesey, is a mesmerising place. Time your visit with low tide so you can walk across to the Church of St Cwyfan, which dates back to the 13th century. During its first couple of centuries, the church was enlarged but eventually fell into disrepair and saw some parts demolished in the 19th century. Restoration work took place in the 20th century and there's a donation box for contributions towards ongoing repairs.

The island itself appears to be a recent addition to the Anglesey coastline – a 17th-century map shows it linked to the mainland. But the surrounding cliffs are formed from boulder clay, a soft material that erodes easily. Graves from the churchyard were disappearing into the sea during the 1800s due to the erosion, so the sea wall was built around Cribinau to protect those remaining in the churchyard. At the back of the church you'll discover one of the most sublime benches in the country. Sit here a while and drink in the isolation enjoyed by this place of worship.

▲ *One of the most intriguing churches in the world, in one of the finest settings.*

HOLY ISLAND

LOCATION: 53.3171°N 4.6402°W

GRID REFERENCE: SH242832

POPULATION: 13,659

SIZE: 346km²

GETTING THERE: Thanks to the busy port linking Wales with Ireland, Holy Island is well served by the road network – both the A5 and A55 wind up here. There is also a regular train service to the island's station.

WHERE TO STAY: The Haven Guest House, Marine Square, Holyhead, LL65 1DG, **T:** 01407 760254, **W:** www.thehavenholyhead.com. The Boathouse Hotel, Newry Beach, Holyhead, LL65 1YF, **T:** 01407 762094, **W:** www.theboathousehotel.com.

WHERE TO EAT: Langdon's Restaurant and Bar, Holyhead Marina, Beach Road, Newry Beach, Holyhead, Anglesey, LL65 1YA, **T:** 01407 762415, **W:** www.langdons.restaurant. Harbourfront Bistro, Newry Beach, Holyhead, LL65 1YD, **T:** 01407 763433, **W:** www.harbourfrontbistro.co.uk.

▼ *Take time to gaze out to sea from the lookout near South Stack.*

Holy Island – Home to Holyhead

Mention Holy Island and people will probably think you're talking about the atmospheric tidal island off the coast of Northumberland. This corner of Wales is better known for its biggest town – Holyhead – but the island it sits on is also called Holy Island. You'll find it off the east coast of Anglesey and it's well connected by bridges carrying road and rail – all because of the ferry terminal that sees regular services leave for Dublin. The island is home to a bustling community, many working in jobs linked to the ferry and tourism. The best way to explore this historic seaport is to head for the oldest lifeboat station in Wales – built in the 1850s – which now houses the fine Holyhead Maritime Museum. Here you can learn all about how important the sea has been for this town over the centuries, and the challenges it has brought with it, including the many ships that have wrecked on the treacherous rocks along this coastline and stories of the lifeboatmen who work tirelessly to save lives. The museum gets right up to date, comparing the technology of modern ships sailing over to Ireland with those making the journey 100 years ago.

Captain Skinner

The most visible landmark on Holy Island also has a maritime theme. High on a hilltop, looking down to the ferry terminal, is a memorial to Captain John Macgregor Skinner. Born in New Jersey, Captain Skinner lost an eye and an arm while serving in the Navy, later moving to Holyhead to become master of packet ships going back and forth over the Irish Sea. He campaigned for improvements to ship conditions and was well known for bringing a ship into harbour during a severe gale. His seafaring life came to a tragic end when he was washed overboard from his ship in 1832.

LLANDDWYN ISLAND

LOCATION: 53.1423°N 4.4076°W

GRID REFERENCE: SH390632

POPULATION: 0

SIZE: <1km²

An Island for Lovers

Making your way along the sandy paths towards Llanddwyn is idyllic enough, but the arrival at the crossing point to the island is sublime. Off-season, you may have much of this area to yourself, and that's such a treat because there are few settings around our islands more magical than this. Sheltered sandy beaches welcome you at every turn, enticing families to paddle. If there are too many people in one area, continue walking along until you find an emptier beach. It's an astonishingly glorious island and a therapeutic place to relax, all in the shadow of the Snowdonia mountains.

The biggest treat is saved until last. At the very tip of the island is a 19th-century lighthouse modelled on the design of local windmills. With a set of steps running up from the beach to the brilliant white tower, this makes for one of the best views on all of the islands around Anglesey. If you experience loved-up feelings on lovely Llanddwyn, there may be a reason why. The island is strongly associated with Dwynwen (the name Llanddwyn means 'church of Dwynwen'), the Welsh equivalent of St Valentine. Her saint's day is 25 January, when many Welsh romantics send cards and gifts.

GETTING THERE: A network of paths works its way down to the coast from Newborough in south-east Anglesey. Once you get to the shore, Llanddwyn Island is accessible at low tide.

WHERE TO STAY: The Anglesey Arms, Mona Road, Menai Bridge, LL59 5EA, **T:** 01248 712305, **W:** www.anglesey-arms.co.uk. Victoria Hotel, Telford Road, Menai Bridge, LL59 5DR, **T:** 01248 712309, **W:** www.vicmenai.com.

Why I Love... Llanddwyn Island...

'Islands can offer us much needed solitude, a chance to reflect inwardly and an opportunity to look outwards to the wider world.'

Rich Edward,
Police Constable

MIDDLE MOUSE

Ynys Badrig

Welcome to the most northerly point of Wales! You won't find any people living on this small island 1km (0.6 miles) to the north of Anglesey, but if you visit in the summer months there are plenty of seabirds, so make sure your camera is constantly poised for action. June and July are popular months to go take a look at the vast population of guillemots that cling to the rock on almost impossible perches. Legend has it St Patrick ran aground here and had to swim ashore. This explains the island's Welsh name – Ynys Badrig, or Patrick's Island.

LOCATION:	53.4352°N 4.4370°W
GRID REFERENCE:	SH382959
POPULATION:	0
SIZE:	<1km²

GETTING THERE: Boat trips to get up close to Middle Mouse are available from Anglesey, including those offered by RibRide (**T:** 0333 1234303, **W:** www.ribride.co.uk).

WHERE TO STAY: Leafy Lane Guest House, Y Graiglwyd, Bull Bay, Amlwch, LL68 9SG, **T:** 01407 831902. Gwesty Gadlys Hotel, Cemaes Bay, LL67 0LH, **T:** 01407 710227. **W:** www.gadlys. co.uk

PUFFIN ISLAND

LOCATION: 53.3180°N 4.0279°W

GRID REFERENCE: SH650820

POPULATION: 0

SIZE: <1km²

A Haven for Puffins

Although it's now uninhabited – by humans, at least – this was not always the case on Puffin Island. Formerly known as Priestholm, there was a monastery here in the 12th century and a hermitage some 600 years before that. Today the island is dominated by birdlife, and especially the puffins that give it its name. After the puffin population was decimated by rats, accidentally introduced to the island in Victorian times, the island was recently declared rat-free and the puffins have been increasing in number ever since. Hundreds of puffins now come here to breed, along with close to 1,000 great cormorants and plenty of guillemots, razorbills and shags. Take one of the pleasure cruises around Puffin Island between Easter and October and you'll also get up close with the local seal colony and, if you're lucky, a dolphin or two.

GETTING THERE: Puffin Island is visible from Anglesey, so take your binoculars to enjoy a better view. Trips around the island get you near to the birdlife. Contact Anglesey Boat Trips for more information (**T:** 01248 716335, **W:** www.angleseyboattrips. com).

WHERE TO STAY: The Bulkeley Hotel, Castle Street, Beaumaris, Anglesey, LL58 8AW, **T:** 01248 810415, **W:** www.bulkeleyhotel.co.uk. Bishopsgate House Hotel, Castle Street, Beaumaris, LL58 8BB, **T:** 01248 810302, **W:** www.bishops gatehotel.co.uk.

SALT ISLAND

LOCATION: 53.3167°N 4.6237°W	
GRID REFERENCE: SH253831	
POPULATION: 0	
SIZE: <1km²	

Worth its Salt

You're only likely to step foot on Salt Island if you're on the way to Ireland, or returning to Wales. In fact, many people don't realise they're on an island in the moments before they board a ferry bound for Dublin, since the road network and bridges make the journey to the boat a seamless experience. The majority of Salt Island is given over to the port of Holyhead. Ferries can berth here, while car and freight drivers sit and wait to be called forth for their voyage across the Irish Sea. The island therefore fulfils a curious role – it's a coming and going type of place, but visitors to it are often filled with anticipation, excitement and other travel-related emotions.

The name comes from a factory based here in the 18th century, which used sea water to process salt. A hospital was also located on Salt Island, initially used exclusively to treat unwell sailors. As well as ferries running their regular service to Ireland, cruise ships also arrive at the harbour during summer months. As many as 25,000 tourists a year come onto land here before heading onward to explore all Anglesey has to offer.

GETTING THERE: To get onto Salt Island, you need to be travelling to or arriving from Ireland on a ferry. Bookings can be made via www.irishferries.com or www.stenaline.co.uk.

WHERE TO STAY: Holyhead Lodge, Maeshyfryd, Holyhead, LL65 2AP, **T:** 01407 769214, **W:** www.holyheadlodge.co.uk. The Boathouse Hotel, Newry Beach, Holyhead, LL65 1YF, **T:** 01407 762094, **W:** www.theboathousehotel.com.

▲ Salt Island is one of Britain's main links with Ireland.
▶ Skerries Lighthouse, surrounded by seabirds.
(Inset) Take a boat ride with RibRide to explore the Skerries.

SKERRIES

| **LOCATION:** 53.4212°N 4.6081°W |
| **GRID REFERENCE:** SH267947 |
| **POPULATION:** 0 |
| **SIZE:** <1km² |

Shipwrecks and Rare Birds

Approaching the collection of islands known as the Skerries, you're grabbed by the dramatic position of the lighthouse and huge numbers of birds darting around in the sky above it. The island's first lighthouse was built in 1716 by William Trench, who tragically lost his son on the rocks. It was rebuilt in 1759 and extended to become the red and white beacon you see today.

As you might imagine, this rocky collection of islands has been the scene of many a shipwreck over the years. For that reason, it's one of the nation's top destinations for diving enthusiasts, who explore the remains of the wrecks in relatively sheltered waters beneath the waves.

Nationally important as a seabird colony, one of the most significant species you'll see here is the Arctic tern. The much rarer roseate tern has also been spotted here in small numbers. The RSPB has a couple of wardens living here for three months of the year, monitoring the tern population. They're the only people allowed to step foot on the islands, but it's well worth taking a boat trip to enjoy this remote bird outpost.

GETTING THERE: A boat trip from Holyhead takes you near the lighthouse on the Skerries and also goes past South Stack. Contact RibRide for more information (**T:** 0333 1234303, **W:** www.ribride.co.uk).

WHERE TO STAY: The Haven Guest House, Marine Square, Holyhead, LL65 1DG, **T:** 01407 760254, **W:** www. thehavenholyhead.com. The Boathouse Hotel, Newry Beach, Holyhead, LL65 1YF, **T:** 01407 762094, **W:** www.theboathousehotel.com.

SOUTH STACK

LOCATION: 53.3070°N 4.6987°W

GRID REFERENCE: SH202822

POPULATION: 0

SIZE: <1km²

RSPB Haven

When you pull up into South Stack car park, you can't see the island and instead are invited to walk along a pretty clifftop path surrounded by gorse and heather. The short stroll over the hill builds anticipation for what is to come, and you won't be disappointed when this beautiful lighthouse in a stunning setting comes into view. The RSPB information centre on the way at Ellin's Tower has huge windows facing out to the Irish Sea and binoculars on hand to spot puffins, peregrines, choughs and guillemots. And then the path continues to the lighthouse, down a gruelling route of no less than 400 steps and across a bridge. The lighthouse was built in 1809 and is maintained by Trinity House. You can visit it to learn about its history and climb the 28m (92ft)-tall tower – visit www.trinityhouse. co.uk for opening times.

Royal Charter Gale

The lighthouse on South Stack has been witness to several tragic events off this rocky shoreline, none worse than the ferocious storm that hit the region in October 1859. An incredible 133 ships were lost over two days of terrible weather and 800 people lost their lives. The most famous ship to be wrecked that night was the steam clipper *Royal Charter*, an emigration vessel on the last part of a return journey from Australia. The passenger list was lost in the accident, but it's thought 459 people were killed. Only 40 people lived to tell the tale, making it the most devastating shipwreck to happen in Welsh waters. The loss of the *Royal Charter* shocked the nation and led to the development of new forecasting techniques, with Royal Navy officer and scientist Robert Fitzroy arguing for the first time that a storm's path could be tracked and predicted.

GETTING THERE: Follow signs for South Stack out of Holyhead, heading west. There's an RSPB car park a short walk away from the island.

WHERE TO STAY: Tan y Cytiau, South Stack, Holyhead, LL65 1YH, **T:** 07494 339180, **W:** www.tyc.house. Blackthorn Farm, Holyhead, LL65 2LT, **T:** 01407 765262, **W:** www.blackthornfarm.co.uk.

AND ON THAT NOTE...

...the cover for Roxy Music's 1975 album *Siren* was shot beneath the bridge and featured model Jerry Hall posing on the rocks.

BARDSEY ISLAND

LOCATION: 52.7547°N 4.7938°W	
GRID REFERENCE: SH115211	
POPULATION: 11	
SIZE: 1.8km²	

GETTING THERE: Boat trips to the island set off from the tip of the Llŷn Peninsula with Bardsey Boat Trips (www.bardseyboattrips.com).

WHERE TO STAY: A small number of cottages are available to rent on the island, providing the opportunity for tranquil overnight stays. Contact the Bardsey Island Trust for more information (**T:** 07904 265604, **W:** www.bardsey.org).

WHERE TO EAT: Ty Pellaf Café serves snacks and drinks on the island. Call 07535 064943 for information.

Island of 20,000 Saints

The Llŷn Peninsula edges away from mainland Wales like a long finger, pointing towards Bardsey Island. Boat trips to this Welsh offshore retreat are magical, giving you around four hours to explore the long, gentle southern half of the island and climb to the 168m (551ft) peak in the north. To savour the solitude, cottages are available to rent through the Bardsey Island Trust. With just a handful of buildings on Bardsey, this is a true island getaway. A small café serves supplies for day-trippers, while the farm next door has the island's free-range eggs for sale, along with locally caught crabs and lobsters. Visitors here share the island with a couple of hundred seals and around 300 sheep. And there could well be more people buried beneath the surface than you'll find walking the local paths. Bardsey is known as the 'island of 20,000 saints' and legend states they all have a resting place on this small piece of land. It might be a bit ambitious to imagine 20,000 saints beneath an island of just under 2 square kilometres (0.8 square miles) but the importance of Bardsey

as a sacred place for druids and monks means there may be a significant number of saints buried here down the centuries. The island marks the end of the 215km (134-mile)-long North Wales Pilgrim's Way footpath, and some reckon it's the resting place of the mysterious Merlin of King Arthur fame.

The Big Apple

When a gnarled, solitary apple tree was discovered by a visitor in 1999, tests revealed it was possibly the sole survivor of an orchard maintained by monks a thousand years ago. Cuttings were taken of what was hailed as the rarest apple tree in the world. The apples borne by the tree are known as Bardsey Apples.

CALDEY ISLAND

Peace, Lavender, Chocolate...

A lovely island with a long monastic history, Caldey makes for a great day trip from Tenby. The short journey across the water brings you to the home of the Caldey Cistercian monks, where their vocation of prayer, study and work continues. The Cistercians took up residence on the island in 1929, but the monastic tradition goes back much further. Caldey was known as Pyro's Island in the 6th century, named after the first known abbot to be based here. By the 10th century the monks had left the island, which may be attributable to Viking raids taking place and focusing on such settlements. But monasticism returned in the 12th century when Benedictine monks established an annexe on the island and remained there until King Henry VIII's dissolution of the monasteries. Private owners held the island until the Cistercians arrived and today it provides a spiritual retreat for hundreds of people who stay here each year. Those who do come to Caldey to experience the solitude of a retreat are encouraged to attend services and help with tasks, like washing up after meals.

The biggest income for the island today is tourism and the monastery is renowned for its gorgeously aromatic lavender products. There'll be plenty of opportunity to grab some lavender soap or perfume before you leave the island. If you've a sweet tooth, you may find the island's chocolate factory more appealing. Here, you can learn how the handmade chocolate bars are produced and, of course, buy a supply for the remainder of your travels.

There are fantastic opportunities to walk the island's paths, a particular favourite being the track that winds to the east of the island and follows the clifftop until reaching the spectacular scene heralded by the lighthouse at the far side of the island. Built in 1828, this impressive structure is flanked by adjoining cottages and was originally designed to help local shipments of limestone and coal reach North Wales. Limestone was mined on nearby St Margaret's Island and has been an important building material here, as you'll see from the houses on Caldey.

LOCATION: 51.6381°N 4.6876°W

GRID REFERENCE: SS141966

POPULATION: 40

SIZE: 2.2km²

GETTING THERE: A fleet of boats make regular trips over to Caldey Island from Tenby harbour between Easter and October, though not on Sundays.

WHERE TO STAY: A retreat house and a guesthouse is available on the island for individuals and groups wanting to spend some days of quiet reflection. Visit www.caldeyislandwales.com/philomenas-retreat-house for more information.

WHERE TO EAT: Caldey Island Chocolate Factory, Caldey Island, SA70 7UH, **T:** 01834 844453, **W:** www.caldeyislandwales.com. There is also a coffee shop in the village.

ST CATHERINE'S ISLAND

Holding the Fort

From the busy seaside resort of Tenby, it's just a short walk at low tide to St Catherine's Island. A towering tidal limestone island, the cliffs of St Catherine's have been eroded into a series of twisting caves. But it's up on the top of this tiny Welsh island where the biggest interest lies, inside a Napoleonic fort that was built in 1867 to protect the nearby ports of Milford and Pembroke. Since its military days, the fort has had a range of uses, and that's what is so fascinating about this historical building. Bought by a wealthy family in 1907, it became a luxury home hosting lavish parties and was even a zoo for a period in the 1960s. Having stood empty since the 1970s, the fort now hosts occasional events such as film screenings and a Christmas grotto.

LOCATION: 51.6706°N 4.6920°W

GRID REFERENCE: SN139003

POPULATION: 0

SIZE: <1km²

GETTING THERE: Visitors can walk to and from St Catherine's Island for around three hours either side of low tide. Observe local signs before setting off, or check them at www.saintcatherinesisland.co.uk/the-fort.

WHERE TO STAY: Giltar Hotel, Esplanade, Tenby, SA70 7DU, **T:** 01834 842507, **W:** www.giltar-hotel.co.uk. Park Hotel, The Croft, Tenby, SA70 8AT, **T:** 01834 842480, **W:** www.parkhoteltenby.com.

ST MARGARET'S ISLAND

Former Home of Quarrymen

Just off Caldey Island sits one of the most important bird habitats in South Wales. St Margaret's is a tidal island named after the chapel that used to stand atop this rock in the middle of Carmarthen Bay. In the first half of the 19th century, the chapel was converted into a house so quarrymen could live close to their work. The industry saw stone cut and distributed around the region for many building projects. Today, the only residents are birds – most notably the largest population of cormorants in Wales. Guillemots, razorbills, kittiwakes and shags are also present on St Margaret's. To conserve the bird population, no public access is allowed. But fear not because you can get a great vantage point with a tour and a pair of binoculars. Boat trips from Tenby get you as close as it's possible to get, and you're likely to see plenty of seals on the visit too.

LOCATION: 51.6429°N 4.7171°W	
GRID REFERENCE: SS120971	
POPULATION: 0	
SIZE: <1km²	

GETTING THERE: Wildlife enthusiasts can take a boat around St Margaret's Island with one of the boat companies in Tenby harbour during the summer months. Look out for the signs displaying departure times.

WHERE TO STAY: Premier Inn, White Lion Street, Tenby, SA70 7ET, **T:** 0871 527 9514, **W:** www.premierinn.com. Heywood Spa Hotel, Heywood Lane, Tenby, SA70 8DA, **T:** 01834 842 087, **W:** www.heywoodspahotel.co.uk.

WORM'S HEAD

A Coastal Gem

Rhossili on the Gower Peninsula is fast developing a reputation as one of the best coastal locations in the country. The long, sandy beach has been voted not only one of the best beaches in the UK, but it's been placed in the top of Europe's coastal gems. Rhossili is also a hot spot for tourism because of the stunning walk along the clifftops and across the rocks to the small tidal island known as Worm's Head. Look at the long, snaky island from a distance and you'll see why it was christened this way; it looks like a sea serpent rising from the water.

Before walking along the clifftop from Rhossili and then again before heading down to the tidal causeway, you'll see prominent displays advising safe times to cross and when you have to be off the island. Take careful note: getting stranded on the island, waiting for the next low tide, is an inconvenience and an experience one young Dylan Thomas did not enjoy.

The walk across the neck of the island to the Outer Head is a joyful stroll and takes you over a magnificent natural rock arch known as Devil's Bridge. Worm's Head is managed by the National Trust and is home to many breeding seabirds. You're asked not to climb to the top of the Outer Head between 1 March and 31 August as it could disturb the nests. While you're standing on Worm's Head, take a look into Rhossili Bay, where you can see the wooden remains of the *Helvetia* near totally covered by the sand.

LOCATION:	51.5643°N 4.3208°W
GRID REFERENCE:	SS392876
POPULATION:	0
SIZE:	<1km²

GETTING THERE: At the southern end of Rhossili Bay, a path leads down from the headland to reach Worm's Head. The island is tidal and only accessible at certain parts of the day. Observe local signs before making the trip over.

WHERE TO STAY: On the mainland, close to the path leading to Worm's Head, you'll find the Worm's Head Hotel, Rhossili, SA3 1PP, **T:** 01792 390512, **W:** www.thewormshead.co.u and Broad Park Bed and Breakfast, Rhossili, SA3 1PL, **T:** 01792 390172, **W:** www.broadparkrhossili.com.

CROSSING TIMES
OUT 08:40
BACK 13:40
OVER-TIDE FISHERMEN
PLEASE TELL N.C.I

COMMEMORATIVE COIN

Think you've seen it before? Worm's Head featured on a silver £5 coin commemorating the 2012 Olympics. The six-coin set symbolised the body of Britain.

FAROE
ISLANDS

Since it's not on the usual tourist trail, most travellers know very little about the Faroe Islands. But they are missing out. Here in the North Sea, an overnight boat ride from both Denmark and Iceland, is a collection of beautiful islands with stunning scenery at almost every turn. Bring your walking boots and hope for good weather so you can explore the many mountain peaks and cascading waterfalls – plenty of which fall straight into the sea from tall cliffs, providing ideal photo material. Many of these attractive islands are linked by tunnels under the sea, making them easy to explore by car in a short break. For others, regular ferries provide essential links for the islanders and the chance for tourists to discover more amazing views. Make your visit during Ólavsøka and you'll be treated to music and singing performances delivered by locals in traditional dress. With many unforgettable maritime stories adding to the Faroese culture, these are truly extraordinary communities.

DON'T MISS

- The exquisite national costumes on display during the Ólavsøka summer festival
- Walking to stunning waterfalls and lakes on Vagar
- Learning about the legend of the Seal Woman beside the statue on Kalsoy
- Walking among the grass-roof buildings that were once part of the Parliament
- Driving up and down the spectacular fjords found throughout these North Sea islands

◄ *Tread the ancient trails of the mountains of Kalsoy.*

BORÐOY

LOCATION:	62.2333°N 6.5500°W
POPULATION:	5,261
SIZE:	96km²

Jolly Good!

The second largest settlement on the Faroe Islands is found here in Borðoy, but don't expect 'bright lights, big city'. Klaksvik is home to only 5,000 people, but manages to boast a decent spread of facilities for its size. The settlement is a good-looking one, the buildings hugging the flat land by the fjord and the water framing it along with the mountains.

If you're looking for a soft drink, you're likely to come across Jolly Cola, as familiar a sight in shops and bars throughout the Faroe Islands as the more popular brands are to us at home. The cool cola comes from a Klaksvik brewery, founded in 1888. This family business is also the origin of well-known Föroya Bjór, a collection of varied beers featuring the company's sheep logo on the front. The brewery's shop sells the drinks along with a range of souvenirs.

GETTING THERE: A tunnel beneath the sea connects Borðoy with Eysturoy.

WHERE TO STAY: Geilin B&B, Geilin, Klaksvik, Faroe Islands, **T:** +298 224104. Hotel Klaksvik, Vikavegur, Klaksvik, Faroe Islands, **T:** +298 457233, **W:** www.hotelklaksvik.fo.

WHERE TO EAT: Angus Steakhouse, Klaksvikvegur, Klaksvik, Faroe Islands, **T:** +298 457777, **W:** www.angus.fo. Carthage Steak, Stoksoyarvegur, Klaksvik, Faroe Islands, **T:** +298 422222, **W:** www.carthage-steak.com.

◀ *Some of the houses have a splash of colour.*

▼ *The cluster of buildings hug the edge of the water in the fjord.*

KALSOY

| LOCATION: 62.2833°N 6.7333°W |
| POPULATION: 76 |
| SIZE: 30.9km² |

GETTING THERE: Ferries arrive at Syðradalur from Klaksvik. For more information, visit www.ssl.fo.

WHERE TO STAY: Various options are available in Klaksvik, including Eysturland Lodge, Traðagøta, Klaksvik, Faroe Islands, **T:** +298 593140, **W:** www.eysturland.fo.

An Island Haunted by Twelfth Night

The short ferry journey from Klaksvik brings visitors to the south of this finger-like island. The main attractions lie in the north, however, so most cars emerging from the ferry head up the island's single road towards incredible scenery and a new, haunting statue. Jagged cliffs, awesome pinnacles and crashing waves caught the eye of the people behind the James Bond movie *No Time to Die* (2021), with scenes shot in the far north making the most of the incredible setting.

The first stop is Mikladalur, a village home to a 3m (10ft) tall statue of the 'Seal Woman'. The story behind this eerie vision tells of a local man who fell in love with one of the seal people who remove their skin and dance on the island every Twelfth Night. Rather than letting her return, he kept her skin locked away and started a family with her. Her life away from the sea continued until she discovered her skin one day, put it on and returned to join her marine family. The tale then takes a dark turn as the men of Mikladalur go out to hunt the seals and end up killing the woman's children. The Seal Woman – or Kópakonan – vows revenge on the land dwellers. She pledges to take men from the sea and mountaintops and won't rest until the number of the dead is enough to link hands around the island of Kalsoy. To this day, any deaths of local fishermen are attributed to her.

Pressing on further north through a narrow tunnel, nothing quite prepares you for the beauty of Trøllanes – called Troll's Peninsula because it is said the mythical creatures would flock here on Twelfth Night. The legend goes that locals were so traumatised by the visits, they abandoned the village and headed for Makladalur for the evening. The walk from the village along the mountaintops to the remote lighthouse at the island's northern tip is exquisite. More of an acquired taste is the local food speciality – Garnatálg is made by kneading intestinal fat from local sheep.

There is a grim tale behind the Seal Woman statue.

KOLTUR

LOCATION: 62.1000°N 7.6000°W

POPULATION: 0

SIZE: 2.8km²

GETTING THERE: Helicopter trips are available all year round from www.atlanticairways.com.

WHERE TO STAY: Accommodation is available in Tórshavn, including Havgrím Seaside Hotel 1948, Yviri við Strond, Tórshavn, **T:** +298 201400, **W:** www.hotelhavgrim.fo.

A Tiny Treasure

Abandoned in the 1980s by the farming community who had tried to make a living from the tiny island, Koltur is a place frozen in time and scheduled to become a national park. To explore the beautiful landscape of Koltur, you'll need to book a helicopter trip or join one of the summer boat trips leaving from Tórshavn. Visitors are easily outnumbered by the sheep that graze the island. But there are two mountains, rugged coastline and a fine beach of white sand to explore here. The stone buildings with grass roofs show how this island was once inhabited. In the 1890s, more than 40 people lived and worked here. Today, fundraising efforts aim to restore all the buildings and celebrate the history of Koltur.

MYKINES

LOCATION: 62.1000°N 7.6000°W

POPULATION: 10

SIZE: 10km²

GETTING THERE: Trips are available from Vagar, but you need to book in advance. Visit www.mykines.fo for details.

WHERE TO STAY: Marit's House B&B, Handan Á, Mykines, Faroe Islands, **T:** +298 286408.

WHERE TO EAT: Mykines Stova, Túalsvegur, Mykines, Faroe Islands, **T:** +298 787515.

Westward Ho!

Of the 18 main islands that make up the Faroes, Mykines is the most westerly and has some of the most dramatic coastal scenery. It's a tiny place and you'll need to book your trip in advance, but making the journey across the sea will leave a huge impact. It's best to see Mykines at the beginning of your Faroe Islands adventure because it's not unheard of for tourists to get stranded here for several days due to unpredictable sea conditions and the small boats used for these trips.

Hiking is the main activity on Mykines and you'll be asked to pay a fee that helps to preserve the local environment. There is a helicopter option for getting to the island, but as it takes just a few minutes it cuts out a lot of the fun – one of the best things about heading to Mykines is seeing the fascinating shape of the cliffs as you approach. The boat gives you longer to savour this and take it in. The one tiny settlement here – also called Mykines – is a delightful place, with buildings topped by grass roofs.

STREYMOY

LOCATION: 62.1333°N 7.0166°W

POPULATION: 24,682

SIZE: 373m²

GETTING THERE: Ferries arrive in Streymoy at Tórshavn from Hirthshals in Denmark. Visit www.smyrilline.com.

WHERE TO STAY: Hotel Føroyar, Oyggjarvegur, Tórshavn, Faroe Islands, **T:** +298 317500, **W:** www.hotelforoyar.fo. Tórshavn Camping, Yviri við Strond, Tórshavn, Faroe Islands, **T:** +298 302425.

WHERE TO EAT: Áarstova, Gongin, Tórshavn 100, Faroe Islands, **T:** +298 333000, **W:** www.heimaihavn.fo. Emilia Fast Food, Eystara Bryggja, Tórshavn, Faroe Islands, **T:** 298 312624.

Tórshavn – Big in Stature

Fewer than 20,000 people live in the city of Tórshavn, making it one of the least populated capitals in the world. Tórshavn – meaning Thor's Harbour – crams many buildings into a small space, making the capital city a busy and vibrant place surrounded by rolling sea and majestic mountains. Interesting buildings are found at every turn, but make sure you pay a visit to the city's cathedral, a beautiful white building established in 1788. On the top of the hill are the floodlights of the football stadium, where the choice 11 players from these tiny islands pitch up against the bigger teams from Europe in qualifying games for the Euros and the World Cup. Although the team loses the majority of its games, the occasional victory – noticeably against Austria in 1990 – invokes much national pride. One of the most atmospheric and visually stunning parts of the capital city is its oldest, Tinganes. The Faroese government was once based here and the Parliament itself dates back to 825, making it one of the oldest in the world. The distinctive grass-roofed buildings built here in the 17th and 18th centuries make this one of the most beautiful areas of Tórshavn.

The famously awe-inspiring cliffs.

SUÐUROY

Grass-roofed houses create a patchwork on a Tórshavn hill.

LOCATION: 61.5333°N 6.8500°W

POPULATION: 4,588

SIZE: 163.7km²

GETTING THERE: Ferries take 2 hours to reach Suðuroy from Tórshavn, with two or three services leaving each day. Visit www.ssl.fo.

WHERE TO STAY: Brim B&B, Vágsvegur, Suðuroy, Faroe Islands, **T:** +298 787876.

WHERE TO EAT: Matstovan í Porkeri, Hòlavegur, Porkeri, Faroe Islands, **T:** +298 223039.

In the harbour, a reminder of the many generations who have served in the fishing industry.

Vestmanna Cliffs

Although the main facilities on Streymoy are in Tórshavn, the biggest tourist attraction is found in the north of the island, at Vestmanna. In recent years the number of visitors travelling to the island has increased and a relatively new campsite now accommodates them. The stunning cliffs of Vestmannabjørgini are the premier pull. A boat trip gives you up close access to the impossibly tall cliffs and the thousands of birds living on them.

Southbound

This island's name translates literally as 'south island' so it's no surprise to find Suðuroy in the lower latitudes of the Faroe Islands. Within easy reach of the capital, Tórshavn, it's a popular destination for tourists who come here for the scenery and remoteness. The people of the Faroe Islands love a good festival, with the capital hosting the biggest –Ólavsøka – at the end of July. It sees bands playing in the street, islanders donning traditional dress, communal singing and fireworks. A smaller version, Jóansøka, takes place on Suðuroy over the last weekend in June and a rowing competition takes place on the Saturday. It's a beautiful island with some amazing walks, but it also hits the headlines for the controversial whale hunts that take place here. Whaling happens in several bays throughout the Faroe Islands, wherever the natural conditions allow. Several places in Suðuroy pull in those involved in the whale hunts – and they attract protestors who object to the practice as well. The scenes are gruesome and unpleasant; the sea turns red with blood and slaughtered whales are lined up on the beach. Supporters of the divisive activity point to the centuries of tradition, how every part of the animal is used and the large numbers of whales in the surrounding seas. It's a conflict that will not easily be resolved.

VÁGAR

Tunnel Vision

The third largest of the Faroe Islands, Vágar is also the most distinctive when seen on a map. This western outpost of the remote Danish island group has the appearance of a dog. On the western coast of Vágar, the bay of Sørvágsfjørður forms the mouth of the dog, while the eye is Lake Fjallavatn. Vágatunnilin, a 5km (3.1-mile) tunnel snaking through the bedrock beneath the sea, links the island to Tórshavn, the capital. It's a formidable connection for an island with such a relatively small population, but you can understand why this significant investment was made when you discover the only Faroese airport is based here. With a runway built up like a grandiose railway embankment, this distinctive landing zone provides a key link with other islands and European nations.

Chasing Waterfalls

There are two big waterfall sights on Vágar that are not to be missed. Incredibly picturesque Múlafossur tumbles over the cliff edge into the sea at Gásadalur, about as far north as you can get on the island. This fabulous waterfall was largely hidden away from the tourist gaze until 2004 when the narrow tunnel was constructed through the hillside and visitors could make their way to this much-photographed spot. It's Lake Sørvágsvatn, though, that steals all the headlines. The lakeside walk to the coast reveals unbelievable views of a body of water that appears to defy logic and hover over the ocean. A waterfall cascades over the cliffs to the sea and there are photo opportunities at every turn. The 4km (2.5-mile) walk from the car park is a controversial one – the landowner charges a hefty fee to gain access to this Faroese gem.

LOCATION: 62.0833°N 7.2666°W	
POPULATION: 3,367	
SIZE: 176km²	

GETTING THERE: Vágar is linked to Streymoy via the Vágatunnilin that dives beneath the stretch of sea dividing the two islands. Planes also arrive at the island's airport – the only one on the Faroe Islands – from various places in Europe. See www.fae.fo.

WHERE TO STAY: Hotel Vagar, Djúpheiðar, Sørvágur, Faroe Islands, **T:** +298 309090, **W:** www.hotelvagar. fo. Vestmanna Guesthouse, 30 Toftavegur, Vestmanna, Faroe Islands, **T:** +298 271142.

WHERE TO EAT: Café Zorva, Ovarivegur, Sørvágur, Faroe Islands, **T:** +298 296969, **W:** www.facebook. com/cafezorva.

▲ Lake Sørvágsvatn seems to float above the sea.
▶ Tumbling Múlafossur is a jaw-dropping find.

NORTHERN IRELAND

A good place to start is the beautiful National Trust island Carrick-a-Rede, separated from the mainland by a rope bridge that would be at home in an Indiana Jones film. Some of the most stunning islands lie off the Atlantic coast, home to incredible clifftop views, a rousing music scene and flourishing wildlife. Save time to travel to Rathlin Island also, to watch the booming bird population and learn about the place where Robert the Bruce was said to be visited by an influential spider.

CARRICK-A-REDE

Bridge Over Troubled Water

A visit to this island is usually combined with a visit to nearby Giant's Causeway on the Northern Ireland coastal tourist trail. And unlike most of the islands in this book, a trip to Carrick-a-Rede is all about how you get there rather than what you do once you arrive. The National Trust manages the site and its fabulous rope bridge, which you'll need to brave to get to the island. Some 30m (90ft) above the waves that crash against the rocks at high tide, the 20m (66ft) long walk across the rickety bridge makes you feel as though you're starring in an Indiana Jones movie. As you'll understand when you're swaying from side to side, the number of people on the bridge is restricted to eight at a time and a huge increase in visitors during the last few years has put pressure on the crossing system. You'll need a timed ticket to enter, which you can book online at the National Trust website.

Salmon Centre

In Gaelic, Carrick-a-Rede translates as the 'rock in the road' and provided a natural obstacle to migrating salmon looking to return to the river where they were born. It's long been a keen place for salmon fishermen to earn their living, with records showing the industry's roots go back to 1620. In those early days, fishing was supported by boats based on the mainland. But in the mid-18th century, passage to the island was transformed when the first bridge was built here. The fishing industry thrived as a result, and remained strong for much of the 20th century too. In the 1960s it was common for hundreds of fish to be caught every day here. Sadly, pollution started to take its toll and the number of salmon returning here declined dramatically. The last fisherman stopped working in these waters during 2002.

LOCATION: 55.2397°N 6.3324°W

IRISH GRID REFERENCE: NR246025

POPULATION: 0

SIZE: <1km²

GETTING THERE: Access to the island is via a National Trust rope bridge, found in Ballintoy, County Antrim, BT54 6LS, **W:** www.nationaltrust.org.uk.

WHERE TO STAY: The Fullerton Arms, Main Street, Ballintoy, Ballycastle, Northern Ireland, BT54 6LX, **T:** 028 2076 9613, **W:** www.fullerton-arms.com. Glenmore House, Whitepark Road, Ballycastle, Northern Ireland, BT54 6LR, **T:** 028 2076 3584, **W:** www.glenmore.biz.

DON'T MISS

- Venturing across the rope bridge to the former fishing hotspot Carrick-a-Rede
- The thriving bird population of Rathlin Island, home of a famous spider legend

▲ *Carrick-a-Rede Rope Bridge.*

RATHLIN ISLAND

LOCATION: 55.2928°N 6.1953°W

IRISH GRID REFERENCE: NR337078

POPULATION: 154

SIZE: 13.7km²

Bays, Bleach and Birds

Within easy reach for a day trip, this boomerang-shaped volcanic island, which contains the most northern point of Northern Ireland, sits 9.7km (6 miles) from the mainland across the Sea of Moyle. The island's history is explored in a series of displays at the museum and visitor centre near the harbour at Church Bay. And it's a rich history, featuring kings, Stone Age tool makers and bleach-making for nearby linen factories. Rathlin's bird population can reach tens of thousands and is a big pull for visitors; over two dozen species of seabird are regular visitors here and the RSPB has established a reserve. When the main industries involved selling fish and seaweed, over 1,000 people were crammed onto this small island. Today the population is a fraction of that, but is slowly growing. Rathlin landscapes are captured in a mesmerising, often dark manner by local artist Yvonne Braithwaite. Visiting her Ballycastle Breakwater Studio is an inspirational way to spend time on the island.

Spider-Man

Several myths and legends are associated with Rathlin Island, the best known being Robert the Bruce's encounter with a spider. The story goes that the Scottish king took refuge on this island after being driven out of Scotland by England's Edward I. One day he spent a while watching a spider try, try and try again to bridge a gap with its web. Once it eventually succeeded, Robert the Bruce was said to be inspired enough to return to Scotland and defeat the English at Bannockburn.

GETTING THERE: Trips can be arranged with the Rathlin Island Ferry Company, **T:** 028 2076 9299, **W:** www.rathlinballycastleferry.com.

WHERE TO STAY: Arkell House B&B, Church Bay, Rathlin Island, BT54 6SA, **T:** 07565 871319, **E:** rathlincottages@gmail.com. The Manor House, Ballycastle, Rathlin Island, BT54 6RT, **T:** 028 2076 0046, **W:** www.manorhouserathlin.com.

WHERE TO EAT: The Water Shed Café, Ballycastle, Rathlin Island, BT54 6RT, **T:** 07517 354990, **W:** www.rathlincommunity.org/eating#cafe. McCuaig's Bar, Ballycastle, Rathlin Island, BT54 6RT, **T:** 028 2076 0011.

IRELAND

Steeped in history and brimming with tales of happiness and torment, the islands off the coast of Ireland have plenty to offer for adventure seekers. On many Irish islands, you'll be able to enjoy the craic in a local bar – many with live music most nights, and weekends being especially popular. Arranmore's Swell Festival takes the musical experience to another level with a programme of traditional tunes. Beautiful coastal scenes come with the territory and everybody will have their own favourites, although the steep limestone cliffs of the Aran Islands are hard to beat. These are the impressive limestone pavements and vertical drops that charmed viewers of *Father Ted* on Craggy Island. Boat trips depart from many islands to go wildlife watching; expect to see several species of seabird on Ireland's west coast, including the adorable puffin. Tourism has increased on many islands over the last decade, but nowhere more so than on Skellig Michael. Since the World Heritage Site was featured as Ahch-to in the *Star Wars* films, visitor numbers have had to be limited to ensure budding Luke Skywalkers do not turn the island over to the Dark Side.

DON'T MISS

- Partaking of a whiskey or two on Inisheer, the island best known for where *Father Ted* was filmed
- Discovering your inner Jedi on Skellig Michael, which doubled up as Luke Skywalker's hideaway in the *Star Wars* movies
- Dancing along to the traditional Irish music festival on Arranmore
- Listening to stories aplenty at the tale-telling festival on Cape Clear Island
- Seeing the fossilised footprints on Valentia

◄ *The coast of Ireland is famous for legendary scenery.*

INISHEER

Craggy Island

Drink! The opening scenes of classic comedy *Father Ted* were shot above Inisheer, giving this small island a curious alter ego as 'Craggy Island'. Don't expect to find the crazy antics of Craggy Island taking place on Inisheer, though – it's yet to see reports of dangerous carnivals or bunny infestations! In fact, many of the outdoor scenes for the hit TV series were filmed on the mainland of Ireland, but those beautiful aerial shots of the island and its limestone landscape are unmistakeably Inisheer.

An enchanting yet swift journey from the west coast of Ireland, Inisheer may only be 8km (5 miles) away but it is like stepping back in time to an Ireland of the past. Don't expect to be spoilt for choice when it comes to facilities, but you can expect a delightful array of views and landscapes on the network of paths that criss-cross the island. Change often reaches Inisheer fairly late in the day, explaining why a reliable electricity supply wasn't available for the locals until 1997. Given the marketing potential to cash in on the island's *Father Ted* links, you may be surprised how low-key the tourist industry is here. True, there may be hundreds of people descending on Inisheer for day trips when the summer sun is shining, but this is a tranquil place during the off-season and when the boats head back to the mainland.

An Iconic Wreck

One of the most familiar-looking shipwrecks in the world is found on the shores of Inisheer, famously seen by millions in the opening credits of *Father Ted*. The rusty old wreck of the MV *Plassy*, run aground on the rocks, is a must-see when visiting the smallest of the Aran Islands. The incident took place in 1960, on a night of stormy seas and strong winds. Thankfully, all crew survived and were hoisted onto the island by local rescuers one at a time.

LOCATION: 53.0655°N 9.5181°W

IRISH GRID REFERENCE: L982027

POPULATION: 260

SIZE: 8km²

GETTING THERE: Ferries leave Doolin on the Irish mainland and take around half an hour to reach Inisheer. For more information, get in touch with Doolin2Aran Ferries (**T:** +353 65 7075949, **W:** www.doolin2aranferries. com). Aran Island Ferries runs a service from Rossaveal (**T:** +353 91 568903, **W:** www.aranislandferries.com).

WHERE TO STAY: An Creagán B&B, Baile Thiar, Inisheer, Co. Galway, Ireland, **T:** +353 86 076 7346. Inisheer Hotel, Inisheer, Co. Galway, Ireland, **T:** +353 99 75020, **W:** www.hotelinisoirr.com.

WHERE TO EAT: Tigh Ned, Inisheer, Co. Galway, Ireland, **T:** +353 99 75004, **W:** tighned.com. Seaweed Café, Inisheer, Co. Galway, Ireland, **T:** +353 87 974 5848.

▼ *The shipwreck has become an iconic sight on the island.*

The island will enthral you with its history.
Inset: Celtic crosses on Inisheer.

INISHMORE

Inishmoreish

Of the three Aran Islands, Inishmore is the largest and has the widest range of physical and human attractions and a sublime ability to draw people back after their first visit. The most striking feature is the island's bedrock. The island is an outlying section of the Burren – a vast area on the Irish mainland known for its rocky landscape. Here on Inishmore, the terrain features some highly distinctive limestone pavements. Best seen from the air, they are also fascinating places to discover on the ground, a lunar landscape even more enchanting for their windswept locations and lack of other tourists. But don't let the charmingly desolate horizon lull you into a false sense of security. These are dangerous places, with deep grikes between the rocks eroded away by water over thousands of years.

The human history of Inishmore meets natural wonder at the stone fort of Dun Aengus. This semi-circular defensive structure sits atop a stunning cliff, 100m (328ft) above the crashing sea. Many argue that this is one of the best prehistoric monuments on the continent and it's hard to disagree when you're up close to one of the incredible walls, some 6m (19.7ft) tall and 5m (16.4ft) thick. The facilities on the island are concentrated around the main village – Kilronan – and you'll likely end up here if you're intending to stay over or find something to eat. You'll arrive here when the boat comes in; to make the most of your time on the island, it might be an idea to rent a bike from the village hire shop (https://aranislandsbikehire.com).

LOCATION: 53.1194°N 9.6658°W

IRISH GRID REFERENCE: L885089

POPULATION: 845

SIZE: 31km²

GETTING THERE: Passenger ferries take around 90 minutes to reach Inishmore from Doolin on the mainland and 40 minutes from Rossaveal. For more information, get in touch with Doolin2Aran Ferries (**T:** +353 65 7075949, **W:** www.doolin2aranferries.com) or Island Ferries (**T:** +353 91 568903, **W:** www.aranislandferries.com).

WHERE TO STAY: Aran Islands Hotel, Kilronan, Inishmore, Co. Galway, Ireland, H91 DH27, **T:** +353 99 61104, **W:** www.aranislandshotel.com. Aran Islands Camping and Glamping, Frenchman's Beach, Kilronan, Inishmore, Co. Galway, Ireland, H91 F65P, **T:** +353 86 189 5823, **W:** www.irelandglamping.ie

WHERE TO EAT: Bayview Restaurant, Krusty Krab Road, Killeany, Kilronan, Inishmore, Co. Galway, Ireland, **T:** +353 86 792 9925. Teach Nan Phaidi, Inishmore, Co. Galway, Ireland, **T:** +353 99 20975.

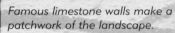

Famous limestone walls make a patchwork of the landscape.
Inset: Horsing around on Inishmore.

'Located off the west coast of Ireland, the Aran Islands are rich in cultural history and natural beauty, and are the jewel in the crown of Galway Bay. Inis Mór in particular offers steep, jaw-dropping cliffs and crashing waves to one side of the island with beautiful calm, sandy beaches and refuge to the other side. Uniquely patterned stone walls cover the island, which are built to withstand the wildest of weather, these a keen favourite with visiting photographers. Coming to the islands is like stepping back in time to old Ireland, where time slows down and being among the local people, enjoying a pint of Guinness and listening to traditional music becomes the order of the day. There is no rush hour on the Aran Islands, only peace and tranquillity.'

Frankie Moran, Manager at Aran Islands Camping & Glamping

ACHILL ISLAND

Wild Atlantic Way

A stunning driving route that winds some 2,500km (1,550 miles) down the west coast of Ireland, the Wild Atlantic Way makes an important diversion onto Achill Island. The popular tourist trail that covers this fabulous Atlantic scenery is generally divided up into five sections to help visitors plan their journey, but those tackling the section arriving at Achill are in for a real treat. Keem Bay is one of the Wild Atlantic Way's Discovery Points, and it's been picked for good reason. The sheltered bay has a wonderful stretch of sand and prominent headlands at either side. The blues and greens of the Atlantic tempt families back to this spot year after year. St Patrick is said to have journeyed here and blessed the bay after seeing the beauty of the place, announcing that nobody would ever drown in its waters. Despite this holy prediction, you are still urged to follow the advice of the lifeguards monitoring the beach during the summer.

LOCATION: 53.9303°N 9.9269°E

IRISH GRID REFERENCE: L734995

POPULATION: 2,569

SIZE: 148km²

GETTING THERE: A bridge over the Achill Sound provides a good link from mainland Ireland via the R319.

WHERE TO STAY: Achill Island Hotel, Illanbelfarsad, Achill Sound, Co. Mayo, Ireland, F28 EA31, **T:** +353 98 45138, **W:** www.achillislandhotel.com. Achill Cliff House Hotel, Keel, Achill Island, Co. Mayo, Ireland, **T:** +353 98 43400, **W:** www.achillcliff.com.

WHERE TO EAT: Hot Spot Takeaway, Main Street, Illanbelfarsad, Achill Island, Co. Mayo, Ireland, **T:** +353 98 20675. Ted's Bar, Cashel, Achill Island, Co. Mayo, Ireland, **T:** +353 98 47234, **W:** www.teds achill.ie.

From tourist diving to fishing, the sea provides a livelihood for many.

Keem is also a hotspot for adventurers wanting to see the marine life in these crystal clear waters. The Snorkel Trail sets out from the southern end of the bay. It's suitable for experts and beginners because the tidal flows are generally calm. If you're lucky, you may spot a porpoise or a basking shark. Keem Bay used to be home to many basking sharks until they were hunted for their oil after the Second World War – but the occasional individual makes a return here. Other species to look out for are the spider crabs parading a few metres down from the beach in the summer.

The Deserted Village

The impact of the 1845 Famine on Achill Island can be seen at the Deserted Village. The stone homes here were once inhabited, but when the food shortages struck the villagers started to leave for the Dooagh, another village by the sea, where they could fish. The village was abandoned in those desperate times and nobody has lived here permanently since.

ARRANMORE

LOCATION: 54.9895°N 8.5308°W

IRISH GRID REFERENCE: B665155

POPULATION: 469

SIZE: 22km²

Gee, That's Swell

There are times of the year when Arranmore is an ideal place to get away from it all, enjoy solitary beach walks and marvel at the remote coastal landscape. And there is also a time when you can head to Arranmore to indulge in good food, family fun, the famous craic, drink perhaps far too much alcohol and listen to some great music. That far more raucous time for revelry is called the Swell Festival, during which folk come together to hear new bands, drink cans of Guinness and break up the action with lengthy strolls on the sand. Swell Festival has grown over the years and both day and weekend tickets are popular. Musicians from all over the world perform at Swell's multiple venues, but there's not the emphasis on headline acts and massive stages like there is elsewhere. Instead it's about coming together and enjoying the stirring sound of traditional Irish tunes. Although the island is quieter when the festival has ended, music remains a key feature at the island's pubs all year round. Early's Bar is a popular place to listen to Irish music, and during summer acts perform here every day – pull up a chair, order food and a drink and prepare for a foot-tapping session like no other! Check local notices to find out who is playing where.

GETTING THERE: The ferry for Arranmore leaves from Burtonport and takes 15 minutes. Contact Arranmore Ferry for more information (**T:** +353 7495 42233, W:www.arranmoreferry.com).

WHERE TO STAY: Arranmore Hostel, Leabgarrow, Arranmore Island, Co. Donegal, Ireland, **T:** +353 87 805 4246, **W:** www.arranmorehostel.ie. Muldowney's B&B, Baile Ard, Arranmore, Co. Donegal, Ireland, **T:** +353 87 908 1277, **W:** www.muldowneysbb.com.

WHERE TO EAT: Early's Bar, Leabgarrow, Arranmore, Co. Donegal, Ireland, **T:** +353 87 805 4246, **W:** www.earlysbar.com.

BERE ISLAND

LOCATION: 51.2182°N 10.8637°W

IRISH GRID REFERENCE: V704431

POPULATION: 167

SIZE: 17.7km²

GETTING THERE: Two ferry services link Bere Island to mainland Ireland. Murphy's Ferry (**T:** 087 2386095, **W:** www.murphysferry.com) arrives at Rerrin Village on the east end of the island and on the western side Bere Island ferries (**T:** 086 2423140, **W:** www.bereislandferries.com) connects islanders to Castletown.

WHERE TO STAY: The Bere Island Hotel, Ballynakilla, Bere Island, Co. Cork, Ireland, P75 RX59, **T:** +353 27 75018. Cottage Heights B&B, Derrymihan, Castletownbere, Co. Cork, Ireland, **T:** +353 27 71743, **W:** www.cottage-heights.com.

WHERE TO EAT: The Lookout, Derrycreeven, Bere Island, Co. Cork, Ireland, **T:** +353 27 75999.

▲ *Isolated houses on Bere Island are a world away from the mainland.*

Seaweed Soak

Many of us don't think twice when we find seaweed on the beach, but for some of our coastal communities the slimy green marine plant is the lifeblood of the economy. On Bere Island, seaweed has been important for hundreds of years and is now a key ingredient of popular skincare products sold here. Seaweed comes in all shapes and sizes, and in a range of fabulous colours. As well as being an ingredient in cooking and fertiliser, the Irish have been using seaweed in bathing for over 300 years. I'd read about the beneficial properties of a seaweed bath a few years ago and, now having indulged in one, I can testify to that. The smell and sand may take a while to get rid of in the hours after, but it's well worth experiencing!

Soaking in a bath of seaweed was considered to be 'the fisherman's cure' due to the healthy attributes of the salty tub, the ingredients of which were pulled from the clean Atlantic waters off the Irish west coast. Ocean Bloom on Bere Island first started harnessing the therapeutic powers of seaweed from the island's shores to help a family member suffering with eczema. Today their organic skincare products help people around the world to manage a range of skin conditions.

FASTNET ROCK

Ireland's Teardrop

For 18th-century emigrants leaving the Emerald Isle to start a new life in North America, Fastnet Rock was the last sight of their Irish homeland. The island's nickname, 'the Teardrop', reflects the sadness of leaving, although there were no doubt mixed emotions as they looked forward to the prospect of life on a new continent. Today, Fastnet Rock is known for its lighthouse, a stunning feat of engineering admired around the world. The lighthouse is constructed from tough Cornish granite block, which is interlocked to make the structure stronger, a necessary feature when you consider it sits atop a remote rock in the middle of the wild Atlantic Ocean. The visitor centre at Mizen Head has more information on this remarkable achievement. The trip to get up close to Fastnet lasts a full day and there are plenty of opportunities to take photos from all available angles.

The first lighthouse tower was built in 1854 but proved too weak to stand the test of the rough waves and did not provide a strong enough light. Work on the replacement started in 1897 and the current lighthouse was first used in 1904. It stands 54m (177ft) tall and its light can be seen some 43km (27 miles) away. Although now fully automated, lighthouse keepers used to live all the way out here. The last three left the island in the 1980s. It's well worth taking a trip to their former home – the environment is so inhospitable when hit by a storm, but when the sun shines on this structure it's truly gorgeous.

LOCATION: 51.3891°N 9.6026°W

IRISH GRID REFERENCE: V885163

POPULATION: 0

SIZE: >1km²

GETTING THERE: Boat trips to the rock are available with Fastnet Tours (**T:** +353 28 39159, **W:** www.fastnet tour.com).

WHERE TO STAY: The Stone House B&B, Lifeboat Road, Baltimore, Co. Cork, Ireland, P81 VP77, **T:** +353 28 20511, **W:** www.thestonehousebnb.ie. Casey's of Baltimore, Ballylinchy, Co. Cork, Ireland, P81 YW66, **T:** +353 28 20197, **W:** www.caseysofbaltimore.com.

INISHBIGGLE

Hills rise steeply from sea level, creating a dramatic landscape.

A Traditional Way of Life

With a little imagination Inishbiggle looks like a horse on a map, trotting away to the mainland from Achill Island. Little Inishbiggle doesn't benefit from causeway access, which is perhaps surprising given how close it is to both nearby landmasses. But it's a very short ferry ride to Inishbiggle whichever way you approach. Once you're on the island you'll immediately feel the impact of being relatively cut off. This is a place to relax, to forget about pressures of life on the mainland and see how life on Inishbiggle differs from it. The community living here has farming and fishing at its heart. A walk along the Inishbiggle Loop is the best way to get a feel for traditional life on the island. It sets off from the pier at Bullsmouth and is a popular route for the small number of visitors making their way here. Plans have previously been drawn up for a cable ferry crossing to make access easier, but this has yet to materialise.

LOCATION:	54.0034°N 9.8858°W
IRISH GRID REFERENCE:	F764076
POPULATION:	18
SIZE:	2.6km²

GETTING THERE: Ferries to Inishbiggle make the short crossing from the mainland at Doran's Point (+353 87 1269618) and from Bullsmouth on Achill Island (+353 86 0612482).

WHERE TO STAY: Inishbiggle is less than 100m (328ft) from Achill Island and there are opportunities to stay at Achill Lodge, Bunnacurry, Achill Island, Co. Mayo, Ireland. **T:** +353 98 47162, **W:** www.achilllodge.ie. Murrayville B&B, Springvale, Achill Sound, Co. Mayo, Ireland, **T:** +353 98 45123, **W:** www.murrayvilleachill.com.

INISHBOFIN

LOCATION: 53.6251°N 10.188950°W

IRISH GRID REFERENCE: L552661

POPULATION: 160

SIZE: 12km²

Pirates, Prisons and Playtime

This small island has a tumultuous history that belies its peaceful surroundings. Ireland's famous Pirate Queen, Grace O'Malley (see Clare Island, page 266), was based here in the 16th century. The pirate clan had a castle at one side of the harbour, while their ally Don Bosco held ground across the water. Working together, they could stop unwanted visitors to the island and board ships they thought had a valuable cargo so they could begin looting. At one point they even had a chain spanning the entrance to Inishbofin's harbour.

After the English Civil War, Cromwell's forces built the star-shaped fort that still stands next to the harbour today. The well-preserved building became a jail for Catholic clergy from all over Ireland after they were declared guilty of high treason in 1655. Following the restoration of Charles II in 1660, he used the fort as part of a military strategy to defend the islands.

Today Inishbofin is thankfully a much more peaceful place. Families come here in summer to take advantage of its clear seas and gorgeous beaches, some of which received the Green Coast Award to signify their high status. They are perfect places to take a walk or spend the afternoon picnicking and playing. You might even time your visit to join one of the organised yoga sessions that take place here. Be sure to visit the Inishbofin Heritage Museum, too, with its photographs of local people through the decades and exhibits of traditional fishing and farming tools.

GETTING THERE: The ferry for Inishbofin leaves three times a day in peak season, dropping to two times a day during the rest of the year. It leaves from Cleggan Pier. For more information contact Inishbofin Ferry (**T:** +353 86 171 8829, **W:** www.inish bofinferry.ie).

WHERE TO STAY: Dolphin Hotel, Knock, Inishbofin Island, Co. Galway, Ireland, **T:** +353 95 45991, **W:** www.dolphinhotel. ie. Inishbofin House Hotel, Inishbofin Island, Co. Galway, Ireland, **T:** +353 95 45809, **W:** www.inishbofinhouse.com.

WHERE TO EAT: The Galley Restaurant, Eastend, Inishbofin Island, Co. Galway, Ireland, **T:** +353 95 45894, **W:** www. inishbofin.com/the-galley-bb. The Beach, Middlequarter, Inishbofin Island, Co. Galway, Ireland, **T:** +353 95 45829, **W:** www.thebeach.ie.

Historic ruins harbour tales of piracy from centuries ago.

INISHMURRAY

The Island of Illicit Distilling

The most impressive feature of a trip to Inishmurray is the 6th-century Cashel – the remains of an early Christian monastic community. Archaeological explorations have also discovered burial sites and carved stones, which suggests people have lived on Inishmurray since prehistoric days. The population has climbed and dipped over the centuries, peaking in the 1880s at just over 100. The lure of a more affluent life away in Sligo, Dublin and England drew many islanders away from a life of farming the island.

One of the more colourful aspects of Inishmurray's long history is the role it played in the illicit distilling of Irish whiskey – and it's also a trade that has helped shape the population and prosperity of the island. Inishmurray's isolation made it the ideal location for such activity and those producing illicit whiskey soon gained a favourable reputation among connoisseurs of the golden tipple. Inishmurray whiskey was considered extremely high quality, and its popularity interested excise officers very much. Officials set about trying to deal with the illegal trade in the 1830s but many visits to Inishmurray were thwarted by poor weather. On the occasions when the police did make it ashore, arrests were made and several men were sent to jail. But the distilling continued until the 1850s, when the authorities came up with a master plan to open a police station on the island. The whiskey trade stopped abruptly but this also saw local incomes plummet and the population decline. When the police officers packed up and left in 1890, it wasn't long before whiskey production resumed and the island started to thrive once more. It was all brought to an end once more by the Second World War and the rationing of sugar, leading to another fall in the number of islanders living here.

LOCATION: 54.4331°N 8.6618°W

IRISH GRID REFERENCE: G571540

POPULATION: 0

SIZE: >1km²

GETTING THERE: Trips to the island can be booked with Inishmurray Island Tours, **T:** +353 87 254 0190, **W:** www.inishmurrayislandtrips.com.

WHERE TO STAY: Moran's Bar and B&B, Newtown, Co. Sligo, Ireland, **T:** +353 87 927 9070, **W:** www.moransofgrange.ie. Ocean Heights B&B, Cloonagh, Ballinfull, Co. Sligo, Ireland, F91 H9T2, **T:** +353 71 912 4907, **W:** www.oceanheightsbnb.com.

Inishmurray is home to archaeological wonders as well as illicit distilling.

INISHTURK

LOCATION: 53.7059°N 10.0920°W

IRISH GRID REFERENCE: L619749

POPULATION: 51

SIZE: 6km²

GETTING THERE: The Clare Island Ferry Company operates daily sailings to Inishturk from Roonagh Point, with the journey taking around 40 minutes (**T:** +353 86 851 5003, **W:** www.clareislandferry.com).

WHERE TO STAY: Ocean View House, Garranty, Quay Road, The Harbour, Inishturk, Co. Mayo, Ireland, **T:** +353 87 631 5805, **W:** www.oceanviewhouse.info. Tranaun House, Beealaum, Inishturk, Co. Mayo, Ireland, **T:** +353 87 761 6582, **W:** www.tranaunhouse.com.

WHERE TO EAT: Caher View Restaurant, Inishturk, **T:** +353 87 1665415.

Scuba Diving and Signal Towers

Surrounded by some of the cleanest, clearest waters in Europe, a visit to Inishturk is all about getting to the coast for some fun. This is one of the most impressive go-to destinations for scuba divers in the British Isles and many dives are organised during the summer to investigate some of the wrecks that are found off these shores. If you're happier staying on land or simply enjoying a paddle in the sea, there are good beaches here that pull families back year after year. Curraun and Tranaun both have lovely sand and impressive views. It's not all about sitting on a beach or taking to the water, though. Rocky clifftop walks fill your lungs with fresh air and afford stunning views out to the nearby islands. A literal high point of a trip to Inishturk is the signal tower, one of 82 built along the Irish coast to ward off Napoleonic ships in the early 19th century. The tower on Inishturk was number 57 and like the others it used a polished steel plate to reflect the sun and communicate in Morse Code.

Rock Lobster

Aside from tourism, fishing remains important to the island's economy. A particular delicacy in these parts is the Inishturk lobster, which, along with the big crabs found off shore, dominates the local catch. It's hard to resist a visit to Caher View Restaurant, where the fresh seafood is served up with cracking views. Those wanting to catch their own fish can check out the options for sea angling, which is another popular pastime for those visiting.

SKELLIG MICHAEL

LOCATION: 51.7719°N 10.5385°W	
IRISH GRID REFERENCE: V247606	
POPULATION: 0	
SIZE: <1km²	

The Force is Strong in This One

Skellig Michael's magnificence came to global prominence when *Star Wars* filmmakers chose it as the location for Luke Skywalker's hermitage Ahch-To. Filming on the island took place in 2014 and 2015 for *The Force Awakens*, *The Last Jedi* and *The Rise of Skywalker*. The dramatic location certainly has an otherworldly feel, with wild waves crashing onto steep cliffs and zigzagging paths that climb up to monastic ruins.

Just as Luke Skywalker was using the island as a hideaway where he could not be troubled by the outside world, so did the early religious settlers who came to Skellig Michael. Around AD 600 many Catholics who were being oppressed came to the island in search of a haven, eventually establishing one of the first monastic settlements in Ireland. Life was simple for those living at St Fionan's Monastery. They settled in stone huts that have the appearance of a beehive, and are incredibly well built and surprisingly watertight because of the way the stones were placed. Each day the monks would walk down over 600 steps to fish and then return to spend the day praying, studying and gardening. After the monks left in the 13th century, Skellig Michael became a place of pilgrimage, which it

remains. Today, though, many of the 11,000 annual visitors come here to pay pilgrimage to their screen heroes. You might even see tourists dressed as Rey or Luke Skywalker, posing for pictures with a lightsaber. To stop tourism overwhelming the island and damaging its unique environment, there is a limit of 180 visitors a day. It's therefore vital that you book your place beforehand.

Tourists have visited Skellig Michael since Victorian times, but it's a tricky place to get to and the rough seas mean trips sometimes have to be called off. It's this isolation and detachment from the mainland, of course, that first attracted those seeking peace and has since helped to preserve the island's buildings. Aside from

GETTING THERE: Trips to Skellig Michael should be booked in advance. Boat companies include www.skelligislands.com, which leaves from the marina at Portmagee, Co. Kerry.

WHERE TO STAY: The Moorings Guesthouse, Main Street, Portmagee, Co. Kerry, Ireland, V23 RX05, **T:** +353 66 947 7108, **W:** www.moorings.ie. Ferry Boat Guesthouse, Portmagee, Co. Kerry, Ireland, V23 E400, **T:** +353 86 398 6984, **W:** www.bandbinportmagee.ie.

the wonder of this UNESCO World Heritage Site, expect to see seabirds teeming overhead. Puffins, gannets, kittiwakes and Manx shearwaters are just some of the species found here.

VALENTIA ISLAND

All Mouth

Announce you're going on a trip to Valentia and your mates might think you're bound for Spain! The name of this charming island on the west coast of Ireland actually comes from the Gaelic meaning 'mouth of the sound' and is a reference to its geographical location.

Footprints with a Backbone

The Valentia Island trackways – a series of prehistoric footprints – are a fascinating insight into life on Earth 385 million years ago. Discovered in 1993 by a geology student, the footprints can be found at Dohilla on the north coast, well preserved in the Devonian era rocks. Way back then, when this island was tropical and a river flowed nearby, an early vertebrate made its way across the sandy surface and left these footprints behind it. After being covered with silt, the footprints were preserved in the rock that formed here over millions of years. The result is an incredible window into the past that gives a glimpse into the lives of one of the earliest creatures with a backbone.

LOCATION:	51.9070°N 10.3361°W
IRISH GRID REFERENCE:	V393753
POPULATION:	665
SIZE:	25.7km²

GETTING THERE: A bridge on the R565 connects Valentia to the mainland from Portmagee. A car ferry service also operates continually back and forth, covering the short distance from Knightstown to Reenard Point.

WHERE TO STAY: The Royal Hotel, Market Street, Knightstown, Valentia Island, Co. Kerry, Ireland, V23 XR88, **T:** +353 66 947 6144, **W:** www.royalvalentia.ie. Horizon View Lodge, Glanleam Road, Knightstown, Valentia Island, Co. Kerry, Ireland, V23 W447, **T:** +353 87 693 6963.

WHERE TO EAT: Valentia Ice Cream Parlour, Kilbeg East, Valentia Island, Co. Kerry, Ireland, V23 D299, **T:** +353 87 349 7385. Fuchsia Restaurant, Market Street, Knightstown, Co. Kerry, Ireland, V23 HF66, **T:** +353 66 947 6051.

Fishing and tourism are two important industries on the island.

Cable Guy

The first transatlantic telegraph cable helped people and companies communicate with each other at much faster speeds than ever before. The cable, set along the ocean floor between Europe and North America, was a historic marker in the development of communications. With its prominent positioning on the west coast, Valentia was an ideal choice as a place to bring the cable ashore. Various attempts at getting this process right were made from the 1850s, but the successful link was eventually made in 1866, with the cable stretching from Foilhommerum Bay to Heart's Content in Newfoundland.

Valentia Slate of Mind

Slate from the island of Valentia has furnished the palaces of the great and the good ever since the mine was opened in 1816 (valentiaslate.com). The quality of slate taken from the quarry here is so high that it attracted the likes of Queen Victoria and the Duke of Wellington. The slate used in the Paris Opera House originated at the mine in Valentia, as did that still found in London's Houses of Parliament. Countless billiard tables have a smooth surface because of this island's slate. Various issues over the decades led to the closure and reopening of Valentia's mine. A rockfall in 1910 caused a lengthy 14-year abandonment. However, slate is still quarried today and a wide range of products are on offer.

The rugged landscape of Valentia is home to a set of prehistoric footprints.

GREAT BLASKET ISLAND

Go West!

You can go no further west in Ireland than the Great Blasket Islands, a group of three islands that sit 4.8km (3 miles) off the Dingle Peninsula. It's the westernmost spot in Europe, a real place of extremes – west of here lies the North Atlantic and North America. Great Blasket Island is the largest of them and although nobody lives here now, it was once home to over 150 people in the early 20th century. Permanent habitation continued until 1953, when severe bad weather lasting many weeks led to the islanders being cut off and eventually requesting evacuation. Ruins of the small village can still be seen. Boat trips leaving from Dingle cruise to the island and allow those on board to spend up to four hours ashore. Guides are on hand to give a tour around the abandoned village, enabling you to gain an understanding into how challenging it would have been to survive here.

Drinking water is limited on the island, so if you arrive on one of the boat trips you are asked to bring as much as possible with you. In recent years, old cottages have been renovated in a simple manner to give people a tranquil place to stay. There are plenty of vantage points to soak up on the island, but make sure you get sight of the brilliant mountainous outline of An Tiaracht out to sea.

LOCATION:	52.1084°N 10.5152°W
IRISH GRID REFERENCE:	V277981
POPULATION:	0
SIZE:	4.3km²

GETTING THERE: Trips to Great Blasket Island can be arranged from Dingle Bay. Visit www.greatblasketisland.net for more details. Booking ahead is advised.

WHERE TO STAY: Self-catering accommodation is available in a small number of cottages on the island. For more information visit www.greatblasketisland.net/accommodation.

◄ *Head to the extreme west of Ireland to spend time wildlife-spotting at sea.*

► *The distinctive ferry bringing arrivals to Cape Clear Island.*

CAPE CLEAR ISLAND

LOCATION: 51.4507°N 9.4646°W

IRISH GRID REFERENCE: V982229

POPULATION: 124

SIZE: 6.7km²

GETTING THERE: Ferries for Cape Clear Island leave from Baltimore on the mainland. For more information call Cape Clear Ferries on +353 28 39 159 or visit www.capeclearferries.com.

WHERE TO STAY: Cape Clear Island B&B, Old Light House Road, Glen, Cape Clear, Co. Cork, Ireland, **T:** +353 28 39160, **W:** www.capeclearbandb.ie. There's also a glamping option at Chleire Haven, Cape Clear, Knockanamorough, Co. Cork, Ireland, **T:** +353 86 197 1956, **W:** www.yurt-holidays-ireland.com.

WHERE TO EAT: Cotter's Bar, North Harbour, Cape Clear, Co. Cork, Ireland, **T:** +353 28 39153, **W:** www.capeclearisland.eu. Séan Rua's Restaurant, North Harbour, Cape Clear, Co. Cork, Ireland, **T:** +353 028 39099, **W:** www.capeclearisland.ie/FoodAndDrink.

Southernmost Island of Ireland

One of the best places in Ireland to escape modern life and find solitude, this is the southernmost inhabited island in the country. Certainly don't expect to be overwhelmed with facilities on Cape Clear Island. But there's also strangely everything you need for a soul-searching getaway. That is, there's a grocery store and a couple of traditional bars the big-city Irish-themed pubs can only dream of emulating. These are concentrated close to the harbour, where you'll find the all-important noticeboards containing information about events and also the paths that criss-cross the island to the lovely inlets, beaches and cliffs. And it's on these paths and tracks where you'll come across the gems of Cape Clear Island – the 12th-century church, the 14th-century castle and the thousands of migrating birds that call briefly as they pass over the island. Learn more about these at the observatory near the harbour.

Are You Sitting Comfortably?

The ancient art of storytelling is taken extremely seriously on Cape Clear. Each year in September some of the most gifted in the art of telling tales arrive on the island for a festival that has people listening in wonderment to the wonderful stories they weave. For more than a quarter of a century the International Storytelling Festival has left people amazed and inspired by the traditional pastime of gathering people around and spinning a good yarn.

Irish Music

On this southern outpost of Ireland's islands, music is at the heart of most social events and Club Cléire is at the centre of it all. There's a small annual membership to pay to gain entry, but the craic inside is more than worth it and you can be sure you'll return before you leave this charming island. There's live music most weekends in the summer and there's a special focus on Bank Holidays. The experience of hearing visiting and local musicians will stay with you forever.

GOAT ICE CREAM? I'M NOT KIDDING!

Drop in to the Cléire Goats Visitor Centre between 10am and noon to see the goats being milked and learn how the milk is made into ice cream. The results are on sale here and a perfect treat for a sunny day.

HEIR ISLAND

LOCATION: 51.4944°N 9.4322°W

IRISH GRID REFERENCE: W005277

POPULATION: 29

SIZE: 1.5km²

An Island of Learning

Some islands in this book are places to let your hair down, others are ideal for solitude. Heir Island is the place to come and learn new skills while enjoying the peace and quiet that this small oasis of calm provides. Heir Island Sailing School (T: +353 87 1488127, W: www. heirislandsailingschool.com) takes advantage of the often-ideal sailing conditions on the picturesque offshore waters to offer a range of courses. You may want to improve your existing skills, test them on an advanced course or perhaps you're just after an introduction to sailing. Places on the courses are suitable for children as young as six, giving primary school kids a taste of the open sea. There are also full-on adventure opportunities for those wanting a five-day camping trip to several different islands.

The Island Cottage (www.islandcottage.com) has a phenomenal reputation for providing delicious meals. Pre-booked trips from the mainland bring passengers here for an evening of culinary delights on the island. Those wanting to sharpen their cooking skills can take part in one- or two-day courses in the kitchen between April and August.

Or perhaps you want to learn yoga, compose music or meditate. All these options to develop your inner self are available at the Heir Island Retreat (www.heirislandretreat.ie), set among the grounds with their several walkways and a lake. Bliss!

GETTING THERE: Passenger ferries run every day to Heir Island from Cunnamore Pier and take just 5 minutes. For more information call Heir Island Ferry on +353 86 8092447 or visit www.heirislandferry.com. A second service is also offered from the busier harbour of Baltimore.

WHERE TO STAY: On the mainland close to the ferry you'll find The Slipway, The Cove, Baltimore, Co. Cork, Ireland, **T:** +353 28 20134.

WHERE TO EAT: Island Cottage offers dinner for those reserving in advance, **T:** +353 28 38102, **W:** www.islandcottage.com.

SHERKIN ISLAND

Island of the Arts

Any artistic community needs an outstanding environment to help it flourish, so it's no surprise that Sherkin has gained a reputation as the 'Island of the Arts'. The beautiful views out to sea, golden sandy bays and ever-changing skyscapes have both inspired those brought up on Sherkin and pulled in talented artists who have gone on to thrive here. Painters, photographers, craftspeople and writers are all part of the scene. Studio visits are welcomed by several of those working on the island. For more information about this and other things to do while you're here, visit the island's website, www.sherkinisland.ie.

The population of this wonderful little island is around a tenth of what it was before the Great Famine rocked Irish communities in the mid-19th century. Since then, it has steadily fallen, although it's up on the low point of the mid-1960s when only around 60 people called this place home. As well as the thriving artistic scene, tourism is now a vital employer on the island. Sherkin is one of the most accessible of all the Irish islands and has the visitor numbers to match. Aside from the artistic attractions, it has more than enough archaeological sites to keep you entertained. There's an Iron Age fort dating back to 600 BC, but the pick of the bunch is on the hill above the pier where the ferry arrives. The castle and the friary are in ruins after suffering heavy damage in 1537 when the island was invaded by residents from Waterford. A dispute over a ship led to tempers boiling over in what was one of the most significant events in the island's history.

LOCATION: 51.4785°N 9.4205°W	
IRISH GRID REFERENCE: W01326C	
POPULATION: 111	
SIZE: 5km²	

GETTING THERE: Ferries for Sherkin Island leave from Baltimore on the mainland and take 10 minutes. For more information call +353 87 911 7377 or visit www.sherkinisland.eu/ferry.

WHERE TO STAY: Sherkin House, Harboursmouth, Sherkin Island, Co. Cork Ireland, **T:** +353 28 20116, **W:** www.sherkinhouse.com. Sherkin North Shore, Sherkin Island, Co. Cork, Ireland, **T:** +353 87 618 5368, **W:** www.sherkinnorthshore.com.

WHERE TO EAT: The Jolly Roger, Farranacoush, Sherkin Island, Co. Cork, Ireland. **T:** +353 85 141 2503.

CLARE ISLAND

LOCATION: 53.8005°N 9.9527°W
IRISH GRID REFERENCE: L714851
POPULATION: 159
SIZE: 16km²

The Pirate Queen of Clare Island

Clare Island has strong links to the O'Malley family – and to one notorious member in particular. Known for miles around as a fearless leader and ruthless plunderer, Grace O'Malley is one of the most feared figures in Irish history. The ruins of the O'Malley tower house on Clare Island go by the name Granuaile's Castle because Grainne – or Grace – was the most significant resident there. It's thought that she was buried in the O'Malley tomb at Clare Island Abbey, which the family founded. When the Spanish Armada went into retreat, one ship wound up wrecked on the island, and the O'Malleys killed everyone on board.

GETTING THERE: Ferries leave from Roonagh on the west coast of Ireland. Contact the Clare Island Ferry Company for more information (**T:** +353 86 8515003, **W:** www.clare islandferry.com).

WHERE TO STAY: Clare Island Lighthouse, Balltoughey, Clare Island, Co. Mayo, Ireland, **T:** +353 87 668 9758, **W:** www.clareislandlighthouse. com. O'Grady's Guest Accommodation, Fawbglass, Louisburgh, Clare Island, Co. Mayo. Ireland, **T:** +353 98 22991, **W:** www.ogradysguestaccommodation. com.

Lighthouse History

The first lighthouse in the north of the island was destroyed by fire in 1813, just seven years after it was built. The new tower was constructed in 1818 and it provided a warning to passing ships until it was decommissioned in 1965, the problem being that it was frequently hidden in the thick sea mists due to its height on the very tall sea cliffs. Today, though, the lighthouse has been put to good use as a boutique hotel for those wanting to mix luxury with heritage high above the crashing waves.

WHERE TO EAT: Sailor's Bar and Restaurant, Capnagower, Westport, Clare Island, Co. Mayo, **T:** +353 98 26307, **W:** www.goexplorehostel.ie. Clare Island Community Centre, Westport, Clare Island, Co. Mayo, **T:** +353 87 770 3976.

Why I Love... Clare Island

'Clare Island is a stunningly beautiful unspoilt island just a mere 30-minute ferry journey from Roonagh pier off Ireland's west coast on the Wild Atlantic Way. I love this jewel of an island! It's still home to 140 full-time residents. It has a wonderful old-fashioned community feel with its own authentic charm. What I really love is the delicate balance of tourism, sheep farming, local craft and natural activities that coexist side by side, making this island a very special place to live and to visit.'

Roie McCann, General Manager, Clare Island Lighthouse

FOTA

LOCATION:	51.9010°N 8.2825°W
IRISH GRID REFERENCE:	W806721
POPULATION:	15
SIZE:	3.2km²

GETTING THERE: Fota lies just to the east of Cork. The N25 road runs close by, with connecting roads linking it to the mainland. Rail services stop on the island at Fota Station.

WHERE TO STAY: Fota Island Resort, Fota Island, Co. Cork, Ireland, T45 HX62, **T:** +353 21 488 3700, **W:** www.fota island.ie. Waters Edge Hotel, Yacht Club Quay, Kilgarvan, Co. Cork, Ireland, **T:** +353 21 481 5566, **W:** www.waters edgehotel.ie.

WHERE TO EAT: Food options are available at Fota Island Resort and inside the wildlife park.

▲ *Fota is a playground with plenty to do – including golf.*

Go Wild!

Sitting in Cork Harbour and home to a luxurious hotel and family attractions, Fota has developed a name as a fun island where people come to relax and play. The Fota Island Resort is set in a 780-acre estate and enjoys a reputation for being a golfing paradise. Several tournaments have taken place here, including the Murphy's Irish Open. Families come here to enjoy a day among the animals at Fota Wildlife Park (www. fotawildlife.ie). Tigers, lions, gibbons, giraffes, rhinos and kangaroos are just some of the creatures living here in what is Ireland's only wildlife park. To enhance your visit, you can book on a range of behind-the-scenes tours and take part in experiences such as feeding the penguins.

Quieter days out can be had at Fota House, a charming 19th-century construction with a well-preserved kitchen and service wings, showing what life was like back in the day. The house also has a stunning collection of landscape paintings and a fully functioning working garden that contains a glasshouse and orchard. This was once the main source of fruit and vegetables for those in the house. Save time for a wander around the gardens, which are well maintained by local volunteers.

GREAT ISLAND

LOCATION: 51.8499°N 8.2954°E

GRID REFERENCE: W796664

POPULATION: 14,000

SIZE: 32km²

A Seafaring History

Situated in Cork Harbour, there's a rich maritime history surrounding Great Island on the south coast of the country. People have lived on this island for the best part of a thousand years, with influential families owning the land from the 13th century. The town of Cobh grew quickly in the 19th century as its strategic position was recognised and several military sites were established in the harbour. Fortifications can also be spotted on Great Island itself, including a string of Martello towers, built to bolster defences.

Shipbuilding has been an important contributor to the island's economy down the years, but now the links with tourism are stronger. Huge cruise ships berth here when stopping off at Cork on a tour of the British Isles. Departing guests visit the island and head into Cork, spending important Euros as they go. Today's keen seafarers can have their own historic adventures by setting out from Great Island on one of the many yacht and dinghy courses offered by Sail Cork (www.sailcork.com). Away from the largest town of Cobh, several saltmarshes are a go-to destination for birdwatchers.

GETTING THERE: Great Island is linked to the mainland by the bridge on the R624. There's also a trainline to the island, terminating at Cobh.

WHERE TO STAY: Waters Edge Hotel, Yacht Club Quay, Kilgarvan, Cobh, Co. Cork, Ireland, **T:** +353 21 481 5566, **W:** www.watersedgehotel.ie. Bella Vista Hotel and Self Catering Suites, Spy Hill, Kilgarvan, Cobh, Co. Cork. Ireland, **T:** +353 21 481 2450, **W:** www.bellavistahotel.ie.

WHERE TO EAT: Grand Italian Pizzeria, Casement Square, Kilgarvan, Cobh, Co. Cork, Ireland, P24 CA47, **T:** +353 21 481 5104. Titanic Bar and Grill, 20 Casement Square, Kilgarvan, Cobh, Co. Cork, P24 Y560, Ireland, **T:** +353 21 481 4585, **W:** www.titanicbarandgrill.ie.

LETTERMORE

Ponies of the Peninsula

Driving across the bleak and barren landscape of Lettermore is for some a means to an end as they press on for the idyllic beaches of Lettermullen. Many folk don't give Lettermore the time it deserves and head beyond the rocky horizon, passing the large boulders and taking the R374 as it meanders down the peninsula that is linked by causeways and juts out into the Atlantic. But there is fabulous coastline to be seen and enjoyed here in Lettermore too, and a good selection of beaches. It's true that the harsh environment of rock, gouged with small lakes, may not be the most inspiring, but the island is home to a special breed of ponies that have learned to thrive here. The Connemara pony is at home among the wilds of Lettermore, thriving on the occasional grassy area and developing a deserved reputation as a tough, resilient animal. Just how these hardy ponies ended up here in Ireland is up for debate. One theory suggests they are the descendants of mighty military Spanish horses that lived on the island after ships in the Spanish Armada ran aground in 1588. Others believe local horses bred with hardy ponies brought over from Scandinavia by the Vikings, or that they are a descendant of the now-extinct Irish Hobby workhorses. Whatever their origin, Connemara ponies are now part of the Lettermore landscape, as well as being a common sight elsewhere in West Galway.

LOCATION: 53.2890°N 9.6550°W

IRISH GRID REFERENCE: L887279

POPULATION: 528

SIZE: 9.1km²

GETTING THERE: Lettermore is linked to the mainland by the R374.

WHERE TO STAY: Costelloe Lodge, Derrynea, Costelloe, Co. Galway, Ireland, **T:** +353 87 226 0065, **W:** www.costelloelodge.com.

Connemara ponies can be spotted all over the island.

LETTERMULLEN

Mind Your Language

Island explorers should head west out of Galway for over 48km (30 miles) to reach Lettermullen, crossing over bridges, causeways and other islands stretching out across Galway Bay. Although the drive may only take you 45 minutes or so, you'll notice a significant change in the language spoken here. You'll find most people on Lettermullen speaking Irish, so much so that the local council has in the past insisted that new residents buying homes here are fluent in the language.

To get to grips with the history of this small island, pay a visit to the local heritage centre that opened in 2009. It's free to get in, though you're asked to make a donation to the upkeep so that the rolling exhibitions can be maintained into the future. As well as photographs of days gone by on this western Ireland outpost, there are several tools and instruments from those who worked as blacksmiths and carpenters here on Lettermullen. It's generally a flat island, but that doesn't mean you won't be treated to good views. There are many places on Lettermullen to enjoy the views of surrounding islands, the mainland and the ocean.

LOCATION: 53.2440°N 9.7260°W

IRISH GRID REFERENCE: L848522

POPULATION: 219

SIZE: 3.2km²

GETTING THERE: Lettermullen is connected to the island of Ireland by the R374.

WHERE TO STAY: Accommodation is available nearby at Bayview B&B, Teeranea, Murvagh Island, Co. Galway, Ireland, **T:** +353 91 551757, **W:** www.bayviewlettermore.com.

INCH ISLAND

Bring your binoculars to Inch Island to spot migrating birds.

Icelandic Arrivals

Perched in Lough Swilly in County Donegal, Inch Island is a small affair – as the name might suggest – but it's worth the lengthy journey made by many birdwatchers. Just like the tourists themselves, the birds are migrating and tend not to stay here too long. But like the visitors, they come from all over. The waterfowl arriving for the winter are of special interest because they stay here in great numbers, allowing for some amazing sights and sounds. The best time to arrive on the island is towards the end of autumn, when different species of geese and swan make their way down from Iceland and take up residence in the surrounding waters. This is, after all, the first land they come across on their journey south so they deserve the rest. The magnificent whooper swan and the Greenland white-fronted goose are two to look out for. Binoculars and recording books are essential for a trip to Inch Island.

LOCATION: 55.0515°N 7.4748°W

IRISH GRID REFERENCE: C336227

POPULATION: 448

SIZE: 13km²

GETTING THERE: Inch Island is connected to the mainland via a causeway.

WHERE TO STAY: There are several options on the nearby mainland. An Grianan Hotel, Speenoge, Co. Donegal, Ireland, **T:** +353 74 936 8900, **W:** www.angriananhotel.com. The Frontier Hotel, Bonemaine, Bridgend, Co. Denegal, Ireland, **T:** +353 74 936 8667, **W:** www.frontierhotel.ie.

INNISFREE

LOCATION: 54.2463°N 8.3585°W

IRISH GRID REFERENCE: G766330

POPULATION: 0

SIZE: >1km²

Literary Inspiration

Anybody who has spent tranquil days around Loch Gill and seen the Isle of Innisfree sitting peacefully in the water will know what thoughts were going through William Butler Yeats' head. He spent childhood summer days around the island and wrote a famous poem – 'The Lake Isle of Innisfree' – in 1888, which describes his longing to be back there. Legend has it that Yeats found inspiration for the poem while walking along busy Fleet Street in London, longing to be whisked away to the Irish loch and iconic island. The 12-line poem begins with the line 'I will arise and go now, and go to Innisfree.' It quickly became a classic, receiving critical acclaim in England and Scotland, and is so loved in his native Ireland that it is featured on the nation's passports. The desire to be somewhere calm and peaceful instead of the pressure-cooker city environment was a pressing issue in the 19th century just as much as it is today. The Yeats tours offered by Rose of Innisfree takes you around this fabulous little island and additional tours visit more places frequented by Yeats during his time here.

GETTING THERE: Sailings are organised in summer months from the jetty at Doorly Park, Sligo, by Rose of Innisfree (**T:** +353 87 610 2822, **W:** www.roseofinnisfree.com).

WHERE TO STAY: Castle View B&B, Faslowart, Co. Leitrim, Ireland, **T:** +353 86 071 6968, **W:** www.leitrimbnb.com. Teach Eamainn B&B, Faughts, Calry, Co. Sligo, Ireland, **T:** +353 71 914 3393, **W:** www.teacheamainn.com.

Haunting Innisfree in the waters of Loch Gill.

ISLE OF MAN

Expect to discover inspiring history, taste delicious seafood and learn how important speeding motorcycles are to the local culture and economy. The Isle of Man is many things to many people; you can get away from it all at a rural retreat or immerse yourself in the bustling streets of Douglas. Whatever you decide to do, you're in for a treat on this group of islands that sits between England and Ireland. Wildlife spotting is a delight down at the Calf of Man, where the attractive scenery leaves you in little doubt as to why many film directors have chosen these islands as film locations. It doesn't take long before you develop a taste for the islands. Fresh seafood is available throughout, with the fishy hotspots of Douglas and St Patrick's Isle being a real delight. And don't forget to sample one of the Fairly Famous Manx Knobs.

DON'T MISS

- Marvelling at the awesome Laxey Wheel after an electric train journey
- Breakfasting in style with a plate of Manx kippers
- Experiencing the intense sights and sounds of the Isle of Man TT races
- Wandering around the castle and sampling seafood snacks on St Patrick's Isle
- Coming face to face with motorcycling history at the Isle of Man Motor Museum

◄ *Peel Castle at night.*

CALF OF MAN

Shear Heaven

Across the swirling and turbulent waters of Calf Sound, this small island is a haven for ornithologists wanting to get away from it all. Basic self-catering accommodation is available for up to eight people at an observatory built in the late 1950s, while day-visitors can make the journey on small boats to spend a few hours among the local bird population. Top of the checklist for many is the population of Manx shearwaters, which take their name from this area, along with puffins and a seal colony making their home on the shoreline.

For nine months of the year, there are two permanent inhabitants on the Calf of Man. Working for Manx National Heritage, these seasonal positions are thought to be among the most isolated jobs in the British Isles. As ornithology and estate wardens, the dedicated pair live in basic conditions, enjoy just one shower a week and have to fetch their own water. It's hard work, but the wildlife, views and isolation keep pulling in applications.

The intriguing Calf of Man is visible from the Isle of Man.

LOCATION: 54.0513°N 4.8141°W

GRID REFERENCE: SC159658

POPULATION: 2

SIZE: 2.6km²

GETTING THERE: Trips around the Calf of Man and those including a landing on the island leave from Ragland Pier in Port Erin, IM9 6JA, **T:** 07624 322765, **W:** www.shonaboattrips.wixsite.com.

WHERE TO STAY: Calf of Man Bird Observatory Self Catering Hostel, Calf of Man, **W:** www.manx nationalheritage.im.

ISLE OF MAN

Douglas

The seafront in Douglas is a delight. The perfectly curvaceous coast is lined with lights and a wide promenade for walkers, joggers and cyclists. At the northern end of the bay, the large 'Electric Railway' sign marks the point of departure for journeys trundling along the coast to Laxey, home of the Great Laxey Wheel – the largest working waterwheel in the world. At the southern side, steam trains head south to Port Erin along the longest narrow-gauge railway in the UK. Running parallel to the sea, Strand Street is the place to shop and has a good range of national chains, reminding us that this is one of the most populated of our islands. There's a confused cosmopolitan feel about central Douglas, as cool cafés and trendy bars sit near to empty units and charity shops. A little way down, you'll find impeccably presented hair salons brushing shoulders with vape shops and a whole host of TT merch. Some hotels have embraced the 21st century, while others are all Fawlty Towers and shared bathrooms. It's an island of contrasts, an island in transition but not exactly sure what it wants to be. Still, there is plenty to keep you busy on the Isle of Man for a few days, and it's easy to fall in love with the place. Whether you come for the roar of the TT or the relative peace and quiet of the closed season, the island manages to feel 'away from it all' while having all the facilities of a decent sized town.

LOCATION: 54.2361°N 4.5481°W

GRID REFERENCE: SC381760

POPULATION: 83,314

SIZE: 572km²

GETTING THERE: The port at Douglas has regular ferries from Heysham, Liverpool, Birkenhead, Belfast and Dublin with the Isle of Man Steam Packet Company (**T:** 08722 992992, **W:** www.steam-packet.com). Flights connect the Isle of Man Airport with London, East Midlands, Manchester and Liverpool (**T:** 01624 821600).

WHERE TO STAY: Englewood Lodge, King Edward Road, Douglas, Isle of Man, IM3 2AS, **T:** 01624 616050, **W:** www.englewoodlodge.com. The Claremont Hotel, 18 Loch Promenade, Douglas, Isle of Man, IM1 2LX, **T:** 01624 617068, **W:** www.claremonthoteldouglas.com.

WHERE TO EAT: Enzo's Restaurant, 52 Bucks Road, Douglas, Isle of Man, IM1 3AD, **T:** 01624 622653. Harbour Lights Café and Restaurant, The Promenade, Peel, Isle of Man, IM5 1AH, **T:** 01624 843543, **W:** www.harbour-lights.com.

▲ *The promenade at Douglas is a delightful place to walk both day and night.*

Kippers and Sweets

On the west coast of the Isle of Man, in the charming town of Peel, you'll find one of the traditional tastes of the island – Manx kippers. The Moore's family factory sits beside the River Neb and it's here the fish are cut, soaked in salt and hung in large chimneys to be smoked in a traditional manner. Factory tours are available and show you the processes involved in the Manx kipper business from start to finish (www.manxkippers.com).

If you've got a sweeter tooth, keep an eye out in local shops for the confectionary specialism of the island. Produced in small batches by a local company, Manx Rock is a perfect treat to take back home. And then there's the wonderfully named 'Casement's Fairly Famous Manx Knobs', an Edwardian seaside favourite sold in lovely tins featuring a behatted gent sporting the three legs of Man.

Three Legs of Man

One of the world's most unusual and noteworthy flags, the three-legged triskelion on a red background has been the official flag of the Isle of Man since 1 December 1932. You'll see the symbol, with its three armoured legs and golden spurs, all over the island.

Time for TT

The Isle of Man TT races have grown into a multi-million pound event and enjoy a worldwide reputation. Those who have witnessed first hand motorcycles whizzing past at bewildering speeds don't forget the sight, and those who wonder what it's all about should go online to see one of the jaw-dropping videos filmed from participants' handlebars. This is what best symbolises the Isle of Man today, and you don't have to look far to find TT merchandise. But these huge events had fairly humble beginnings in the early 20th century, following a decision to ban road races in Britain and introduce a 20mph speed limit. With the Manx Government being a lot more lenient, the first Tourist Trophy races were held in 1907 for two categories of motorcycles. To learn more about the island's history of road racing, head to the Isle of Man Motor Museum on the site of former RAF Jurby. This is a private collection of cars and motorcycles, opened to the public in a brand-new building in 2015. Vehicles from all over the world make up this glorious visitor attraction, which manages to balance the fast and the furious with the cute and indulgent. The detailed history of motorcycles used in TT races should keep all racing fans entertained.

The races have come at a large cost to human life over the decades. Since 1907, there have been 260 deaths during race events on the island. The deadliest year was 1970, when seven racers sadly lost their lives.

Isle of Hollywood

The diverse scenery on the island has turned the heads of several film directors as they realised Manx locations could stand in for many other countries on the big screen. In 1995, a major initiative was launched to make actors and directors welcome on the island. Since then, Isle of Man Film has completed over 100 movie, television and animated projects. Well-known films to originate in Manx landscapes include *Waking Ned* (1998), *Thomas and the Magic Railroad* (2000), *Harry Potter and the Chamber of Secrets* (2002), *Churchill: The Hollywood Years* (2004), *Mindhorn* (2016) and *Where Hands Touch* (2018).

▼ *A world class collection of motorbikes is on display at the IOM Motor Museum.*

HE TT DOWN THE YEARS

1907 First races
1914 Crash helmets compulsory
1927 Sidecar races begin
1957 First 100mph lap
1962 First time a woman competes in a solo race
1989 New Lightweight lap record of 130.02mph
2001 Races cancelled due to foot and mouth crisis
2014 Peter Hickman makes fastest ever debut

The Laxey Wheel is the largest working waterwheel on the planet.

ST MARY'S ISLE

Tower of Refuge

Looking out to sea from the promenade in Douglas, a small and curious island grabs your attention near the ferry terminal. The treacherous rocks that form St Mary's Isle (also known as Conister Rock) claimed several ships in the early 19th century. Sir William Hillary, who helped to set up the Royal National Lifeboat Institute, was living on the Isle of Man and realised something had to be done. He suggested building a safe haven, where shipwrecked sailors could seek safety from the sea until help came. The iconic Tower of Refuge was built in 1832 – part funded by Hillary – and was kept well stocked with supplies of fresh water and bread in case sailors needed to stay there in stormy conditions. During a restoration period in 2008, the tower was repaired and had lighting installed, which makes it a distinctive feature of the town's night-time skyline.

LOCATION: 54.0901°N 4.2807°W	
GRID REFERENCE: SC388755	
POPULATION: 0	
SIZE: <1km²	

GETTING THERE: People are discouraged from making their own way because of the risk posed from fast incoming tides. A sponsored walk takes place in August each year, which allows people to cross safely in an organised group.

WHERE TO STAY: Halvard Hotel, Loch Promenade, Douglas, Isle of Man, IM1 2NA, **T:** 01624 844040, **W:** www.halvard.co.uk. Ellan Vannin Hotel, Loch Promenade, Douglas, Isle of Man, IM1 2LY, **T:** 01624 674824, **W:** www.ellanvannin hotel.im.

The unmistakable historic castle is easily spotted from Douglas.

ST PATRICK'S ISLE

Bountiful Isle

For a relatively small lump of rock in the Irish Sea, St Patrick's Isle has a long and interesting history. Settlers are first thought to have arrived here 8,000 years ago, and made use of the shelter and plentiful supplies of fish. Legend has it that St Patrick stepped ashore here from Ireland, bringing Christianity to the Isle of Man and establishing a monastery and several churches. In the 10th century, Vikings were attracted to the wealth on this coast and targeted the land in their Irish Sea raids. A fort was built on the hill by King Magnus Barelegs and so began centuries of fortification under different rulers. Although the pendulum of power swung between different kings, the castle and church stood firm until the 18th century. But when the garrison was moved inland and the church roof was stripped for its lead, soldiers and hymn-singers made way for seabirds and howling winds to take over.

After exploring the castle, foodies must save time to walk along the harbour wall and sample a snack at one of the popular food kiosks dotted around this area. It's a great chance to pick up some tasty Manx delicacies freshly caught in local seas. Scallops in a chilli dip, Manx crab, and kipper baps are just some of the marine treats on offer.

LOCATION: 54.2258°N 4.7017°W

GRID REFERENCE: SC241845

POPULATION: 0

SIZE: <1km²

GETTING THERE: A causeway connects St Patrick's Isle to the Isle of Man, allowing road and pedestrian access.

WHERE TO STAY: The Waldick Hotel, Marine Parade, Peel, Isle of Man, IM5 1PB, **T:** 01624 842410, **W:** www.waldickhotel.co.uk. The Fernleigh, Marine Parade, Peel, Isle of Man, IM5 1PB, **T:** 01624 842435, **W:** www.isleofman-bedandbreakfast. com.

WHERE TO EAT: Several seafood kiosks are found on the island.

▲ *Remember to order seafood on your trip.*

◄ *The castle on St Patrick's Isle has a prominent coastal position.*

ISLES OF SCILLY

Much of the summer accommodation on this group of islands is booked up six months in advance – testament to how popular the Isles of Scilly are. As soon as the *Scillonian III* passenger ferry or the helicopter from Cornwall drops you off on the island of St Mary's, it quickly becomes apparent that you've arrived at a special place. The pace of life slows, the weather generally improves and most activities are centred on bustling little harbours as boats arrive and depart for the other islands. Each of the Isles of Scilly has a unique feel and if you spend a week or two here you'll be able to sail to most of them to discover the beaches, scenery, crafts and food they have to offer. The artistic hub of St Martin's is a great place to find souvenirs to take back to the mainland, while the unique microclimate of Tresco allows a jaw-dropping collection of plants and trees to thrive. The small island of Bryher is a favourite for many tourists, a place criss-crossed with sandy paths and honesty boxes where you can buy fresh vegetables and plants. Wherever you stay, keep an eye on harbour displays to catch the latest information about boat trips to other islands, sample the islands' many restaurants and watch the famous gig races.

DON'T MISS

- Watching the summer gig races from a spectator boat on the ocean
- Wandering around the varied and forever-flowering gardens on Tresco
- Setting up a tent and letting troubles slip away on Bryher
- Walking along the long, deserted beaches on St Martin's
- Choosing your flavour of locally made ice cream while strolling around St Agnes

◄ *The Isles of Scilly are an idyllic and very popular location – plan your visit well in advance.*

ANNET

Bird Island

The second largest of the uninhabited Isles of Scilly, Annet has a worldwide reputation for its bird population. Indeed, it's sometimes known as 'Bird Island' due to the sheer numbers involved. The entire island is a bird sanctuary and the biggest bird-breeding site in the Isles of Scilly. The range of species and number of birds on Annet is bewildering. On a trip around the island's waters you can expect to see shags, Manx shearwater and warblers. There are also nearly a thousand pairs of the European storm petrel on Annet, the Isles of Scilly being the only place in England where they breed.

Because of its importance as a breeding location and a Site of Special Scientific Interest, there is no landing on Annet. But there is potential to take a boat on a tour around the island or stand and gaze across the water from nearby St Agnes. Pack your binoculars and a camera with a zoom lens.

LOCATION: 49.8962°N 6.3726°W

GRID REFERENCE: SV864087

POPULATION: 0

SIZE: <1km²

GETTING THERE: There is no landing allowed on Annet, although you can go on a boat trip to see the island's wildlife from a distance. Contact St Mary's Boatmen's Association for information (**T:** 01720 423999, **W:** www.scillyboating.co.uk). You can also enjoy stunning views of Annet from St Agnes.

WHERE TO STAY: Stay in Hugh Town on St Mary's before taking a day trip to visit Annet. The Atlantic, Hugh Street, St Mary's, TR21 0PL, **T:** 01720 422417, **W:** www.atlantic innscilly.co.uk. Tregarthen's Hotel, Garrison Hill, TR21 0PP, **T:** 01720 422540, **W:** www.tregarthens-hotel.co.uk.

BRYHER

LOCATION: 49.9560°N 6.3497°W

GRID REFERENCE: SV881152

POPULATION: 84

SIZE: 1.3km²

Why the Whales Came

After arriving at St Mary's and transferring to the smaller boat bound for Bryher, I noticed a familiar face on a seat close to me. Former Children's Laureate Michael Morpurgo is a regular visitor to Bryher and during our summer stay was often spotted on the sandy lanes criss-crossing the island. He used Bryher as the setting for his 1985 children's story, *Why the Whales Came*, a tale about ten-year-old Gracie, who embarks on an adventure centred on visiting narwhals. When it was turned into a film in 1989 – *When the Whales Came* – shooting took place on the island. A former telephone box on Bryher has been turned into a small museum about the story. Squeeze inside to see the original manuscript typed by Michael Morpurgo and photographs of Helen Mirren and David Suchet on the island during filming.

Incredible Camping

Having camped in many places while writing this book, the experience of pitching a tent on Bryher was particularly memorable. Taking a tent to this island is both exhilarating and rejuvenating, and will make you want to return time and time again. Many campers on the Bryher site are return visitors and pitches get booked for much of the following year when they are made available in November. It's worth planning ahead so you can add this unforgettable camping trip to your to-do list. The most liberating thing about Scilly camping is that you don't bring a car. Everything you want to have with you must be carried onto the *Scillonian III* passenger ferry in Penzance – tent, cooking equipment, clothes, toiletries, the lot. On arrival at St Mary's your baggage is transferred to the smaller boat bound for Bryher, where the campsite owners will meet you with a tractor. Bags are put in the trailer and you walk behind as the equipment is taken to your camping pitch. The whole experience is a celebration of Bryer's beautifully remote setting.

GETTING THERE: Tresco Boat Services operates services from St Mary's and connecting journeys are timed to meet the *Scillonian III* passenger ferry (**T:** 01720 422849, **W:** www.tresco.co.uk).

WHERE TO STAY: Bryher Campsite, Bryher, TR23 0PR, **T:** 01720 422068, **W:** www.bryhercampsite.co.uk. Hell Bay Hotel, Hell Bay, Bryher, TR23 0PR, **T:** 01720 422947, **W:** www.hellbay.co.uk.

WHERE TO EAT: The Crab Shack, Hell Bay, TR23 0PR, **T:** 01720 422947, **W:** www.hellbay.co.uk/dining-with-us/crab-shack. Fraggle Rock Bar, Bryher, TR23 0PR, **T:** 01720 422222, **W:** www.bryher.co.

Fudge it...

Sampling the fudge from Veronica Farm is a must before you leave the island. Using Scillonian milk, butter and clotted cream, the vanilla fudge is freshly handmade on Bryher. It's available in the Bryher shop and on some of the other islands, too. The best place to make a purchase, though, is at one of Bryher's honesty stalls, which also sell eggs, vegetables, plants and other local produce. You'll come across these little stalls on the sandy lanes that cut across the island and they're a perfect place to have a browse and pick up something special for dinner.

▶ *Boats are an integral part of life on Bryher.*
▼ *Waiting for the ferry – planning journeys in advance is essential here.*

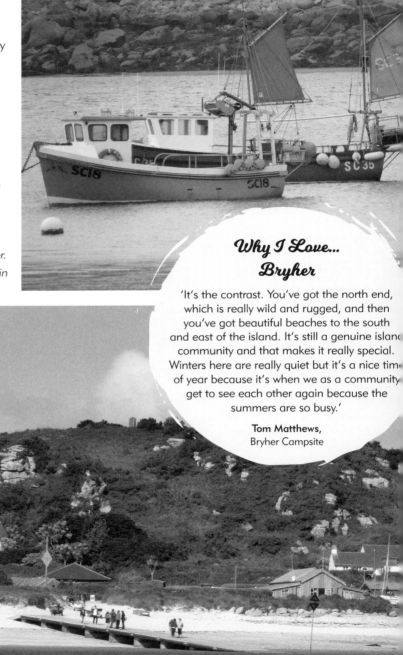

Why I Love... Bryher

'It's the contrast. You've got the north end, which is really wild and rugged, and then you've got beautiful beaches to the south and east of the island. It's still a genuine island community and that makes it really special. Winters here are really quiet but it's a nice time of year because it's when we as a community get to see each other again because the summers are so busy.'

Tom Matthews,
Bryher Campsite

BURNT ISLAND

LOCATION: 49.8961°N 6.3550°W

GRID REFERENCE: SV873086

POPULATION: 0

SIZE: <1km²

GETTING THERE: At low tide, you can walk across to Burnt Island and Tins Walbert from Periglis beach on the island of St Agnes. From St Mary's, day trips to St Agnes are advertised on the boards at the harbour (**T:** 01720 423999, **W:** www.scillyboating.co.uk).

WHERE TO STAY: See St Agnes, page 293.

WHERE TO EAT: Take a picnic with you on the trip. Or head to nearby St Agnes for dining options (see St Agnes, page 293).

The warning beacon on Burnt Island is still important today.

Shipping Aid

This small tidal island is fairly easy to reach at low tide, walking over the exposed rocks on an adventurous outing to experience scillonian solitude. Burnt Island and adjacent Tins Walbert provide a good view of St Agnes and Annet, and attract plenty of seabirds. Tins Walbert is also home to a relatively recent addition by Trinity House

to help local shipping. The large navigational marker is the most obvious feature of Tins Walbert island, and was added in 2002 to mark the north-west passage following an incident involving a German cruise liner. On 16 May 1997, the *Albatros* was being guided out by a local pilot when it hit a ledge and sustained a 60m (200ft) long gash. Over 500 passengers

were on board and were taken to Penzance on the *Scillonian III* passenger ferry before continuing their journey home overland. The resulting concrete aid to shipping is used in combination with the St Agnes lighthouse for safe entry to and exit from the islands. Another important aid to shipping in the area, the iconic Bishop Rock Lighthouse, can be seen out to sea.

GUGH ISLAND

LOCATION: 49.8960°N 6.3330°W

GRID REFERENCE: SV889083

POPULATION: 3

SIZE: <1km²

GETTING THERE: Gugh is a tidal island joined to St Agnes. Day trips to St Agnes can be arranged from St Mary's Quay and other islands but do not run every day. For boat trips originating from St Agnes, visit www.stagnesboating.co.uk.

WHERE TO STAY: See St Agnes, page 293.

WHERE TO EAT: See St Agnes, page 293.

Especially for Gugh

As your boat arrives at St Agnes, you'll be told by the captain what time of day you're able to walk across the sandy stretch to Gugh Island. Pay attention to these times and make sure you don't get stuck, as the island gets cut off at high tide. Hopefully, though, the tides will be kind during your visit and you'll have a few hours to enjoy a circular walk around this beautiful place. Head past the Turks Head pub, which is always handy for grabbing a beer at the end of your walk. You can call in here on arrival as well to order a Cornish pasty or two, which will be ready for you to collect later. After passing the Turks Head, go down the slope to the tombolo known as the Bar.

St Agnes is remote enough, but when you cross the sand to Gugh you're entering a whole new level of out-of-the-way. Technically, this could be described as the sixth inhabited island of the Scillies because there are a handful of folk who call this place home, but often it gets coupled together with St Agnes. You'll only see two houses on Gugh and these are located close to the Bar. Once you're beyond them there's a round walk that takes you through beautiful countryside with stunning sea views. You'll also encounter plenty of seabirds, with numbers on the increase thanks to a successful operation that eradicated non-native brown rats. When bird numbers started to plummet because the rats were eating their eggs, a team of 30 volunteers began the rodent removal programme. Today, there are no signs of rats on Gugh, but wildlife enthusiasts are anything but complacent; you'll see several signs around the island telling you who to get in touch with if you do happen to come across one.

◄ *The walk around Gugh Island is delightful, but the island is cut off at high tide.*

▼ *Rugged stones are found at the top of the island's hill.*

HANGMAN'S ISLAND

Rock Legend

On the eastern shore of Bryher, Hangman's Island is a prominent rock commanding a view of the channel out towards Tresco and haunting the area with a set of gallows at the summit. Legend has it that Admiral Blake used the island as an execution site during the English Civil War. Blake was a renowned naval commander who successfully led a force to the Scilly Isles to remove Sir John Grenville, a governor appointed by Charles II. Some historians suggest the name of the island comes from the Cornish *an men*, which means 'rock'.

Eerily named Hangman's Island is best viewed from the pub on Bryher!

LOCATION: 49.9594°N 6.3498°W

GRID REFERENCE: SV881156

POPULATION: 0

SIZE: <1km²

GETTING THERE: Accessible from Bryher at certain low tides, or enjoy the view towards Hangman's Island and Tresco from the shore. Boats to Bryher leave St Mary's daily through Tresco Boat Services (**T:** 01720 422849, **W:** www.tresco.co.uk).

WHERE TO STAY: On Bryher you'll find Hell Bay Hotel in Hell Bay, TR23 0PR, **T:** 01720 422947, **W:** www.hellbay.co.uk.

WHERE TO EAT: Dining options are available on Bryher.

RAT ISLAND

The Rat Pack

This tiny, unremarkable island punches well above its weight because it forms part of the biggest quay on the Scillies. Although not scenically inspirational or geologically fascinating, most people who come and go from the Isles of Scilly cross Rat Island. For some, it's gone by in the blink of an eye as they push on to stay at one of the other islands. But for others it's an important hub of information where one can book boat trips, get shipping timetables and grab a drink as you wait for departure.

Many people have their first experience of the Isles of Scilly when stepping from the *Scillonian III* passenger ferry – nicknamed the 'Vomit Comet' – in rough seas. It can be a hectic experience. When you get on board in Penzance, luggage is sorted into different containers depending on which island you're going to be staying on. There are scenes of organised chaos as the luggage is taken off and loaded onto the smaller boats. If you're not staying on St Mary's, which is joined to Rat Island, you'll need to make sure you're on the correct boat for your final destination. And then your brief visit to Rat Island is complete. As you move on to explore St Mary's or float away to one of the other islands, you'll start to get a feel for how each of the Scilly Isles has a totally different character.

Hugh Town's Harbour Wall

The harbour wall joins Rat Island to Hugh Town, the largest settlement on St Mary's. The Lord Proprietor of the Isles of Scilly, Augustus Smith, made the wall one of his first priorities when he took up the post in 1834. A few years later, the new wall was complete and bigger ships were able to arrive here with increased frequency. Further expansion of the quay in 1889 was carried out because the flower trade on the isles was booming.

LOCATION: 49.9178°N 6.3180°W

GRID REFERENCE: SV901108

POPULATION: 0

SIZE: <1km²

GETTING THERE: The *Scillonian III* passenger ferry arrives here after its journey from Penzance. Contact Isles of Scilly Travel to book (**T:** 01736 334220, **W:** www.islesofscilly-travel.co.uk).

WHERE TO STAY: Just off Rat Island you'll find Schooners Hotel on Town Beach, St Mary's, TR21 0LN, **T:** 01720 422682, **W:** www.schoonershotel.co.uk.

WHERE TO EAT: At the end of the harbour wall is the Mermaid Inn, close to Rat Island on The Bank, St Mary's, TR21 0HY, **T:** 01720 422701, **W:** www.mermaidscilly.co.uk.

Gig Racing

The harbour wall makes a brilliant vantage point for the best spectator sport on the Isles of Scilly – gig racing. Throughout the summer months, regular races of these small rowing boats are held in the ocean between the islands. The high point of the season is the Gig Racing World Championship, where teams come from all over the world and accommodation is hard to come by. Different types of races are held throughout the year, with some having the finish line at the harbour wall – to the delight of the cheering crowds gathered there. The best way to see a race, though, is to get on board one of the spectator boats. It's not too expensive, and the rules will be explained to you if it's your first time.

Gig racing is a popular sport here, with people using the harbour on Rat Island to view the finish line.

Inset: Boat tours are available that try to keep up with the action.

SAMSON

Twin Peaks

Nobody has lived on Samson since 1855, meaning you'll have much of the island to yourself if you decide to head there on a trip. Enjoy solitude, walking on beaches and exploring the spectacle of ruined cottages that remain from when Samson had a small population. From the sea and other islands, Samson is one of the most recognisable of all the Isles of Scilly. Two distinct hills protrude from the waters, rising to Samson's famous twin peaks. Climbing up either the North Hill or South Hill allows a good vista of the surrounding islands.

LOCATION: 49.9326°N 6.3535°W

GRID REFERENCE: SV876127

POPULATION: 0

SIZE: <1km²

GETTING THERE: From St Mary's, day trips to Samson allow you to spend time experiencing the solitude of the island. Contact St Mary's Boatmen's Association for information, **T:** 01720 423999, **W:** www.scillyboating.co.uk.

WHERE TO STAY: Stay in Hugh Town on St Mary's before taking your day trip across. The Atlantic, Hugh Street, St Mary's, TR21 0PL, **T:** 01720 422417, **W:** www.atlanticinnscilly. co.uk. Tregarthen's Hotel, Garrison Hill, TR21 0PP, **T:** 01720 422540, **W:** www.tregarthens-hotel.co.uk.

The distinctive two-peaked outline of Samson is easily recognised from surrounding islands.

ST AGNES

LOCATION: 49.8919°N 6.3447°W

GRID REFERENCE: SV881430

POPULATION: 82

SIZE: 1.5km²

GETTING THERE: Day trips to St Agnes can be arranged from St Mary's, the largest island in the Isles of Scilly. Other islands also have day trips running to St Agnes, but they do not run every day. For boat trips originating from St Agnes, visit www.stagnesboating.co.uk.

WHERE TO STAY: Places to stay on St Agnes are limited. There is a campsite at Troytown Farm, St Agnes, TR22 0PL, **T:** 01720 422360, **W:** www.troy town.co.uk.

WHERE TO EAT: The Turks Head, The Quay, St Agnes, TR22 0PL, **T:** 01720 422434. High Tide Seafood Restaurant, Old Lane, St Agnes, TR22 0PL, **T:** 01720 423869.

Day-trippers head to the slipway for the journey back to St Mary's.

Extremely Scilly

Of all the inhabited Isles of Scilly, St Agnes is the most outlying, south-westerly. There's a real sense of being at the outer limits of the archipelago, at the edge of the Earth. From your approach where you can see the vast emptiness of blue sea behind it, through to stepping foot onto the small, sloping jetty, St Agnes is all about peace and quiet, tranquillity and mindfulness. On a warm, sunny day, wandering around the island's twisting lanes and beautiful coastal paths is idyllic. You can comfortably stroll right around St Agnes and build in some relaxing time on the beach during a day trip from one of the other islands. If you're lucky enough to be staying overnight on St Agnes, be prepared to enter a completely different time zone, where the pace of life is far less stressful than on the mainland. It's like living in another dimension. The island is so compact that as you walk, you'll inevitably hit all the main attractions.

Weaving and Wood Art

This wild outpost has a busy, creative farming community with a growing number of products on sale to visitors. Discover traditional methods of handweaving during a workshop at Twisted Bobbins, where you could order a bespoke piece of fabric. Handmade wooden art is designed at Wood Tattoos, and save time to visit Pot Buoys Gallery, which showcases the work of talented local artists. The only licensed distillery on the island at Westward Farm is the perfect place to sample some locally produced gin. There's also apple juice, cyder and a range of soaps – all made using produce grown on the island.

Mazes and Milk

The lighthouse standing in the centre of St Agnes dates back to the late 17th century and has warned ships away from the Western Rocks ever since. Although the Peninnis Lighthouse on St Mary's replaced the light shone here in 1911, it has continued to serve as a day beacon. Head down a country lane from the lighthouse and you'll reach Troytown, home of a rare kind of turf maze with confusing defences around its outer layer. The maze here is thought to be the work of a lighthouse keeper in the 1790s. The mazes were built to send fair winds to sailors out on the ocean. The Troytown dairy farm is a great place to stop at the end of a busy day exploring the island. The cows are milked in a small parlour before buckets of milk are walked down the lane to be pasteurised and bottled. Some is made into delicious local produce like yoghurt, clotted cream and ice cream.

With a limited amount of indoor space, a trip to St Agnes is largely weather dependent. Pick your day well and you'll never look back, sampling local produce and indulging in the fine environment enjoyed by this island community. Go on a day with strong winds and driving rain, however, and it could be one of the longest days of your life. Fortunately, the microclimate of the Isles of Scilly is favourable and you shouldn't have to wait long for the sunshine.

▼ *The turf maze at Troytown. Inset, left: The buildings on St Agnes look like they're on the film set of a period drama. Inset, right: Farming is an important industry on the island.*

ST HELEN'S

LOCATION: 49.9724°N 6.3250°W

GRID REFERENCE: SV900170

POPULATION: 0

SIZE: <1km²

Quarantine Island

Uninhabited St Helen's sits between Tresco and St Martin's and contains a number of significant ruins that can be explored on foot. The largest ruined building you see on the island is known as the Pest House and is the grim remains of an isolation hospital built in 1764. Sailors who arrived in the Scillies with suspected plague were brought here to quarantine, and you can only imagine the suffering and anxiety that was experienced inside. On the southern side of St Helen's is an early Christian site, thought to be the remains of an 8th-century chapel where St Elidus lived and was buried. The chapel was enlarged in Norman times. A service to mark the feast of St Elidus is held here annually. The St Helen's Site of Special Scientific Interest is designed to protect the rare flora and the eight species of seabirds breeding here. St Helen's is often grouped together with the three other islands that are close and easily seen from the northern shore. These are Golden Ball, Men-a-Vaur and, most notably, Round Island with its lighthouse.

GETTING THERE: Boat trips and chartered boats are available to visit St Helen's, especially in the summer months. Check the boards in St Mary's harbour for details or find a boat company at www.visitislesofscilly.com.

WHERE TO STAY: Stay in Hugh Town on St Mary's before taking your day trip across. The Atlantic, Hugh Street, St Mary's, TR21 0PL, **T:** 01720 422417, **W:** www.atlanticinnscilly. co.uk. Tregarthen's Hotel, Garrison Hill, TR21 0PP, **T:** 01720 422540, **W:** www.tregarthens-hotel.co.uk.

WHERE TO EAT: Take a picnic with you on the trip.

ST MARTIN'S

LOCATION: 49.9631°N 6.2836°W

GRID REFERENCE: SV925159

POPULATION: 136

SIZE: 2.4km²

Producing the Goods

Each of the Isles of Scilly has a completely different feel, something that becomes apparent after spending only a short time here. St Martin's has an affectionate character of being a creative community hard at work. There are still fewer than 150 people living on the island and plenty of ways to experience splendid Scilly isolation on beaches, but there are also more places to buy local products than the other outlying islands. This is evident when you disembark at Higher Town Bay and see the collection of boards advertising local businesses, each one tempting you in and well worth a look. Scilly Billy is a popular place to start. A local clothing company, it's taken the name of the archipelago and created a fun range of T-shirts and jumpers. You'll undoubtedly see people wearing 'Scilly Billy', 'Scilly Moo' and 'Scilly Ass' designs. Adam's Fish and Chips is a great place for lunch, serving up fish caught around the island and using potatoes that have been grown on the nearby farm. Fay Page has a jewellery shop selling a wide range of pieces that have been locally made in their workshop and are themed around shells and sea creatures. In the south-east of the island, St Martin's Vineyard gives the island a Mediterranean presence, with slopes covered in grape vines and a well providing the water needed for wine production. The first vintage was bottled here in 2000 and the business continues to grow.

GETTING THERE: Boat trips from St Mary's to St Martin's are advertised on boards at Hugh Town harbour. Information about boats to and from St Martin's is available from Scilly Boating (**T:** 01720 423999, **W:** www.scillyboating.co.uk).

WHERE TO STAY: The Stables, Highertown, TR25 0QL, **T:** 01326 563811, **W:** www.thestables-stmartins.uk. Karma St Martin's, Lower Town, TR25 0QW, **T:** 01720 422368, **W:** www.karmagroup.com.

WHERE TO EAT: Sir Cloudesley Shovell Restaurant, Lower Town, St Martin's, TR25 0QW, **T:** 01720 422368, **W:** www.karmagroup.com. Adam's Fish and Chips, Higher Town, St Martin's, TR25 0QN, **T:** 01720 423082, **W:** www.adamsfishandchips.co.uk.

Why I Love...
St Martin's

'Once you've experienced the Isles of Scilly, they get into your heart and never leave. Their unique blend of unspoilt natural beauty, genuine caring community and relaxed pace of life are intoxicating. I was blessed to live here when I was a kid, and I understand why people are always drawn back. After travelling the world and living in New Zealand, I still returned, and re-met the Scillonian boy I went to school with, who is now my husband. I created Scilly Billy with Scilly-inspired designs to embody the charm, fun and characters of these magical little islands.

Stephanie Moakes,
Founder of www.scillybilly.com

Life's a Beach

The beaches on St Martin's are thought by many to be the best the Isles of Scilly have to offer. Even on the busier days, when boatloads of visitors arrive, you don't have to walk far to find a quiet stretch of coastline to get away from it all. It's possible to walk all the way around the island on a day trip here, but save time to linger in Great Bay and Little Bay. These are wonderful spots to paddle in the sea, play in the sand and relax as you watch boats out to sea.

On a warm summer night, the beaches are special places to hang out and you're in for a treat if there are clear skies. The lack of light pollution makes St Martin's a

fantastic place to observe the glory of the night sky – it's designated as a Dark Sky Discovery Zone for this reason. Astronomers have built two observatory domes here, which you can visit during the weekly open evenings.

A Clifftop Beacon

The path that circumnavigates St Martin's is an inspiring way to get a feel for all the island has to offer, but the views of rugged coastline get more dramatic as you climb the cliffs in the north-east, towards the island's highest point. As you get closer, what appears to be a huge red pencil comes into view. This is the St Martin's daymarker, used as a beacon for shipping since it was built in 1683. It hasn't always had the distinctive red and white stripes – initially it was painted all-white, then in the early 19th century it was changed to a red daymarker until the stripe design seen today was adopted. It's a striking landmark and makes for some great photographs, standing over 6m (20ft) tall and with a diameter of nearly 5m (16ft). On a clear day, this red and white tower can be seen from the mainland and it is one of the most familiar sights in the Isles of Scilly. Close by, marking the highest point on the island, is the Ordnance Survey triangulation pillar – the only one on St Martin's.

▲ Of all the islands in this group, many say St Martin's has the pick of the beaches.

▼ The pencil-like beacon acts as a shipping guide.

ST MARY'S

LOCATION: 49.9250°N 6.2987°W

GRID REFERENCE: SV915115

POPULATION: 1,723

SIZE: 6.6km²

GETTING THERE: The *Scillonian III* passenger ferry brings people from Penzance to St Mary's during the holiday season. Flights are available to St Mary's from Land's End, Newquay and Exeter, taking much less time but costing more money. To book, call 01736 334220 or visit www. islesofscilly-travel.co.uk.

WHERE TO STAY: Schooners Hotel on Town Beach in St Mary's, TR21 0LN, **T:** 01720 422682, **W:** www.schoonershotel.co.uk. The Atlantic, Hugh Street, St Mary's, TR21 0PL, **T:** 01720 422417, **W:** www.atlanticinnscilly.co.uk.

WHERE TO EAT: Dibble and Grub, Porthcressa Beach, St Mary's, TR21 0JQ, **T:** 01720 423719, **W:** www.dibbleandgrub.co.uk. Pilot's Gig, The Bank, St Mary's, TR21 0HY, **T:** 01720 422654.

Garrison

No visit to St Mary's is complete without a walk up to the Garrison walls, a short trek from the harbour. As you walk around what are some of the finest and best-preserved coastal defences in the British Isles, it's easy to get lost in the history of this place and imagine you're on the film lot for *Pirates of the Caribbean*. The Isles of Scilly were highlighted as a target for attack during the reign of Queen Elizabeth I, but little was done to prepare them for the risk. But after the 1588 attack of the Spanish Armada, a second wave of enemy ships was anticipated and so work started to fortify St Mary's. The prominent headland called The Hugh was chosen, and defences were constructed to deal with the Spanish threat, with the centre of the project being the Star Castle, now a hotel. The second armada never came, but the garrison went on to play an important role during the English Civil War. Initially a Royalist garrison, the future King Charles II stayed here in 1646 before moving on to Jersey. Royalists on the island surrendered to Parliament, but a later revolt saw it once again become a stronghold for 800 Royalists. In 1651, Parliamentarian Admiral Blake turned his full attention to hitting St Mary's and finally took the island. The outer walls were later extended because of threats from the French in the 17th and 18th centuries, eventually covering most of the headland. During the world wars, soldiers were stationed here and it was used as a signal station. Walking along these remarkable walls is to take a stroll through the nation's military history. And the cannons are ideal for the obligatory photo that all kids seem to have at some point in their childhood.

▲ *St Mary's is a great place to get to grips with the military history of the islands.*

▶ *We will rock you – impressive formations on the coast of St Mary's.*

Hugh Town Galleries

The seascapes and varied nature of the Isles of Scilly are unsurprisingly an inspiration to many local and visiting artists. Hugh Town is the place to indulge your artistic needs in a range of galleries and seek something lovely to take home. There are items for all budgets, from postcards to original works of art. The Tamarisk Gallery on Hugh Street contains glasswork, pottery, felt, jewellery and paintings from local artists. It's a showcase for how creative a place the Isles of Scilly are.

Head Out to Sea

When you're staying on St Mary's, wandering down to the harbour and checking out the boat trips is a real delight. Noticeboards at the entrance to the harbour list times and prices of all the trips on offer during that day – they're updated every morning so make sure you know what is available on the day you intend to go. The options here for a bit of island exploration are extensive. You can hit the ocean for a spot of fishing, see one of the

The Scillonian III provides a vital link with the mainland.

much-loved gig races (see Rat Island, page 290), join a wildlife cruise, or board a tour that takes in all the islands at once or is a day trip to one of the other islands. The options for boat trips are greatest when you're staying on St Mary's, the hub of the Isles of Scilly with the largest population of all the islands.

TEÄN

LOCATION: 49.9680°N 6.3123°W

GRID REFERENCE: SV908164

POPULATION: 0

SIZE: <1km²

Tropical Teän

Make the most of the generous microclimate enjoyed in the Isles of Scilly and head to Teän when the sun is shining. This glorious uninhabited island close to St Martin's is the nearest you'll get in England to imagining you're on a tiny tropical island. The beaches are fabulous, the water is so calming and the solitude inspiring. It's possible to find small corners of the island with views out to sea that make you feel a thousand miles away from other humans.

Exploring Teän is a joyful experience and you should look out for Bronze Age settlements and an early Christian chapel. To gain a perspective of Teän's place within the Isles of Scilly, climb up to the granite tor known as Great Hill. Rising to 40m (131ft) above sea level, there are fine views to be had of the other islands from here, as well as some of the secret places on Teän you may have missed.

GETTING THERE: Teän sits just 300m (984ft) off the western shore of the island of St Martin's and guided tours are available to help you explore its history (www.visitislesofscilly.com).

WHERE TO STAY: There are several places to base yourself on nearby St Martin's (see St Martin's, page 296).

Take a guided tour to learn about Teän's rich history.

TRESCO

LOCATION: 49.9514°N 6.3330°W

GRID REFERENCE: SV893421

POPULATION: 175

SIZE: 3km²

Plant Diversity

Spring comes early to Tresco and summer stretches out into a very late autumn. The near total lack of winter weather means the island has an exceptional climate, which sets it and the other Isles of Scilly apart from anywhere else in the British Isles. It's the subtropical weather on Tresco that allows a stunning variety of vegetation to grow, creating a naturally occurring version of Kew Gardens out in the middle of the Atlantic Ocean. Many of the trees and plants on display in the stunning Tresco Abbey Garden would not stand a chance on the Cornish coast – just 48km (30 miles) away. But exotic plants from all over the world thrive here, and no matter what time of year, this is an inspiring place to wander around – from the blooming spring flowers that burst to life earlier than on the mainland through to the blaze of colour in autumn. There are still more than 300 species of plant in flower on the winter solstice! At least a couple of hours can be spent taking in the diversity of the garden, and then there's a café to reflect on the flora of Tresco.

Tresco is an island famed for its plant diversity.

GETTING THERE: Boats to and from Tresco are advertised on the boards at St Mary's harbour. One of the main operators from the island is Tresco Boat Services, **T:** 01720 422849, **W:** www.tresco.co.uk.

WHERE TO STAY: The New Inn, New Grimsby, Tresco, TR24 0QQ, **T:** 01720 423006, **W:** www.tresco. co.uk/staying/the-new-inn. Sea Garden Apartments, Old Grimsby, Tresco, TR24 0PW, **T:** 01720 422849, **W:** www.tresco.co.uk/staying/sea-garden-apartments.

WHERE TO EAT: The Flying Boat serves food on the site of an old flying boat station at New Grimsby Harbour, Tresco, TR24 0QQ, **T:** 01720 424068, **W:** www.tresco.co.uk/eating/flying-boat. Ruin Beach Café, New Grimsby, Tresco, TR24 0PU, **T:** 01720 424849, **W:** www.tresco.co.uk/eating/ruin-cafe.

▲ *Tresco has some fabulous beaches.*
Inset: The museum at the Abbey Gardens features figureheads from local wrecks.

▶ *The Abbey Garden Arch, beckoning visitors to explore the delights of the displays.*

Why I Love... Tresco

'Tresco is the most varied in vegetation and geology of the Isles of Scilly. It's the second largest, but it's got the most variation. And it's also got the Abbey Garden, which is unique in British horticulture. The garden is Premier League in world terms because we can grow plants from places that nobody else can really grow in Britain. We can grow from every Mediterranean climate zone in the world, and from California, Chile, South Africa, Australia, New Zealand. This is unusual because a lot of these places either have a lot of rain or no rain. But the way the garden is built, with microclimates and shelter, we can do something quite extraordinary.'

Mike Nelhams, Garden Curator,
Tresco Abbey Garden

Civil War History

The islands were fought over during the English Civil War and plenty remains from that key period in British history. In the north of the island, King Charles's Castle dates back to the 16th century and was occupied by Royalists during the war. After, parts of it were dismantled and used to build Cromwell's Castle in the early 1650s. The Old Blockhouse in Old Grimsby was a gun tower during the war and was used to defend the nearby harbour.

Valhalla

The small museum about local shipwrecks situated inside Tresco Abbey Garden houses one of the most unusual and intriguing maritime collections. You'll see many well-preserved figureheads that have been salvaged from boats wrecked on the Isles of Scilly down the centuries.

On Yer Bike...

You can comfortably walk around Tresco on a full day visit, experiencing the gardens, beaches and rugged terrain that this island of contrasts has to offer. To have more time to idle in cafés and lounge on the beach, you can hire bikes next to Tresco Stores and explore the many paths on the island with the freedom that two wheels allow.

An Island for Foodies...

Whether you're looking for a picnic or some produce to cook up a treat in the evening, Tresco Stores has a wide range of food available and much of it has an island influence.

Locally caught fish, Tresco beef and Isles of Scilly ice cream should all be on your culinary radar when visiting the island.

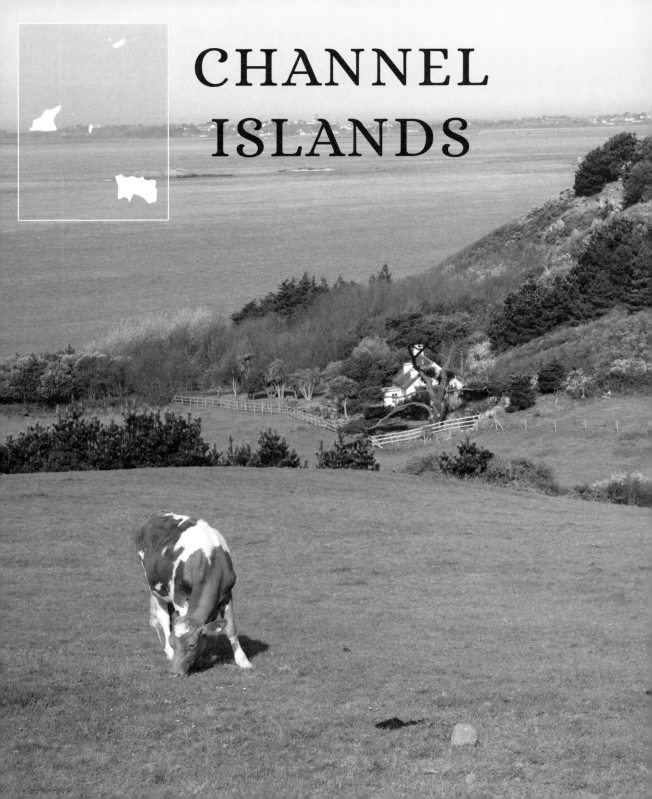

CHANNEL ISLANDS

With a memorable coastline, a generous helping of sunshine and a fascinating history, the chances are you won't have time to cover all you want to in the Channel Islands. A return trip to Jersey, Guernsey, Sark or Alderney will be high on your list once you become hooked to everything on offer on these stunning islands off the coast of France. With the weather on your side and a sense of adventure in your heart, a visit here can also satisfy hardcore adrenaline hunters. Sign up for an afternoon of coasteering or take to the waters in a kayak to see the islands from a different angle. When you've dried off, explore the range of museums that deal with the Nazi occupation during the Second World War. Each island had a different experience during these difficult years, with some populations being evacuated and some adapting their way of life while having their freedoms taken away. Liberation Day is still celebrated on the streets each year on 9 May. The Channel Islands are also a real treat for foodies. There are numerous places to enjoy the latest catches from the sea, and sweeter snacks to follow are made on Sark by renowned chocolatier Caragh. Being close to France, the favourable climate allows vineyards to thrive so washing down your meal with a locally produced wine is a must.

DON'T MISS

- Sampling locally made wine and gin while soaking up the sun on Jersey
- Coming to terms with how Nazi occupation changed life on these islands
- Jumping into the sea on an adventurous coasteering trip on Guernsey
- Indulging in the chocolatey heaven of delicious sweet treats made on Sark
- Enjoying the views as you paddle around the bays of Alderney on a kayak

◀ *Guernsey cattle on the island of Herm.*

ALDERNEY

Sun, Sea and Sand

Alderney is relatively small when compared to Jersey and Guernsey but it sure packs a lot in when it comes to facilities and beaches. West-facing Clonque Beach is perhaps the best place to start. The long beach contains sandy and shingle areas, with a section that's ideal for exploring rock pools. Make sure you stay here into the evening to enjoy one of the finest sunsets on the Channel Islands. In south-east Alderney, another cracking beach to discover is Longis. The sand stretches for over half a mile, but the biggest feature on this stretch of coast dates back to the Second World War. The huge anti-tank wall stretching across the beach was built during the German occupation of the island. The waters in the bay are popular for holidaymakers looking to paddle, swim and kayak.

The Larder

When the Channel Islands fell to the Germans at the beginning of the Second World War, Alderney had a key role to play for the occupiers. The first two years saw the island act as the 'larder to the Channel Islands' because it was so important for the growing of food consumed by islanders and German troops. In 1942, though, Hitler changed Alderney's role and ordered a fortress to be built here. Prisoners from Russia, Poland, France, Spain and further afield were put to work

LOCATION: 49.7133°N 2.2058°W

GRID REFERENCE: WA572070

POPULATION: 2,039

SIZE: 7.8km²

GETTING THERE: The Little Ferry Company provides a service that links the island to Guernsey (**T:** 01481 724810, **W:** www.thelittle ferrycompany.com.).

WHERE TO STAY: Braye Beach Hotel, Braye Street, St Anne, Alderney, GY9 3XT, **T:** 01481 824300, **W:** www.braye beach.com. Victoria Hotel, Victoria Street, Alderney, GY9 3UG, **T:** 01481 822471, **W:** www.thevictioria.gg.

WHERE TO EAT: Braye Chippy, Braye Harbour, Alderney, GY9 3XX, **T:** 01481 823475. Cantina No. 6, Braye Street, Alderney, GY9 3XT, **T:** 01481 824063.

– and sadly many died during construction. Bunkers, tunnels and anti-tank walls were built, many of which are still visible today.

Unlike the other Channel Islands, Alderney was evacuated when war broke out. Early on 23 June 1940, the church bells rang out to let locals know Royal Navy ships were on the way. They had just hours to get their belongings together and were prevented from returning before 15 December 1945. That's a day still marked on the island with a Bank Holiday.

GUERNSEY

Gorgeous Guernsey

Stunning coastlines, favourable weather and brilliant outdoor activities in a fabulous location bring families back to Guernsey year after year for memorable holidays. The continental influences and centuries of history make the island a truly unique destination and it's relatively easy to reach from the British mainland.

German Occupation

The only part of the British Isles to come under German control during the Second World War were the Channel Islands and there are plenty of historic sites to remind visitors of those dark times. You will not fail to notice the German military buildings that regularly appear along the coastline. Seek out more information by visiting the underground war museum at La Vallette. Located in a bunker built to house fuel for German U-boats, it's packed with a gripping military collection that tells the story of the island's occupation. The Germans arrived here at the end of June 1940. Britain had decided that the Channel Islands offered no strategic benefit so declared them a demilitarised zone. Around a quarter of the population – including many schoolchildren – were evacuated to the UK. More can be discovered at the German Occupation Museum (www.germanoccupationmuseum. co.uk), which tells some grim stories about daily life during the war.

LOCATION: 49.4600°N 2.5352°W

GRID REFERENCE: WV336786

POPULATION: 62,729

SIZE: 65km²

GETTING THERE: Condor Ferries operates routes to Guernsey from Poole and Portsmouth, with sailing times from three to seven hours. Call 0345 609 1024 or visit www.condor ferries.co.uk for more information. Flights arrive at Guernsey Airport from several UK airports (**T:** 01481 237766, **W:** www.airport.gg).

WHERE TO STAY: The Farmhouse Hotel, Route Des Bas Courtils, St Saviours, Guernsey, GY7 9YF, **T:** 01481 264181, **W:** www.thefarm house.gg. La Barbarie, Saints Bay Rd, St Martin's, Guernsey, GY4 6ES, **T:** 01481 235217, **W:** labarbariehotel. com.

WHERE TO EAT: The Kiln, Les Gigands, Guernsey, GY2 4YT, **T:** 01481 245661, **W:** www.thekiln. gg. Old Quarter Restaurant, Mansell Street, Guernsey, GY1 1HP, **T:** 01481 727268, **W:** oldquarter.co.uk.

▲ *Castle Cornet, Saint Peter Port.*

Thousands of islanders were sent to internment camps in Europe. Wireless radios were confiscated. As the Germans lost control of France following D-Day in 1944, food supply became a severe issue on Guernsey and eventually a Red Cross ship was sent to help. The island's Liberation Day on 9 May 1945 is still marked today with a range of parades and events.

The Great Guernsey Outdoors

Adventurous visitors to the island will love a trip out with Outdoor Guernsey (www.outdoorguernsey.gg). Several trips leave each day, but you'll need to book them in advance because these popular activities fill up – especially in the school holidays. If you're looking to get out of your comfort zone, have a go at climbing, abseiling or the exhilarating experience of coasteering. For a gentler excursion, you can hire kayaks and explore the coastline at your leisure. One of the island's best walks focuses on the clifftop paths in the south-west of Guernsey. Pleinmont rewards you with far-reaching views across to Jersey and even to the coast of France on a clear day. Dominating the skyline is the Second World War observation tower, which is open to the public during the summer.

Castle Cornet has guarded Saint Peter Port for 800 years.

HERM

LOCATION: 49.4666°N 2.4500°W

GRID REFERENCE: WV398794

POPULATION: 60

SIZE: 2km²

Tying the Knot

With a favourable climate, a good hotel at its heart and a halo of serene beaches at the island's northern shore, Herm is an ideal location for couples wanting an island wedding. The gleaming waters provide an ideal backdrop for those all-important pictures of the special day. Ceremonies take place at the beautiful St Tugual's Chapel, which dates back to the 11th century and can hold 50 people. Its stained-glass windows are jaw-dropping and have a special local character. Designs show Guernsey cows with Noah's Ark and even Jesus having a chat with fishermen at Herm harbour.

Operation Huckaback

Herm became the focus of a British Commando raid during the Second World War, with the objective of capturing German prisoners to seek information on their Channel Island operation. However, the mission, in February 1943, found only abandoned buildings and no evidence of German occupancy.

GETTING THERE: Passenger ferry The Travel Trident leaves from Guernsey for the 20-minute journey to Herm. Contact Condor Ferries (**T:** 0345 609 1024, **W:** www.condorferries.co.uk) for more information.

WHERE TO STAY: The Seagull Campsite, Herm Island, **T:** 01481 750000, **W:** www.herm.com. The White House Hotel, Herm Island, **T:** 01481 750000, **W:** www.herm.com.

WHERE TO EAT: The Conservatory Restaurant, Herm Island, **T:** 01481 750075, **W:** www.herm.com.

JERSEY

Family-friendly

With by far the lion's share of the Channel Islands' population, Jersey enjoys the facilities and attractions of a leading tourist destination. When the weather conditions are suitable – as they so often are – it's time to head outside to the beach and the sea. And when the grey clouds gather there's plenty to occupy the curious minds in any family. Jersey is simply one of the most idyllic islands to visit.

Pick a Pearl

If you're looking for the perfect Jersey souvenir, the island has a pearl of an experience waiting for you. At Jersey Pearl (www.jerseypearl.com) you can pick jewellery from many unique designs as well as choose your own special pearl from a sustainably grown oyster. Guided tours are available to learn more about the process and you can see pieces being made in the workshop. You'll find all this in the stunning setting of the bay at St Ouen.

LOCATION: 49.1900°N 2.1100°W

GRID REFERENCE: WA648489

POPULATION: 107,800

SIZE: 118.2km²

GETTING THERE: Condor Ferries operates routes to Jersey from Poole and Portsmouth, with sailing times taking from 4 hours 30 minutes (**T:** 0345 609 1024, **W:** www.condorferries.co.uk for more information). Flights arrive at Jersey Airport from several UK airports (**T:** 01534 446000, **W:** www.jerseyairport.com).

WHERE TO STAY: Radisson Blu Waterfront Hotel, Rue de l'Etau, St Helier, Jersey, JE2 3WF, **T:** 01534 671100, **W:** www.radissonhotels.com. The Lyndhurst, La Route de la Haule, Jersey, JE3 8BA, **T:** 01534 720317, **W:** www.thelyndhurstjersey.com.

WHERE TO EAT: Bistro Rosa, Beresford St, Jersey, JE2 4WX, **T:** 01534 729559. Mark Jordan at the Beach, La Route de la Haule, St Peter, Jersey, JE3 7YD, **T:** 01534 780180, **W:** www.markjordanatthebeach.com.

Pleasure craft – yachts, cruisers and speedboats – moored at St Aubin's Bay.

Garden Splendour

The privately owned Botanic Gardens make for an essential day out in Jersey (www.samaresmanor.com). Created in the 1920s and superbly maintained, they are an inspiring place to wander through. It's easy to lose your thoughts amid the diverse plant species and have your senses enhanced in the Japanese Garden. The standout section is the Herb Garden. It's one of the best in the world and bombards you with breathtaking aromas. There's a café, play area and customary gift shop.

Amazing Grape

Set in 20 acres of land with a fabulous backdrop of the English Channel, the La Mare Estate is an idyllic place to learn about the production of wine, Jersey apple brandy and gin (www.lamarewineestate.com). Tours are available that show how some of the island's legendary drinks are crafted. Stroll through the vineyard to see the year's grapes growing and then head inside for a tasting session as you learn about the process of winemaking. Save time for a cream tea in the restaurant and visit the shop to take a bottle home with you.

Remembering the Occupation

Remnants of the German Occupation are still to be found throughout the island. Millions of tons of concrete were used to fortify Jersey during a period that dramatically changed island life. The huge building project carried out by the occupiers took place as local folk tried their best to continue with their daily lives. Dealing with loss of freedom and, as the war progressed, food shortages, some islanders risked their lives trying to escape. History tours of the island (www.historyalive.je) bring the period to life by visiting key sites and telling the stories of the ordinary people who lived through it.

SARK

LOCATION: 49.4330°N 2.3608°W

GRID REFERENCE: WV463757

POPULATION: 492

SIZE: 5.5km²

GETTING THERE: Sark Shipping has a busy timetable of services between Guernsey and Sark (**T:** 01481 724059, **W:** www.sarkshipping.gg).

WHERE TO STAY: Stocks Hotel, Sark, GY10 1SD, **T:** 01481 832001, **W:** www. stockshotel.com. La Sablonnerie, Little Sark, GY10 1SD, **T:** 01481 832061, **W:** www.sablonneriesark.com.

WHERE TO EAT: Shenanigans Café, Le Grand Fort, Sark, GY10 1SH, **T:** 01481 832827, **W:** www. shenanigans-cafe.business.site.

Sarktastic!

There are some lovely footpaths around Sark, with the best known and most atmospheric route being La Coupée. It's a fabulous causeway along a high ridge 80m (262ft) above the sea, linking Big and Little Sark together. The waves down below are constantly eroding parts of the cliff and experts believe the causeway will eventually fall into the sea. This will ensure Little Sark becomes an island in its own right, and deserve a separate chapter in future editions of this book! More adventurous hikers may want to scramble over rocks to discover Venus Lake – an idyllic rock pool with clear waters that is seen when the tide has gone out. However, the most inspiring way to explore the island is to sign up for one of the horse and carriage tours. The jolly trips last either one or two hours and up to ten people can be pulled along the historic streets. The route treats you to the best views of the island and it's also a great way to learn about Sark's history, as the driver tells local stories and will answer any of your questions.

Chocs Away!

There's always something magical about visiting a chocolate shop, enjoying the smells and tastes that it has to offer. Sark's chocolate of choice is Caragh – available throughout the Channel Islands and further afield. You can visit the kitchens to see the chocolatiers hard at work pouring the deliciously sweet confectionary into moulds and dipping truffles. This is also a learning experience, though, and you'll come away stuffed with chocolatey facts. Visit www. caraghchocolates.com to get a taste.

Wildlife Haven

There's plenty for nature lovers to explore on Sark. Listen out for a range of different warblers and in the summer check out the many different butterflies and moths found here. The island is also home to dozens of wildflowers, which are fabulous when in bloom.

Horse and carriage cross La Coupée narrow track between Little Sark and Sark.

INDEX